D0529428

The English Climate

NEW SCIENCE SERIES

General Editors

SIR GRAHAM SUTTON, C.B.E., D.Sc., F.R.S.

Director-General, Meteorological Office.
Formerly Dean of the Royal Military College of Science, Shrivenham,
and Bashforth Professor of Mathematical Physics

and

PETER WHITTLE, M.Sc., Ph.D.

Professor of Mathematical Statistics,
University of Manchester

THE ENGLISH VOTER
A. J. Allen, B.Sc. (Econ.)

THE CONTROL OF PAIN
F. Prescott, M.Sc., Ph.D., M.R.C.P. (Lond.), F.R.I.C.

SCIENCE AND THE SKIN
A. Jarrett, M.B., Ch.B. (Birm.), F.R.C.P.Ed.

The English Climate

H. H. LAMB
Meteorological Office

THE ENGLISH UNIVERSITIES PRESS LTD
102 NEWGATE STREET
LONDON · E.C.1

First edition by C. E. P. Brooks 1954
Second edition (rewritten) 1964

New edition Copyright © 1964
H. H. Lamb and Mrs D. L. Brooks

PRINTED AND BOUND IN ENGLAND
FOR THE ENGLISH UNIVERSITIES PRESS LTD
BY HAZELL WATSON AND VINEY LTD, AYLESBURY

General Editors' Foreword

SOME ten years ago the late Dr. C. E. P. Brooks wrote a typically delightful book called *The English Climate*, in which he gave the reader the benefit of his immense knowledge of the vagaries of our weather and discussed not only historical storms and other memorable events but also what meaning we should attach to words such as 'summer' and 'winter' in relation to the British Isles.

In this new edition Mr. Lamb has used a wider canvas and has considered our weather as part of a whole, that of the Northern Hemisphere. This is the modern approach. The subject of dynamical climatology relates the long-term average of weather to the global motions of the atmosphere, and this philosophy is the mainspring of the present book.

Mr. Lamb is a scholar of wide learning who has always been as deeply interested in the story of man's struggle with his environment as with the physical properties of the atmosphere. This book should attract and fascinate not only those who make the weather their trade but also geographers, historians and economists, and indeed all who love to talk and speculate about our climate, surely the most interesting in the world. It is to be recommended as an authoritative account of what lies behind our favourite topic of conversation.

Contents

Illustrations

Preface to the New Edition

THE title 'The English Climate' has been preserved in this new edition, although the book deals with wider fields. In reality the climate of England cannot be understood in isolation any more than the country's history or trade can. As in the case of the late C. E. P. Brooks's original text, the chief aim of this work is to take a fresh look at England's climate and explain what makes it what it is, not just in terms of average conditions but with all the vagaries of the weather thrown in. In the course of explaining how these come about we shall consider many processes and principles which are just as relevant to neighbouring countries. And the writer's friends in Scotland, Wales and the Irish Republic in particular will find that an effort has been made to cater for their interests rather more than was done in the first edition.

In revising the work a certain amount of interesting anecdote and reminiscence has had to be cut out to make room for more attention to the physical basis of climate and Britain's place in the world scheme of things. The useful historical material has, however, been retained (even added to) and gathered together in an appendix, as a calendar of historic events. This form of presentation makes it easy to compare the occurrences listed with what the text has to say about the normal round of the seasons and the atmospheric processes that accompany it.

Since the first edition of this book appeared, the Meteorological Office has adopted the Centigrade scale of temperature, which now appears in weather forecasts and on the maps published in newspapers and in the Daily Weather Report which are explained in this book, as well as being heard on the radio. A new edition is therefore an opportunity to make this scale—by far the simplest one for the layman—more familiar. In other ways too the opportunity is used to further the cause of simplification of units. To go over now to the standard units in international use, wherever these are already well known in this country, is to bury the last remnants of the chaos of the past when barometer and thermometer scales were almost as numerous as countries. There was a time when even the mile had a different length in different parts of England, and that was no small hindrance to the making of intelligible maps!

Conversion figures and diagrams are given in an appendix at the end of the book: units used for temperature, rainfall and other elements of the weather are included. As regards temperature, however, there is much to be said for learning to 'think in Centigrade'. On this simple scale, on which 0° is the freezing point and 100° the boiling point of water under normal conditions, 10° is the level of much of our mildest weather in winter, 20° is attained in good warm weather in spring and 30° represents a rather strong heat wave. By international usage, days with maximum temperatures of 25° C (77° F) or more are counted as good 'summer days', and the numbers of these in different places and different years give an interesting measure of climatic differences. 20° C (68° F) is also a really acceptable water temperature for bathing in most people's estimation, though sea water at this temperature never lasts for long anywhere in Europe outside the Mediterranean. (The nearest approach is in the still waters of Oslo Fjord in July and early August.) A map (fig. 21) shows that this figure is not normally achieved for as long as a month in summer in this country, although along the more favoured bits of our coast it occurs freely in the shallows in shorter periods of warm weather and may be comfortably surpassed when the tide comes in over sun-heated sand. It is also by no means uncommon in open-air swimming pools during the best of the summer and in still or sluggish inland waters, though not where the water is too deep.

In spite of these admissions that the times for really enjoyable sea bathing are limited in these islands, the facts presented in this book surely add up to an unarguable case that—apart from atmospheric pollution in some areas—there are no better climates in which to live and work and enjoy a full life than that of England and neighbouring lands in these islands and across the narrow seas between southern Scandinavia and northern Italy. Southeast England is near the centre of this favoured region.

The author's thanks go to the Director-General of the Meteorological Office for his interest in the plan of the new edition, and to Mr. J. Maitland of the English Universities Press who was unfailingly helpful at all times. The new author appreciated his real interest in the book and his accommodating attitude about its progress, which was held up by various things including the need to incorporate results of current research in Chs. 9, 10 and 11. Help given by the author's colleagues, Messrs. A. Bleasdale, R. W. Gloyne, F. E. Lumb and H. C. Shellard of the Meteorological Office who supplied valuable information, is gratefully acknowledged. The medical allusions in the original edition were checked by Dr. L. S. F. Woodhead, M.B.E. Any changes and additions in this field in the new edition have been discussed with Dr. G. S. C. Sowry, Edgware General Hospital, to whom the author's thanks are due.

Acknowledgments are due to the Controller of Her Majesty's Stationery Office for permission to reproduce figs. 10, 11, 13, 14, 15, 16, 19, 22 and 24 which are based on maps in the *Climatological Atlas of the British Isles* (published 1952) and two Daily Weather Report maps. Figs. 17 and 18 appeared in the earlier edition by permission of the then National Smoke Abatement Society (now National Society for Clean Air). Fig. 21 appears here by the kind permission of the International Council for the Exploration of the Sea, Charlottenlund, Denmark. Fig. 25 originally appeared in the *Quarterly Journal of the Royal Meteorological Society*, 1950 (p. 400), and permission to reprint it here is acknowledged with thanks. Information supplied by Dr. M. Clifton of the Warren Springs Laboratory, Stevenage, by Mr. J. Catlow of the Ministry of Housing and Local Government and by Mr. Hicks of the Automobile Association is also gratefully acknowledged. For detailed production of the text and diagrams the author acknowledges the help of Mrs. Y. M. G. Dean, Mrs. C. A. E. Baker and Miss D. Fishlock of the Meteorological Office.

The author of the present edition expresses his thanks to Mrs. C. E. P. Brooks for facilitating the preparation of the work in its present form.

Finally, the author records his thanks to his wife for assistance with the proof reading and in many indirect ways, not least some months of late hours while the new edition was being compiled. Without her help this book could not have appeared.

1

Introduction — What we mean by Climate

AN Englishwoman, reproached by a friend with not having visited her for ten years, replied: 'But my dear, look what weather we've been having!' That joke is typical of the way the English speak of their climate, but is it a true bill?

We must distinguish between climate and weather. Weather changes from day to day, while climate goes on all the time. The distinction may be illustrated by the example of a man's bank account. His average balance depends on his annual income and expenditure—that is, his financial climate. In some months income regularly exceeds expenditure; in others, such as the Christmas season, the reverse holds, so that his financial climate, like the natural climate, has an annual variation. But his balance will also fluctuate from day to day, depending on more or less casual windfalls and expenses, and these fluctuations represent his financial weather. Climate is thus the summing up of all the day-to-day changes of weather. In the early days of meteorology, climate was represented mainly by averages: average temperature, the average rainfall of the month, the average number of hours of bright sunshine, and so on. These were presented either in the form of tables of figures, or of maps showing lines along which specified elements had specified values, such as the isotherms (lines of equal temperature), isohyets (lines of equal rain), etc. A recent fine example of information of this kind is the *Climatological Atlas of the British Isles*.[1]

Maps and tables like these are indispensable for many purposes, such as agriculture and engineering, but the calendar month is not a natural unit of time and averages cannot tell the whole story. Their popularity is due to the fact that till quite lately averages were the only statistics that it was practicable to compute. In many cases it is not really the average state of affairs but the frequencies of this or that condition that are of interest. One cannot sensibly speak of an *average* wind direction, for example, but the changing *frequencies* of northeast and southwest winds matter to everybody.

Figures soon accumulate in a weather register, and the longhand

1. London, Air Ministry, Meteorological Office, *Climatological Atlas of the British Isles*. London, H.M. Stationery Office, M.O. 488, 1952, £2 12s. 6d.

calculation of averages for each set of figures (temperature, humidity, pressure, wind speed, etc.) over different periods of time strained the resources and patience of the early observers. Some of them saved work by taking, instead of the average, a middle value half-way between the extremes. It happens that in the case of temperature the middle value for each day $\frac{1}{2}$(max. + min.) is usually, but not always, within a degree or so of the average obtained from hourly observations. But over the range of a month, for temperature or pressure, this does not work at all well. The extreme low temperatures on a cold night (like the lowest pressures when a depression centre is near) are liable to occur rather briefly, as the situation passes. Most of the time the thermometer (or barometer, as the case may be) stands rather above the midway point of the range. And the average of all the daily observations would probably be above the midway point too. So we see that distributions are important: the range of variation, the frequency and duration of occurrence of particular conditions of temperature, pressure or what you will.

The two most obvious and fundamental variations in our climate are the diurnal and annual changes with their more or less regular and dependable effects. Average temperatures go down at night and in the winter, just as surely as our fuel demands go up. But there are some other chapters in Nature's story. Sometimes the sky changes from hour to hour; but often, as we know, the weather comes in spells lasting some days or even several weeks and not uncommonly accounting for all we remember afterwards of the character of a whole season. We shall see later that this tendency for the weather to come in spells appears to mark out a regular calendar of natural seasons. But the differing nature of the spells, and in some years and seasons the fact that the weather never settles down for long, very largely marks the difference between one year and another.

This undependable aspect of our climate—its alleged 'fickleness'— is one of the most frequent jibes levelled against it. But considerable differences from year to year are characteristic of all climates outside the tropics, and disastrous seasons are commoner in many countries than here. Moreover, it is arguable that a truly tropical régime suffers from monotony. The climates of the temperate zone present constant challenges to us to make the best of things, but rarely face us with hazardous extremes —especially here in England. Our health may even be toned up by the subconscious adaptations of the body to frequent slight changes of physical circumstance. This incidentally is probably one of the chief virtues of holidays by the sea and on the hills.

The extreme range of temperatures reliably observed in Britain, between about $+38$ and $-27°$ C ($+100$ and $-17°$ F), is under half the range between the world extremes of $+58$ and $-88°$ C[1] (from Tripolitania and Antarctica respectively) and little over half the observed range at one and the same place in Siberia (Verkhoyansk). The range of temperatures occurring here in Britain in most individual years, between about $+30$ and -15 to $20°$ C, is also about half that in Siberia. Our greatest rainfalls, 11 inches (279 mm.) in the day and 257 inches (6,528 mm.) in a year, are about a quarter of the corresponding world extremes. The heaviest falls in any individual year anywhere in the British hills are characteristically between a quarter and a half of those at the world's wettest place, Cherrapunji, high in the mountains of Assam. It is true that tropical-style thunderstorms and tornadoes on the American model, or winters like those in Russia, are not quite unknown here. Instances of these occurrences will be found in our calendar of historic weather (App. I), but they are made the more striking by their rarity and they are never as severe here as the worst cases in the places where these phenomena more properly belong.

The climate of these islands, then, is moderate as climates go, though its continual changes of mood are interesting and may help to keep us sprightly. This book is largely concerned with what makes our climate what it is. To come to grips with the matter we must first consider Britain's place in the physical world. The next three chapters are concerned with this physical setting and with the passing atmospheric systems that are part of it.

1. The Fahrenheit equivalents of these world extremes are $+136$ and -127 (not that there is much point in memorizing these high numbers that have no homely connotation). Average world temperature, so far from being mid-way between the extremes, is about $59°$ F ($+15°$ C).

2

The Roles of Sun, Atmosphere and Oceans

JUST as it is true that English history cannot be understood apart from world history, so to understand the English climate we must first learn what generates the various climates of the world.

The heat supply from the sun and how it is distributed

All the heat comes ultimately from the sun. The climate of any place depends on how it stands in relation to (i) direct receipt of solar radiation (a question of latitude), and (ii) receipt of heat transported by winds and ocean currents from other parts of the world. This is not just a question of how much heat is received by either route but of *net* gain or loss, since heat is also lost—radiated out to the sky and carried away by winds and water, etc. As regards direct receipt of radiation from the sun, places on south-facing slopes have some of the characteristics of more southern latitudes; north-facing slopes are in this respect equivalent to level sites in more northern latitudes. But for length of day, types of weather and warmth of the winds these places, of course, share the characteristics of their own neighbourhood.

The beam from the midday sun falls upon the Earth's surface at different angles in different latitudes and at different times of the year. At London this angle varies from 62° to 15°, at the June and December solstices respectively, and in Shetland from 53° to 7°. The lower the angle of the beam, the greater the area of surface over which each unit of its heat and light is spread, and the less heat and light is received by each particular square centimetre of a horizontal surface. (This point may be appreciated by considering the sizes of the shadow thrown by a roughly round object like the crown of an oak tree according to whether the sun is high or low in the sky.) But although the angle of the incoming solar beam is never high in high latitudes, the summer days are very long. On the longest day the sun is 16 hours 40 minutes above the horizon at London, 18 hours 40 minutes in Shetland. The figure is 24 hours everywhere from northern Iceland to the Pole. This gives time in June for even more heat to be received by each unit area near the Pole than is available at the Equator, though in fact the heat is largely wasted by reflection from the snow and ice and clouds. In mid winter no heat at all is received direct from the sun in the Arctic, and its beam is quite feeble in our own latitudes.

The amount of heat that would be received in different latitudes in the course of a year if the atmosphere were entirely transparent has been calculated by Angot: at the Poles it is 40% of the figure for the Equator. In the latitudes of Britain the proportion ranges from 57% in Shetland to 67% in the south. But, when the angle of the incoming beam is low, it has to pass through much more of the atmosphere before reaching the surface. Some of the heat and the lethal concentration of ultra-violet rays are in any case absorbed in the high atmosphere and never reach the ground. But the slanting beam encounters vastly more water vapour, clouds and pollution in the lower atmosphere than when the sun's elevation angle is high. So the heat reaching the surface in the higher latitudes is still further weakened.

Actually under half (42%) of the incoming solar energy, on a world-wide average, reaches the Earth's surface and is absorbed there as heat—so much is lost, mainly by reflection from cloud tops and from the surfaces of oceans and ice and snow. Only about another 18% is absorbed directly in the atmosphere, chiefly by the clouds, the water vapour and the ozone in the stratosphere. As this implies, the lower air picks up the bulk of its heat from the Earth's surface. And in high latitudes the proportion of the available heat which is actually absorbed is a great deal lower than the world-wide average.

These things mean that the Earth's surface is continually more strongly heated in the tropics than in higher latitudes, the difference being greatest in winter. And so a gradient of temperature from Equator to Pole is set up.

We have mentioned that the polar ice reflects away most of the great supply of heat available in the 24-hour days of summer: it is just this which keeps the polar regions colder than other places at that season. In fact, all different kinds of surface—sea and dry land, swamp, grassland and forest, etc.—behave differently as regards absorption of the radiant heat that falls upon them. They each reflect and waste a different percentage (this figure is called their 'Albedo'). For this and other reasons they heat up by different amounts even when exposed to the same amount of solar heat. If we examine world maps of temperature distribution, however, we see that by far the strongest thermal gradients are those between different latitudes. Important thermal contrasts are found between land and sea and especially near the limit of frozen surface—sea ice or snow-covered land: the latter intensifies and tends to localize in a particular zone a great part of the temperature difference between Equator and Pole.

The atmospheric circulation

It is this unequal heating of different parts of the Earth which sets the atmosphere in motion. To see how this comes about, let us start by supposing that the air is everywhere at rest on the Earth's surface. This means that the atmospheric pressure would have to be everywhere the same at sea level: for where a pressure gradient exists, there is a force to move the air and cause a wind. The air must, however, become less dense, and expand vertically, over the warmer regions than over the places where it is cold and vertical columns of air contract. This means that, if we consider the situation at any particular height above the Earth's surface, there will be more of the atmosphere above this height over the warm regions of the Earth than over the cold regions. So a pressure gradient will be bound to exist in the upper air, from high pressure over the tropics to low pressure over the Poles.

These pressure gradients are just the pattern we do find prevailing through a great depth of the atmosphere from 2 or 3 km. (say 6,000–10,000 feet) above sea level up to 15–20 km. Pressure throughout this range of heights is generally high over the tropics and low over the polar regions. It is also relatively low over the colder regions in each latitude zone. Another way of describing all this is to say that the height above sea level at which atmospheric pressure falls to any chosen value is normally greater over the warm than over the cold regions. This is illustrated by figs. 1(a) and 1(b) which show the average contours of the level of constant pressure 500 millibars (about half the pressure of the atmosphere at sea level) over the northern hemisphere in January and July. We see that the prevailing pressure patterns in summer and winter at this sample height of 5–6 km. (around 18,000 feet) are very simple and consist of a single low pressure region in high latitudes, surrounded by increasing pressures as far as the tropics. We also see troughs of low pressure over cold regions like northeast Canada, and ridges over the warmer waters of the North Atlantic and Pacific Oceans. The gradients are much stronger in winter than in summer, as shown by the closer spacing of the contours.

The differences of pressure represent a force which starts the air moving. But a state of balance is soon approached between this force and others, such as centrifugal effects and the deviating force of Earth rotation, which act upon the air once it gets under way. The result is that the wind blows nearly along the lines of equal pressure ('isobars')—or along the contours of a constant pressure surface, as shown in figs. 1(a) and (b)—counter-clockwise around regions of low pressure in the northern hemisphere. Its speed increases with the steepness of the gradient. Hence, as these maps indicate, the main wind current aloft is a single great vortex of more or less westerly winds blowing around the low pressure centre over the polar regions. This basic circulation is far stronger in winter, when the temperature contrasts between tropics and Poles are greatest, than it is in summer. Because of the great range of heights through which the flow

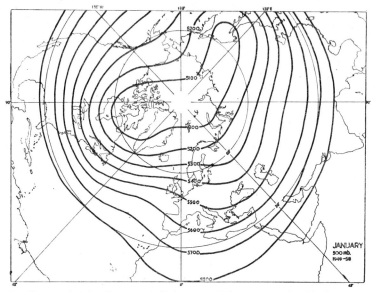

(a) Contour heights (in metres) of the 500 millibar pressure level in January.

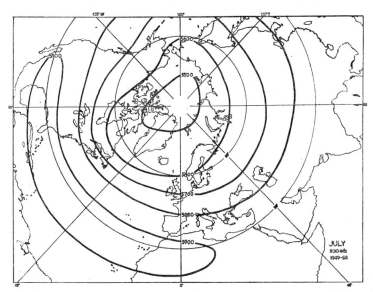

(b) Contour heights (in metres) of the 500 millibar pressure level in July.

FIGURE I. Pressure distribution in the middle atmosphere over the
northern hemisphere, average for 1949–58.

resembles that at the sample height shown, most of the mass of the atmosphere is involved in the prevailing upper westerly winds.

So it is not just a modern fashion[1] to start with the upper air in explaining meteorology and climatology—nor a tiresome fad of certain writers! The wind system which we find between 2 and 20 km. above the Earth's surface is, in fact, the mainstream of the general atmospheric circulation, the most massive flow, carrying most of the momentum. It also presents a far simpler pattern than the surface weather maps with their many separate 'cells' of high and low pressure, which we call anticyclones and depressions. Moreover, paradoxical though it may seem, the simple pattern of the upper wind flow reflects the general surface temperature distribution over the Earth.

As the upper winds circle the Earth, they pass from regions of weak to regions of strong pressure gradients and vice versa. Hence the air undergoes acceleration in one part of the map and has to slow down in another. The temporary disequilibrium between the forces acting upon the air in either case causes some departure from strict flow along the pressure lines (contours or isobars). This is the origin of those shifts of mass which create the anticyclones and depressions of the surface weather map. These familiar features develop and decay in response to changes in the upper wind pattern over them and are carried along with the general direction of the massive flow of the mainstream of the upper winds.

High pressure at the surface is the dominant development along the warm flank (equatorward side) of the strongest upper flow, illustrated at the 5 km. level in fig. 1, and produces elongated anticyclones or a belt of anticyclones there. Low pressure is correspondingly produced by the dynamical effects prevailing along the cold (poleward) side of the main flow. The strongest upper flow at any given moment is represented by great concentrations of high wind speeds in 'jet streams' in parts of the strong wind belt, called 'frontal zones', where the temperature contrast is particularly strong. Speeds of 100–150 knots are fairly commonplace at heights of 5–10 km. in winter, and 200 knots is sometimes exceeded at

1. The reason why emphasis has only lately been switched to the upper air is that not enough was known of the upper winds before the invention of the radiosonde—an automatic instrument with a radio transmitter carried by balloon. This instrument, which has only come into general use since 1940–45, has made it possible for the first time to carry out regular observations of pressure, temperature, humidity and wind up to great heights several times a day in all weathers. (An interesting, short historical review of progress towards understanding the general wind circulation was given by Sir Graham Sutton, entitled 'Theories of the Circulation of the Earth's Atmosphere', in the 1960 Halley Lecture at Oxford and published in *The Observatory*, Vol. 80, No. 918, pp. 169–190, London (Royal Greenwich Observatory, Herstmonceux), October 1960.)

10–12 km., in the core of the jet stream. The accelerations of the air on entering and decelerations on leaving jet streams are considerable. A reverse distribution of surface pressure developments, with high (anti-cyclonic) to the poleward side and low (cyclonic) development to the equatorward side, tends to appear over limited sectors of the hemisphere, in the neighbourhood of the acceleration at the confluences to the strongest parts of the windstream aloft.[1] Figs. 2(a) and 2(b) give the average pressure distribution in January and July respectively over the northern hemisphere for nearly the same group of years as the upper maps in fig. 1. If we examine and compare figs. 1(a) and 2(a), 1(b) and 2(b), we shall see that the developments described in this paragraph explain the main features of the prevailing pattern of surface pressure and winds over the hemisphere.

We may distinguish the following principal features of the pressure field:

(1) a **sub-tropical belt of high pressure,** divided into separate anticyclone cells over the oceans (and over central Asia in winter).

(2) a **sub-Arctic belt of low pressure,** which is also most marked over the oceans in winter, though in summer the regions of lowest pressure are more generally over the land.

(3) in summer the continent of Asia is dominated by the **monsoon low pressure** centred near 30° N. This is actually part—a displaced and invigorated part—of the **equatorial low pressure zone,** which is also present in winter, though farther south. Over the oceans the equatorial low pressure zone is known as the **Doldrums** belt, the winds being light except in thunder squalls.

(4) a region of **rather high average pressure near the Pole,** and some extensions of this over regions of cold surface, especially over the northern parts of the continents in winter. These extensions sometimes occur as separate anticyclones right in the sub-polar zone of prevailing low pressure, where they are known as '**blocking anticyclones**'. Their development is related to the confluent parts of the pattern of jet streams aloft, in the manner mentioned above. Besides the regions of relatively high average pressure over Canada and Siberia in the zone near 60° N, seen on figs. 2(a)

---

1. Departures from balanced flow of the upper winds in the senses required to produce the surface pressure developments here described have been established over Britain and Germany respectively by R. Murray and S. M. Daniels in 'Transverse flow at entrance and exit to jet streams', *Quarterly Journal of the Royal Meteorological Society*, Vol. 79, pp. 236–241, published London 1953, and I. Reinecke in 'Untersuchungen über die Abweichungen vom Gradientwind in der oberen Troposphäre', *Abhandlungen in Meteorologie und Geophysik, Nr. 1, Inst. für Met. der Freien Universität Berlin*, published 1950.

(a) January.

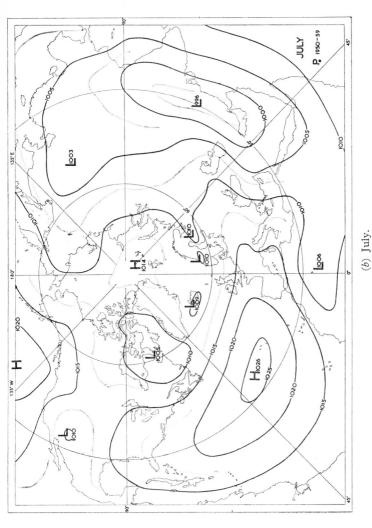

FIGURE 2. Pressure distribution at sea level, average isobars (pressures in millibars) for 1950–59.

(b) July.

and 2(*b*), blocking anticyclones are quite common over Greenland, Iceland and Scandinavia. They bring about a reversal of the prevailing winds, and a change of general weather character, that is a very striking feature of the climate of the temperate zone, including this country. We shall return to this topic.

Corresponding to the general pattern of barometric pressure prevailing over the hemisphere, as described, the surface winds are very largely organized in latitude belts over which either west winds or east winds prevail. The world wind distribution is shown in very much simplified form in fig. 3, the main features being the same in both hemispheres. Actually the idealized wind pattern in fig. 3 is closer to reality in the southern hemisphere because of its simpler geography. We recognize the following principal wind belts:

(i) the **Trade Winds,** mostly NE winds in the northern hemisphere, prevailing between the subtropical anticyclones and the Equator.
(ii) the **Westerlies** prevailing in middle latitudes, between the anticyclones near 30° N (or S) and the depressions near 60° N (or S). Because of the effects of the travelling depressions the westerlies are more variable in direction and speed than the Trades. The whole of Britain lies in the zone of prevailing westerlies.
(iii) in higher latitudes, between the main depression belt and the Pole, rather variable though generally easterly winds are found. These are sometimes called the **Polar Easterlies.**

Surface winds register the effects of friction exerted on the air by the roughness of hills, buildings, trees and sea waves, etc. Friction upsets the balance of forces under which the free air generally moves. When the wind is slowed down, the pressure gradient force overweighs the centrifugal and other forces associated with the air's motion. In consequence, the surface winds blow more or less across the isobars from high towards low pressure. This means that in the northern hemisphere the prevailing surface winds are from SW or WSW rather than W and from NE or ENE rather than E. This effect is taken account of in fig. 3, which should be compared with the rather less simple average pressure patterns in figs. 2(*a*) and (*b*).

The change-over of the Indian monsoon winds from NE in winter to SW in summer can be understood as due to the seasonal movement of the equatorial low pressure belt (and wind convergence zone). In summer this becomes situated so far north over India—its axis is near 30° N in July—that it takes on the nature of a northern hemisphere depression with SW winds prevailing on the side nearer the Equator.

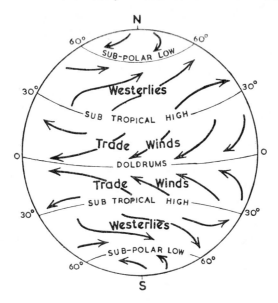

FIGURE 3. General pattern of surface Pressure and
Winds over the Earth.

A similar change-over of the prevailing winds takes place in the latitude
of the British Isles whenever a 'blocking anticyclone' develops in the
subpolar depression belt in this sector. At such times instead of the more
usual SW winds easterly winds prevail. The radically different character
of the accompanying weather is partly due to the fact that the winds
reaching this country then have come over continental tracks instead of the
more usual long tracks over the ocean. The abnormal situation may last
anything from a few days to several weeks. Our usual oceanic climate is
exchanged during that time for a much more continental one.

The role of the ocean

To understand the differences of climate between the continents and
oceans we must consider several more factors. The sea's response to energy
falling on it from the sun is different in a number of ways from the response of dry land. The sea surface reflects (and thereby wastes) a rather
higher percentage of the solar beam at the lower angles of incidence than
do most land surfaces except those covered by snow and ice. But the sea
surface also heats and cools much more slowly than dry land for other
reasons: the incoming radiation penetrates to some depth; wave action,

conduction and convection in the water, besides, ensure that any changes of heat content are spread through a deep layer of the water, which moreover has a great specific heat. This all means that, even under the calmest and most favourable conditions, the sea water surface hardly ever warms up by more than 1 to 2° C in the course of a long summer's day in our own latitude, whereas a dry rock or sand surface may change its temperature by 30° C or more from night to day. The greatest seasonal changes from winter to summer in the surface temperature of the Atlantic Ocean and of the ground in central Asia in 50 to 60° N are in about the same proportion.

The sea strongly influences the temperature of the winds passing over it, which rapidly approach the temperature of the sea surface. The vast store of heat in the ocean, and even in partly enclosed seas like the North Sea and the Baltic, ensures that cold air is heated quickly, sea water chilled in the process sinking and being soon replaced by less cold and less dense water from below the surface. In typical cases of cold winds in January reaching the coasts of Britain with temperatures near the freezing point, the air is warmed up 10–12° C in the course of a 24-hour passage from Iceland and 5–7° C in a 12-hour crossing of the North Sea from Denmark to southern Scotland: the latter figure may even be attained during the shorter crossings of the southern North Sea between Holland and East Anglia when the winds are light. Owing to convection this warming is characteristically spread through the lower atmosphere up to heights of 3–6 km. (10,000–20,000 feet) or more. Cold winds which reach us after still longer trajectories over the ocean, for instance from Canada, however cold their origin, normally arrive with temperatures only 2° C or so below that of the sea surface underlying the latter part of their journey. The effect upon winds that are warmer than the sea is rather different. Chilling of the air from underneath inhibits convection, so the cooling directly attributable to the sea tends to be concentrated in the bottom kilometre or so (3,000–5,000 feet): hence the temperature of warm air over the sea approaches that of the sea surface very quickly. Warm air from the Azores region of the North Atlantic usually comes in on our southwest coasts with temperatures close to that of the sea surface in summer or winter. 11–14° C (52–57° F) is typical in winter. The same thing happens with warm continental air crossing the North Sea; this is liable to produce air temperatures on the coast of Scotland as low as 9–12° C (48–54° F) in June and 13–16° C in August (55–61° F) in air which was causing a heat wave (25–30° C) in Germany. These situations commonly bring sea fog in the Channel or North Sea respectively, known as 'sea-fret' in Cornwall and 'haar' on the east coasts of Scotland and England. At other times low cloud prevails instead of fog, though in the warmer seasons of the year there is always a tendency for sunshine to break the cloud, as the ground heats the air and temperature rises, inland.

One may summarize these effects by saying that the seas around our shores effectively spare us the extremes of temperature to which continental places in this latitude are exposed.

The ocean plays another role quite as important as its property of assimilating the temperature of the air over the water to its own temperature. It also transports heat from lower latitudes. In all these things the action of wind upon the ocean is involved as well as the effects of the ocean upon the wind. The great wind circulation, generated over both hemispheres in the way we have discussed, exerts a drag upon the sea surface, especially where the winds are strong enough to make the sea rough. The upper layers of the ocean are therefore impelled to move with the wind. The effect of the rotating Earth would be to slew the direction of the water motion off to the right (in the northern hemisphere) of the wind force impelling it; but this produces a tendency for the water to pile up in the central regions of anticyclones, and this slight 'head' of water is enough to check the deviation of more water towards the same region. The outcome is that the world's great ocean currents are set up, moving nearly everywhere in the same direction as the usual winds but at speeds of the order of 10 miles a day—or a fiftieth to a hundredth of the prevailing speeds of the winds. The most rapid movement is that of the water near the surface, but the deeper water is carried along in the same general direction down to probably several hundred fathoms, involving enormous masses of water. In this way, a great store of heat is moved towards higher latitudes in the North Atlantic and the North Pacific. It so happens that the configuration of the coasts on the western sides of these ocean basins helps to guide the currents into a northward course to an extent that does not happen in the southern hemisphere. This is particularly important in the Atlantic. The 'nose' of Brazil near 5° S actually splits the westward-moving Equatorial Current (that is driven by the Trade Winds of both hemispheres) and diverts some southern hemisphere water to the north: thus most of the Equatorial Current in the Atlantic is headed into the Gulf of Mexico, from which it emerges as the powerful Gulf Stream.

Fig. 4 maps the Gulf Stream and illustrates the process just described. The strength of the stream emerging through the Florida Strait into the North Atlantic, some 50–70 miles a day, is partly attributable to the head of water built up in the Gulf of Mexico. Sea level on the west coast of Florida is about $7\frac{1}{2}$ inches higher than on the Atlantic side of the peninsula. But once out in the open Atlantic this warm water is carried forward in a general northeasterly direction by the winds. At this stage it is known as the North Atlantic Drift. The integrated effect of the winds over the ocean and over longish periods of time seems to be involved: it produces the highest water velocities near the western side of the ocean and near the boundary of the warm water current all along the fringe of the cold water of Arctic origin. In these areas movements of about 20 miles a day are common. There are many eddies and swirls, caused partly by variations of the winds from day to day, but particularly pronounced where the warm

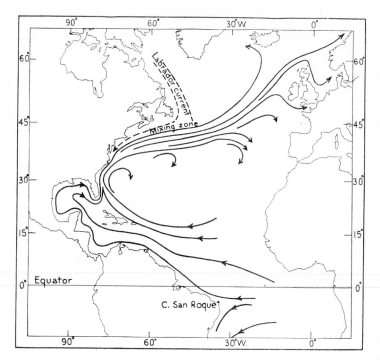

FIGURE 4. The Gulf Stream and North Atlantic Drift currents.

current impinges sharply on the cold Labrador Current and interaction occurs due to the sharp differences of water density. Differences in the strength or prevalence of the SW winds from year to year, or decade to decade, also appear to cause quite important variations in the strength and course of the warm North Atlantic Drift. But ultimately some of it reaches our shores, as well as the coasts of Iceland and Norway, whilst its farthest branch heads towards Spitsbergen and the Barents Sea, sinks beneath the less saline ice-bearing waters and spreads right across the Arctic basin at levels below about a hundred fathoms. In 1941 traces of this water were found beyond the Pole at 80° N 174° W with temperatures above 0° C in depths between 250 and 900 metres below the pack-ice.

The ocean currents in the North Atlantic alone convey about 7% of the total heat that is carried across the parallel of 55° N from lower latitudes. The effect is most pronounced in the northeastern parts of the North Atlantic, where the climate over and near the waters of Gulf Stream origin is much warmer than the average for the same latitude. The coast of Co. Kerry, in southwest Ireland, and of Cornwall, with a mean annual air temperature of 11° C (52° F), is about 6° C warmer than the average for 52° N, and about $7\frac{1}{2}°$ C above the average for 52° S where there are no such favourable water currents and no extensive land surfaces to heat the air. (The climate of the Falkland Islands in 52° S is similar to that of the Faeroes in 62° N.)

Fig. 5 illustrates how the average annual temperatures of places in the latitude of England depends on the proximity of the oceans to the west.

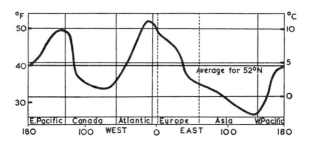

FIGURE 5. Variation of Average Temperature for the year round the Earth in 52° N.

Broken lines on the figure indicate the positions of the southern North Sea which divides Britain from the continent and the longitude of the Urals which conventionally mark off Europe from Asia. Both the Pacific and the Atlantic Oceans show the same effect in only slightly differing degrees. The climates are warm for the latitude over their eastern halves towards which the warm water currents, as well as the prevailing winds, are directed. The western halves of the oceans are chilled by cold winds off the continents. The difference of many degrees between the average temperatures of the eastern and western parts of both continents and oceans is clearly due to the prevailing westerly winds in these latitudes.

The warmth of the climates of countries in 50–60° N near the eastern shores of the great oceans is untypical of the latitude. Fig. 5 shows that this warmth penetrates farther east across Europe than over North America. This is because the mountain wall of the Rockies is a very effective barrier to invading warm air from the west in winter. In Europe an equally sharp west to east climatic gradient from oceanic to continental climates exists only in the mountains of Scandinavia and the Balkans, though fig. 5 indicates that even the Pennines and the mountains of Scotland, Wales and Ireland are not without a similar effect. We shall see that not only in terms of temperature, but in many other ways, such as relative freedom from extreme winds, our eastern lowlands are already distinctly more continental in climate than western districts of the British Isles. In looking at fig. 5 it is well to remember that it is not only higher average yearly temperatures which distinguish the more oceanic climates. In central Canada, and still more in Siberia, the average temperature for the year has little meaning; for while the summer is hot, the winter is long and intensely cold. Irkutsk at 52° N in Siberia has the same average July temperature (18° C) as London, but its average for January is $-20°$ C and in a normal year there is snow lying for five months or more. Even at Berlin, in much the same latitude and at a height corresponding to that of Hampstead, snow lies for about 40 days in most winters. There is a change in the same sense in the frequency of snow cover between Cornwall (2–3 days a year generally) and Cambridge (average 11 days in the 1950s) and between the Hebrides (under 5 days in Barra) and Perth (15 days). In the Hebrides and much of the Atlantic fringe of our islands the seasonal range is so modest that a bad day of wind and rain in July may produce identical temperatures, and a similar scene except for leaves and flowers, to the mildest days of drizzle and rain from grey skies in January. A little reflection on this point may make us thankful for the variations that keep our weather interesting, yet never as severe in summer or winter as those parts of Illinois and Kazakhstan in 41–46° N which have about the same annual mean temperatures as England.

3

Weather Systems

WHAT we are really concerned with here is the nature of the flow of the wind, its structure in terms of airstreams and their convergence, turbulence, convection cells, and eddies of all sizes. In the course of this motion our weather is produced.

Wind flow revealed by tracers

Whoever has watched the smoke from a bonfire on a windy day knows something of the shape of turbulent flow. He has seen the wind pour over bushes and bigger obstacles, has watched parts of the smoke trail caught up into the higher air and parts torn asunder by some fresh obstacle beneath; he may have seen how plunging, forward thrusts of the air go with gusts, and noticed the smoke near the ground stealing back the 'wrong way', or at least being overtaken by the smoke above in a sort of rolling forward motion, during lulls. On calmer days it is easy to see how the smoke (and air heated by the fire) rises into the layers overhead, owing to the difference of density between the heated air and its surroundings. Larger smoke sources enable us to track the air over greater distances. The writer once had the opportunity to fly over the great trail of smoky air from Glasgow right through the Lowlands, out over Fifeshire and the Firth of Forth to the North Sea, where it was caught into the sea breezes of the east coast of Scotland and blown ashore again as a thick haze—of mysterious origin to the local inhabitants—between Montrose and Aberdeen; it went on farther inland, till it was dispersed upwards over the Grampians, rising with the upslope breezes of a warm summer's day.

The minute droplets of which clouds are formed also travel with the wind; they have such negligible rates of fall through the air that they too reveal its motion. The cloud particles moving against a mountainside and over a precipice repeat, on a larger scale, the behaviour of the bonfire smoke blown over small obstacles. But cloud motions sometimes show us great rising columns of air when convection is vigorous, as in shower or thunder clouds, moving almost vertically upwards at speeds up to five to ten times the speed of a fast lift. The spacing (horizontal distance) between neighbouring cloud columns, or convection cells, generally increases with the vertical scale of the convection and may be anything from a mile or two to 50 or 100 miles. The tops of the biggest thunder clouds may be as much as eight to ten miles high. Other clouds reveal a long succession of waves or ripples in the path of the wind.

There are other 'tracers', too, which enable us to follow the wind in its progress through the very largest scale circulation features which encompass the entire hemisphere, and sometimes the whole world. In September 1950 a great pall of smoke from Northwest Canadian forest fires reached heights at which it was carried around the ridges and troughs in the upper westerlies right across the Atlantic and Europe, where both sun and moon appeared pale and bluish-white in colour. There are many cases on record where ash from volcanic eruptions has revealed the course of the upper winds, the moderate-sized particles falling out as a noticeable deposit far from the point of origin and the finest ones spreading around the Earth as a thin veil at heights up to 30 km. in the stratosphere, where it may persist for a year or two. Our very first knowledge of the winds at such high levels was gained in this way. It is interesting that dust-veils from eruptions in Iceland seem never to have been observed farther south than Syria, whereas dust from volcanoes in the equatorial belt is known to have spread over the whole world. There is a suggestion in this that in the upper atmosphere, in addition to the main easterly and westerly flow, there is a slower net transport of air towards the Poles. In the last few years we have had evidence of similar behaviour from nuclear fission products, 'injected' into the high atmosphere by bomb tests. This new material is another 'tracer' of atmospheric motion. Yet another is the ozone produced at heights of 15–50 km. in the stratosphere by the sun's ultraviolet rays.

The meteorologist has had to invent still further methods of tracing the wind flow, in the horizontal and the vertical plane, to give continuous coverage and complete the picture. This is done by calculating quantities derived from temperature and humidity measurements which specify the temperature that any unit of air would have if brought down to a standard pressure level (pressure 1,000 millibars) near the ground. Quantities of this kind keep a constant value over long periods while the particular air sample being studied may have moved many hundreds of miles and changed its height above sea level remarkably. Techniques like this, of course, depend upon regular upper air ascents with balloons carrying instruments. Latterly balloons have also been developed which keep to a constant pressure level and can be tracked right round the world.

From all these types of evidence, and from the instantaneous patterns of flow seen by plotting wind observations on a synoptic weather map (see Ch. 12), our knowledge of the wind systems, large and small, that are responsible for our weather has been built up and is being continually improved.

The reader may by now have reached the view that it is surprising that weather can be forecast at all, if it depends so much upon the often erratic and turbulent flow of the wind. Fortunately, the larger wind systems have a good deal of persistence and continuity in their growth and decay. And climate (as distinct from the instantaneous weather) is mostly concerned with large-scale systems, whose 'life-cycle' is rather long and which set the pattern of weather developments for some time. When discussing climate we can afford to take a purely statistical view of the smaller and more evanescent wind systems, considering them in the mass like the eddies in a stream (or the sheep in a flock): it is the behaviour of the stream itself that we wish to look at.

The main flow in the troposphere; waves in the upper westerly windstream

The mainstream of the upper westerlies, as we saw in the last chapter, is kept in being by the permanent thermal gradient from Equator to Pole. This is fundamental, and the upper west wind system is ever present in consequence, though its strength, latitude and degree of distortion (meandering) vary. The main variation is a pretty regular seasonal growth (intensification and broadening) to about mid winter and a weakening from then until May or early June. Chains of lateral waves, or meanders, are set up in the west wind stream by passing over, and partly round the north of, the Rocky Mountains and the great high plateaux of Asia, that lie athwart the path of these winds. We have also seen (Ch. 2) the great 'troughs' and 'ridges' that may be attributed to thermal effects of the coldest and warmest regions in each latitude zone. The effects of disturbance of the direction of the main wind flow by the Rockies and the thermal nature of Arctic Canada, Hudson Bay and the ice-filled channels and straits farther north, generally reinforce one another; so that it is impossible to say that either is pre-eminent in causing the great trough nearly always present in the flow of the upper westerlies over Canada and the train of successive waves downwind from there—over the Atlantic, Europe and northern Asia. When the dynamically controlled wavelength (longitude spacing) of the wide meanderings of the upper westerlies downstream from the Rockies happens to fit the regions of persistent warm and cold surface round the hemisphere, we probably have a very stable arrangement of the large-scale wind flow. This may be the explanation of those long spells of set type of weather, which are well known in this country and elsewhere in the temperate zone—the zone of the upper westerlies. In such cases, the great ridges and troughs in the upper wind flow stay more or less fixed as an 'anchored' pattern. The biggest meanders in the mainstream of the upper westerlies span 20°–40° of latitude. The spell may only break down when the season ends—that is, when neither the changed distribution of solar heating nor the altered energy content of the winds any longer fits the wave-length which was formerly so harmoniously established.

So far, both in this chapter and the last, we have been considering the winds in the 'troposphere', that part of the atmosphere—70–90% of the atmosphere by mass—which receives most of its heat from the Earth's surface and is stirred by air currents (horizontal, slanting upwards or vertical) in frequent communication with the Earth's surface. The upper limit of this region of the atmosphere, at a normal height of 10–20 km. over the Poles and 17 or 18 km. over the Equator, is called the 'tropopause'. Above the realm of the troposphere and its massive wind streams there is the stratosphere, which develops its own independent circulation—also a hemisphere-wide system—at heights of 20–25 km. and above, involving up to 10% of the mass of the atmosphere. The stratosphere develops an independent circulation because it has its own heat source—the atmospheric ozone that is formed at heights between 15 and 50 km., absorbing all the solar radiation of certain wave-lengths, 7% of the total energy of the incoming beam.

The flow of the stratosphere

As in the case of the lower atmosphere, the winds in the stratosphere in winter circulate around a cold polar region: the cold core is the unheated region of winter darkness, the long polar night, and the strong westerly winds that blow around this at heights of 25 km. and above are known as the 'polar night jet stream'. In summer, the sun heating of the ozone in the stratosphere is actually strongest over the Pole, where it is continuous. This makes the Pole the warmest place at those heights at that season, and accordingly we find easterly winds all over the hemisphere circulating around a warm polar core—quite unlike the situation in the lower atmosphere, where the unmelted ice and snow reflect away much of the solar radiation and, with the cold sea, keep the air cold.

The winter wind pattern in the stratosphere, with its strong winds more or less in line with (and possibly reinforcing the energy of) the main westerlies in the troposphere, commonly breaks down abruptly towards the end of the winter: something like the summer pattern with a warm stratosphere and winds unlike those below quickly emerges. It is uncertain as yet whether, or how much, this circulation in the stratosphere affects the lower atmosphere. There is reason, however, in the theory which suggests that when the stratosphere is warm, it tends to grow (or extend) down to rather lower levels: this, and the easterly winds developed at the same time at high levels, may act as something of a check upon the scale of the largest possible developments in the lower atmosphere. Paradoxically, this should mean that early break-down of the winter westerlies in the stratosphere (as occasionally occurs in mid winter) should tend to weaken the circulation in the lower atmosphere, thereby possibly favouring the development of severer winter cold in temperate and polar lands, though later also favouring the gentler circulation patterns of spring. E. Frogner[1] of the Norwegian Meteorological Institute has produced some evidence that the stratospheric events here discussed really do sometimes influence developments in the lower atmosphere in the manner mooted.

Travelling weather systems

After the great circumpolar vortex of upper westerly winds embracing the entire hemisphere, and the long waves or meanders in this flow—usually only three to five waves around the hemisphere—the next biggest atmospheric circulations are the anticyclones (high pressure regions) and depressions (low pressure regions), familiar on the surface weather map. Examples of both are shown in the maps in Ch. 12. A stable anticyclone, such as the systems commonly occupying the Azores region of the North Atlantic, is characteristically 2,000–3,000 km. (say, 1,200–2,000 miles) or rather more in length along its major axis. The individual centre (or 'cell') has a 'life' of just four to five days in most cases, but is commonly renewed or rejuvenated by the incursion of a fresh airmass of cold origin for another period of days not far from the same position. The larger depressions on the North Atlantic are typically 1,500–2,000 km. (say, 1,000–1,500 miles) in diameter. The normal life cycle is only two to three days from the first small beginnings as a fast-travelling disturbance to the decay stage of a slow-moving large depression. But the major centres of low pressure are commonly 'fed' with cyclonic vorticity, and repeatedly rejuvenated, by younger secondary depressions following similar paths to the earlier members of the same depression series (or 'family') and running into the stagnating primary centre, which they have overtaken.

Speeds of a thousand miles a day (about 40 knots) are fairly typical for travelling disturbances, which means that it is rather common for one to pass in a day. If they happen to come in close succession, places in their path experience similar weather on successive days. This is the explanation of some rhythmic sequences that may be noticed in bad weather, with wind and rain occupying roughly the same hours of successive days or nights, separated by clear spells measured in hours or half a day. Sometimes it is the days, sometimes the nights which get all the fine weather

1. Frogner, E., 'Temperature changes on a large scale in the arctic winter stratosphere and their probable effects on the tropospheric circulation', *Norske Videnskaps-Akademi, Geofysiske Publikasjoner*, Vol. XXIII, No. 5, Oslo, 1962.

in these sequences. With slower speeds of travel slower rhythms may be noted within a similar repeating pattern, giving a sequence of storms every second or third day. The periodic rejuvenations of the anticyclones in times of good weather may also give rise to noticeable repeating patterns, such as a tendency for thundery disturbances or threatening sky every four to five days. Alternating influence of anticyclones and depressions in the same sequence is apparently involved in a seven-day rhythm, which occasionally impresses both meteorologists and laymen and has received some scientific study. Housewives have often been aggrieved by periods of weeks at a time when it rains every Monday and spoils the washing, though the weekend has been fine; the contrary case upsets still more people! All through the severe frost of February 1956 a slight thaw came with a northwest wind each weekend. But none of these repeating cycles ever seems to persist for more than a few weeks at most. Then the prevailing position of the controlling features—the major thermal pattern and upper wind flow—shifts, and the sequences of low and high pressure systems generated at the surface no longer affect the same places as before.

As explained in Ch. 2, the shifts of mass which produce anticyclones and depressions at the surface occur where the air in the main windstream aloft gets out of balance with the forces acting upon it. This occurs particularly near points of sharp curvature of the upper windstream, near upper troughs and ridges, and where the speed of the flow changes rapidly, at the entrance and exits to the strongest parts of the flow, known as 'jet streams'.[1] In the region of acceleration of the upper winds at the entrance to the jet stream, cyclogenesis (surface pressure fall) occurs at the warm (lower latitude) side of the mainstream of upper westerlies, anticyclogenesis (surface pressure rise) at the cold (high latitude) side. In most other places there is anticyclonic development at the warm side and cyclonic development at the cold side of the jet stream. Both high and low pressure systems usually develop a somewhat elongated form, with their major axis roughly parallel with the main current of upper winds.

The jet stream and the polar front

The upper circulation has been explained as basically a thermal wind system, strongest where the thermal gradients are strongest. The jet stream is therefore associated with a concentration of temperate gradient across the stream. Now, at the surface, friction causes the winds always

1. Readers who wish to know more about the principles of location of anticyclonic and cyclonic development should consult R. C. Sutcliffe and A. G. Forsdyke: 'The theory and use of upper air thickness patterns in forecasting', *Quarterly Journal of the Royal Meteorological Society*, Vol. 76, pp. 189–217, London, 1950.

to blow somewhat across the isobars towards the low-pressure side, so that there is general convergence of the surface winds in regions of low pressure and cyclonically curved isobars. Hence, the subpolar low-pressure region, and the cyclonic disturbances formed near the jet stream, are regions where the temperature contrasts between the air on either side are subjected to sharpening by the general convergence of the surface winds bringing the unlike windstreams closer together. Some configurations of the isobars which arise between depressions and anticyclones ('frontogenetic cols') appear to be particularly favourable for sharpening the thermal gradient by drawing surface air from widely separated regions together along a line.[1] At the surface therefore a sharp 'front' develops at the line between airstreams of unlike character.

Viewed in three dimensions a front consists of a wedge of colder, denser air always tending to cut in, spread and flatten out under the less dense, warmer air. Slopes from one in fifty to one in five hundred are typical for frontal surfaces, which normally become less sharply defined with increasing height. The steepest slopes occur in cyclonic situations where the cold air is thrusting vigorously forward ('cold fronts'): the general convergence of the surface winds in a depression requires a compensating upward motion that hinders the cold air flattening out. The flattest frontal surfaces occur in anticyclonic situations, where there is divergence of the surface winds compensated by general downward motion. The cold air is then quiescent (as regards convection within it), and may be undergoing modification (heating) in the sunshine. The cold air is also quiescent, and the frontal surface shelving at low angles, at those points where the warm air is advancing ('warm fronts') and overrunning the upper surface of the retreating cold air.

The northern temperate zone is the meeting place of surface airstreams from the Arctic and tropical zones, which have respectively emerged some days previously from the polar and sub-tropical high-pressure regions. The front at which these airstreams meet is commonly called the Polar Front. The name was given in 1917 by Norwegian meteorologists at Bergen under the leadership of Prof. Vilhelm Bjerknes, who first discovered the front and the way it is involved in the formation of cyclones (or depressions, as they are now more often called). The front is a line of interaction between the two airmasses leading to the growth of frequent disturbances. Hence, the name 'front' suggested itself by analogy with the battle fronts of the first world war, then in progress.

1. For a simple presentation of the formation and life-history of fronts the reader is recommended to consult a series of three articles by the writer, in the *Meteorological Magazine*: H. H. Lamb, 'Essay on Frontogenesis and Frontolysis', *Met. Mag.*, London, **80**, 1951, pp. 35–46, 65–71 and 97–106.

Frontal waves and depression development

The first signs of cyclonic development at the surface are the appearance of a small wave in the line of the front and a corresponding bulge in the cloudsheets in the warmer airstream overlying the wedge of cold air. The succeeding stages in the development of the cyclonic circulation are illustrated in fig. 6. The wave begins as a slight northward bulge of the warmer airmass with the cold air present before it and after it. Initially the cold air may be moving either from an easterly point as shown in the figure or from the west, if it has already travelled round a major ('parent') depression to the north of the point of wave development; the new frontal wave in the latter case represents the first appearance of a secondary depression. The surface winds around the wave soon develop a cyclonic rotation (fig. 6(b)), and all the time the denser cold air is tending to under-cut the warm air incursion, whilst the latter (owing to its lesser density) spreads over the cold air around the developing frontal wave aloft. While this goes on the winds gain kinetic energy, as the centre of gravity of the system falls. At the same time the bulge of warm air, the so-called 'warm sector' of the developing depression, narrows into a tongue (fig. 6(c)) and goes on narrowing until the warm air is lifted entirely off the ground (or 'occluded' from the surface). This process called 'occlusion' is seen completed in fig. 6(d). About this stage most depressions have their maximum vigour and begin to decay. The successive stages in the life cycle of the storm do not take place at a fixed point; the whole system is being carried along, usually eastwards or northeastwards by the main-stream of the upper winds.

Frontal waves grow in regions determined as cyclogenetic (i.e. liable to depression development) by the pattern of upper flow. Waves commonly appear just where the surface winds circulating round the main anti-cyclone in the warm air are directed against the advancing cold front. Resistance to the advancing cold air is greatest there and probably varies with a slight diurnal or semi-diurnal (24- or 12-hourly) rhythm in the strength of the anticyclone, tending to initiate waves at periodic intervals. Waves also form where mountain barriers distort the windstreams suffi-ciently. But no such initiating mechanism will lead to cyclonic develop-ment unless the general situation favours cyclogenesis, as for instance to the right of a jet stream entrance aloft or just east of a marked upper cold trough, and is also suitable as regards spacing from other growing features. Neighbouring waves along a front can hardly grow unless they are at least 1,200 miles apart.[1] This imposes a time interval of the order of a day or

1. Criteria for the formation of new waves on fronts are to be found in the report of a Meteorological Office Discussion opened by J. S. Sawyer, *Met. Mag.*, London, Vol. 79, 1950, pp. 146–149.

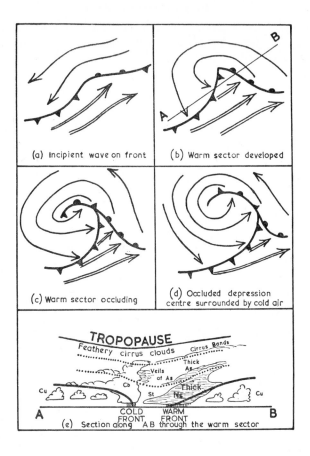

(a) Incipient wave on front

(b) Warm sector developed

(c) Warm sector occluding

(d) Occluded depression centre surrounded by cold air

(e) Section along A B through the warm sector

Key to symbols:

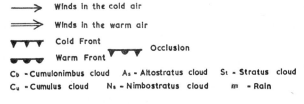

→ Winds in the cold air

⟹ Winds in the warm air

▼▼▼ Cold Front

●●● Warm Front

▼●▼● Occlusion

C_b = Cumulonimbus cloud   A_s = Altostratus cloud   S_t = Stratus cloud

C_u = Cumulus cloud   N_s = Nimbostratus cloud   ⫶⫶⫶ = Rain

FIGURE 6. The life history of a frontal Depression.

more between the formation of successive waves of any importance. A factor notably favouring cyclonic development is the energy available wherever a cold airstream suddenly comes over warm sea. This is important over the Gulf Stream waters of the North Atlantic and in the Mediterranean in winter, though the most striking examples appear to be in the Gulf of Alaska.

As the developing waves are carried along with the strongest winds in the jet stream aloft, the commonest paths of low-pressure centres ('depression tracks') on the surface weather map follow rather closely the line of the mainstream of the upper winds. This is why depressions crossing the Atlantic towards Europe most frequently follow the line (northeast or eastnortheastwards from the American coast near Newfoundland) indicated by the closest spaced contours in figs. 1(a) and 1(b). The next commonest routes for depressions near the British Isles are from about northwest to southeast, following the line of the upper flow east of the ridge whose average January position is clearly indicated in fig. 1(a).

Although the frontal wave is a smaller-scale phenomenon than the great meanders in the flow of the upper westerlies, the winds circulating around a vigorous depression or anticyclone in the lower atmosphere do sometimes transport so much warm air north and cold air south that the temperature pattern of the hemisphere is considerably distorted. This distortion then diverts the flow of the upper winds and changes the steering of the depression or anticyclone in question, which usually becomes slow moving in such cases. If it happens that the sweep of warm or cold air involved comes over a suitable region (e.g. warm sea or land which becomes and readily remains snow-covered), the change of thermal pattern may persist. With this goes a new disposition of places favouring high or low pressure, and corresponding new depression paths, so that a lasting change in the prevailing weather pattern results.

Some idea of the stages of development of a normal frontal depression and the distribution of clouds and weather[1] can be gathered from fig. 6, especially from the cross section through the warm sector and both fronts which appears as fig. 6(e). The warm air advancing and sliding up the frontal surface (thick line in the section) reaches cloud level, its temperature having fallen owing to the reduction of pressure; its moisture is condensed as cloud, which forms a deep, extensive layer up to 200–400 miles ahead of the front, as the warm air spreads gradually higher over the

1. Studies of the cloud structure near fronts and within a depression have been given by M. H. Freeman in 'Fronts investigated by the Meteorological Research Flight', *Met. Mag.*, **90**, 1961, pp. 189–203, and by J. S. Sawyer in 'The free atmosphere in the vicinity of fronts', *Geophysical Memoirs*, **12**, No. 96, London (Meteorological Office), 1955.

cold air wedge below. Rain or snow falls as the front approaches. At the cold front, the 'nose' of the advancing cold air has a more abrupt slope, occasionally even overhanging slightly, becoming unstable and collapsing at the tip; all this results in generally stronger convergence of the airstreams than at the warm front, and over the line of the surface cold front the warm air is commonly induced to rise in great cloud-filled columns almost vertically. Heavy rain sometimes results from the abundant and rapid condensation of moisture in the vertical air current. A recent study by M. K. Miles[1] indicates that fast-moving rather warm dry air aloft overtaking and descending over the oncoming surface cold airmass commonly brings an abrupt clearance and cessation of the rain behind the cold front cloud wall. Other points where cloud formation is common are seen in fig. 6(e). Since there is a general tendency for convergence and uplift in the progressively shrinking warm sector, the air in it also tends to slide upwards along any minor discontinuity surfaces aloft, as illustrated by the dotted lines in fig. 6(e). These are sometimes old, minor fronts. Further cloud layers develop at them, though usually thinner than the main layer. The other clouds depicted are due to convection, turbulence and the moistening of other air layers by falling rain or snow.

Anticyclones and anticyclonic weather

In anticyclones fronts are much less noticeable than in depressions. Perhaps for this reason, there has been much less attention devoted to fronts in connexion with anticyclonic than with cyclonic development. The airmass movements (uplifted warm air, undercutting cold air) characteristic of fronts make no positive contribution to the energy of an anticyclone; the tendency (often quite noticeably) is the other way, so that a front which happens to find itself in the middle of a big anticyclone remains discernible as a narrow zone of disturbance, anything from fifty to two hundred miles in width, the sky often overcast with somewhat inactive cloud, sometimes with drizzle or occasional light rain. Often, however, all that marks a front in an anticyclonic region is a sharp change in the direction of the light breeze and a perceptible change in the feel of the air—its temperature, humidity and so on. There may be little or no cloud, especially in our longer fine spells. Nevertheless, meteorologists have long been aware that when a weakening anticyclone is rejuvenated, the new centre commonly develops after the passage of a cold front—i.e. within the fresh cold airmass. This applies to high-pressure systems in the Azores region of the North Atlantic as well as to systems over this country

1. M. K. Miles, 'Wind, temperature and humidity distribution at some cold fronts over SE England', *Quarterly Journal of the Royal Meteorological Society*, Vol. 88, pp. 286–300, London, 1962.

or the continent. In summer fine spells it commonly accounts for the familiar sequence of a sultry day or two, becoming increasingly cloudy, followed by a thunderstorm and then a recovery of the fine weather, starting with the air feeling notably cool. It has been suggested by Wexler[1] that the frontal surface aloft, usually in these cases at a height of only a few thousands of feet (1–2 km.), plays an important part indirectly in the anticyclonic development. The air accumulating over a region of rising pressure may be pictured as being ejected from the mainstream of the upper winds, especially about the heights where they are strongest (10 km. or more). The accumulation is not so much dissipated by friction when this development goes on above a smooth surface of airmass change (i.e. a discontinuity surface within the atmosphere) as if it were in direct communication with the ground. The quiescent frontal surface acts as a 'shielding layer'.

It is instructive to consider the prevailing pattern of vertical motion of the air in an anticyclone. This is conveniently illustrated by the shape of the surface of a well-marked front involved in anticyclonic development in the region of southern England and Ireland (see fig. 7). This was a case where a new ridge of high pressure developed strongly northeastwards from the Azores towards our southwest approaches after the passage of a cold front with wave developments upon it. The next depression on the front was 'cut off' and became nearly stationary as a 'cold pool' off Portugal. The map (fig. 7) shows the topography of the frontal surface by bold lines, whilst the lighter surface isobars indicate the positions of the anticyclone and depressions. Frontal topography maps like this are regularly used in some meteorological services, but they must be viewed with an awareness that the frontal surfaces generally become weaker and more diffuse with height, especially where upward motion of the air is occurring. Downward motion, however, makes for sharp surfaces of discontinuity which check convection currents and turbulence rising from the ground—acting rather like an invisible lid or ceiling. The interesting feature of fig. 7 is the way in which the cold air layer becomes shallower in the region of anticyclonic development—not only shallower than it was in its source region to the north, but also by comparison with the other cyclonic region to the south. Details differ from one case to another, but the presence of warm subsided air right down to a shielding layer at no great height appears to be common. The frontal surface has been replaced by a descending 'subsidence surface', though turbulence and convection will not allow this to descend below about three to five thousand feet (1–1·5 km.) except on rare occasions of very still, cold surface weather in winter. Just occasionally in winter

1. See H. Wexler on 'Anticyclones', pp. 621–629 in the *Compendium of Meteorology*, published by the American Meteorological Society, Boston, Mass., 1951.

the ridges of isolated hills, and more particularly the higher mountains, penetrate the very clear, dry, rather warm, subsided air.

We can now understand some characteristic differences between the development of clouds and weather in the anticyclonic and cyclonic regions. There is no cloud in the gently subsiding air in regions of anti-cyclonic development, all the way down from the level of strongest upper

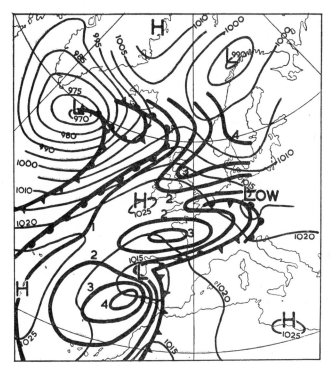

FIGURE 7. Depth of surface cold air during the formation of an Anticyclone over southern Britain.

Bold lines contours of the upper limit of cold air (heights in kilometres). Narrow lines isobars (surface pressure in millibars).

winds (where the development is mainly generated) to the ceiling of the ground turbulence and convection. An absence of cloud in what are known as the middle (or medium) levels between 2–3 and 10–12 km. is therefore characteristic of anticyclonic weather. The discontinuity surface at the base of this may be marked by a visible layer of gathered haze and smoke, checked in its rise from the ground or by an extensive sheet of rather quiescent cloud. This cloud at the top of the surface air layer, which is moister than the air above, is liable to make anticyclonic weather grey or gloomy in winter. The subsiding air above is, however, so dry and so transparent that anyone who has stood in it on the tops of the hills in winter will have had a memorable experience of extreme visibility. By contrast, in the prevailing upward motion in cyclonic regions, clouds, convection and turbulence from the ground are all encouraged to extend upwards.

Whereas a weak cold front and shallow incursion of fresh cold air commonly accompany the renewal of an anticyclone, if deep cold air arrives the case is quite different. The thermal pattern is altered and strengthening upper winds around the advancing cold tongue (or trough in the pressure pattern) are liable to carry the decaying anticyclone away. The deeper the cold air that arrives, the less likely is it that settled anticyclonic weather will return. Convection clouds will be able to develop up to considerable heights, producing an increased likelihood of showers; and the next (warm) frontal system is also likely to be an active producer of clouds and rain, since its cloud systems will be driven to develop up to medium and possibly higher levels. To the keen observer the whole appearance of the sky is seen to have changed after deep cold air has displaced an anticyclone. Cloud development becomes quite frequent in those middle levels (approximately 2–10 km. up) that were persistently clear whilst subsidence was going on; haze usually decreases markedly at, and near, surface level but a thin haziness becomes noticeable higher up. Humidity is also transported upwards. All these changes produce quite different optical effects, especially of sky colour, and make the setting sun paler than before. By such signs as these the practised layman may judge for himself how radical is the change in the weather, and those who know enough of the physics of the atmosphere may reason out in more detail what is going on.

'Cut-off' depressions or cold cyclones

The case of the cut-off depression stagnating as a revolving whirlpool of cold air off Portugal in fig. 7 is of some interest in our own climate. Similar systems are occasionally formed near this country when there is strong anticyclonic development still farther north. The cyclonic region draws in a continued supply of cold air from the neighbouring anticyclone and elsewhere, and deepens this cold air as an effect of the general convergence of surface airstreams in depressions. This situation is capable of maintaining unseasonably cold, miserable weather with massive cloud development up to considerable heights for several days over the region affected.

Tropical cyclones or hurricanes

There is another class of depressions which is an occasional visitor to these islands. Occasionally, over the warmest part of the Atlantic, where the ocean surface is over 27° C and the air correspondingly humid, such massive convection clouds develop over a broad area that the rising air can only be supplied by a system of surface winds rotating and converging spirally inwards from a still wider region of ocean. At first a sluggish whirl, the tropical cyclone is liable to develop into a hurricane. The main cloudbelt, possibly originating at the equatorial (or 'intertropical') convergence between the Trade Winds of both hemispheres at times when this has become displaced more than five degrees of latitude north of the Equator, soon takes the form of a cyclonically (counterclockwise) coiled spiral, leaving a clear space—the 'eye of the storm'—at the centre. These tropical cyclones disrupt the usual monotonous regularity of the Trade Wind zone in the most violent manner. They have a normal 'life' there of three to ten days at most, usually drifting slowly westwards with the upper winds which prevail south of the subtropical high-pressure belt. They are liable to do great damage on the southeastern and southern coasts of North America, but usually soon start to decay over land—owing to friction and loss of the surface moisture supply. If the polar front happens to be near the American Atlantic seaboard, however, the upper winds associated cause the tropical cyclone to turn northwards. It then encounters the front, which the surface winds draw into the circulation of the hurricane. This then acquires a frontal pattern like that of any other depression, derives fresh energy from the juxtaposition of cold and warm air side by side and the sinking and spreading of the cold under the warm. The storm turns further to travel swiftly east or northeast with the jet stream in the temperate zone. This sequence produces some of our deepest depressions and most destructive winds. The great storm which swept across southern England on 6–7 December (New Style) 1703 with a depression centre passing from Wales to Nottingham, and which still ranks as probably the most destructive gale ever reported, was apparently of this type. Another did great damage on the coast of Ireland on 16 September 1961. In both these cases it has been suggested that, by some rare configuration of the wind field, the tropical hurricane centre reached these islands without having fully engaged the polar front—that is, the centre was still within the tropical air: this point, however, appears to have no more than curiosity value, since the encounter with the temperature gradient of the frontal zone is an added source of energy. And some of this energy had doubtless been tapped, at least in the outer parts of the storm circulation in both cases.

Gusts and squalls

This chapter must end by returning to the smaller scale wind systems with which it began, though one of these includes the most violent wind phenomenon of all. We explained 'gusts' and 'lulls' as the fluctuations of strength and direction of the horizontal wind at the ground from minute to minute (or even over a few seconds) caused by friction. The gustiness depends on the scale of the irregularities causing the friction. The ratio $\left(\dfrac{\text{gust speed } minus \text{ lull speed}}{\text{average wind speed}}\right)$ is called the 'gustiness factor'. Winds straight from the sea have a factor of less than a half, which means that in a wind of, say, 20 knots the gusts are about 25 knots and the lulls about 15 knots. Inland, the factor rises to one, so that the difference between gusts and lulls is equal to the average wind itself. In towns with high buildings the factor may even reach two, so that the wind may jump from calm to twice its average speed in a few seconds. This does not mean that gusts are stronger in towns than on the seashore, but that lulls are weaker. Even the gusts are generally weaker inland than on the coast. A 40-knot gale on the open coast might vary in gusts and lulls from 50 to 30 knots. In hilly country some miles inland the range might be from 38 to 12 knots, and in a city from 35 knots to momentary calm. The fluctuations of direction are broadly proportional to those of speed; on the coast a few degrees only, while in a town the wind swings right round the compass.

A 'squall' is an increase of wind speed lasting for several minutes; it may be due to a temporary local concentration of the wind, to the passage of a front or to a downblast which is a feature of violent convection, common in thunderstorms and big shower clouds. It is often accompanied by a rise of the barometer. Squalls commonly consist of a short series of violent gusts and lulls.

The strongest gusts measured by anemometers on standard 33-foot (10 metres) high masts are liable to reach 100 knots (115 m.p.h.) once in ten or twenty years at a number of exposed places around the western and northern coasts of the British Isles from Scilly to Shetland and on bare hill-tops. Fig. 8 shows the instrument record of one of the strongest gusts ever measured by a Meteorological Office anemograph, 101·5 knots on the Hebridean island of Tiree on 26 February 1961. This was the strongest gust in a violent squall accompanying a veer of wind at the passage of the occluded front of an intense depression, the centre of which was passing quite near. Still higher speeds, up to 140–150 knots, have been claimed for measurements by unofficial instruments, particularly on exposed hills at Saxa Vord, Shetland and Grimsetter, Orkney. At the other extreme, in many very sheltered spots, particularly in the more wooded districts

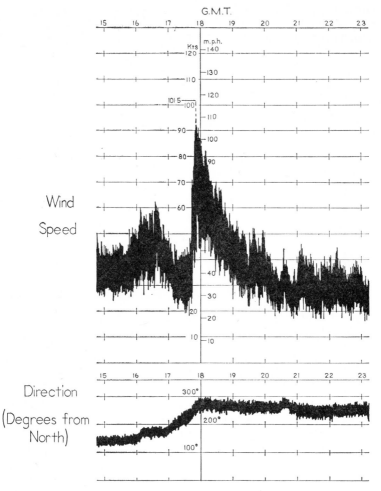

FIGURE 8. Squall at Tiree on 26 February 1961.
(Anemogram—pressure tube anemograph record.)

inland in southeast England, no gust of 100 knots or over may have occurred for several thousand years.

Tornadoes and whirlwinds

Wind speeds as great as this, and even more, may however occur briefly anywhere that is struck by a tornado. These violent whirlwinds are rather rare in this country, but are relatively commonest in the south and south-east, as indicated by the map of tornado trails (fig. 9). Their occurrence is related to thunderstorms (whose frequency distribution is shown in fig. 16), since the essence of the tornado is a violent convection current materially

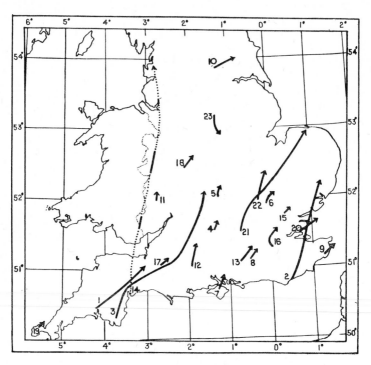

FIGURE 9. Tornado trails in England and Wales.

Key: 1. 31 Oct. 1638   9. 24 Oct. 1878   17. 6 Dec. 1929
     2. 20 May 1729   10. 8 Mar. 1890   18. 15 June 1931
     3. 19 Oct. 1870   11. 26 May 1894   19. 13 Jan. 1934
     4. 25 July 1872   12. 1 Oct. 1899   20. 20 Oct. 1949
     5. 30 Nov. 1872   13. 2 Aug. 1906   21. 21 May 1950
     6. 12 June 1875   14. 27 Oct. 1913   22. 21 May 1950
     7. 28 Sept. 1876   15. 26 Oct. 1916   23. 19 May 1952
     8. 10 Aug. 1877   16. 22 Oct. 1928

stronger than the minimum strength required to produce thunder clouds. A very strong up-current, proceeding from ground level and capable of lifting heavy objects, can only be kept supplied with air by rapid con-vergence of the surface winds organized in a 'corkscrew' twisting motion.

The most unambiguous evidence left by the passage of a tornado is the twisting off at the trunk of the whole tops of trees. The commonness of this type of destruction in cases of tornadoes gives a useful indication of the dimensions of the wind system. The trees are twisted because of the very great difference of wind speed between one side and the other of the crown of a single tree which is caught in a tornado. The central core of the whirl consists of a 'solid' rotation about a centre which moves forward only at the speed of the system, commonly 20–40 knots. (At radius r out from this centre the wind speed v is given by $v = cr$, where c is a constant.) This rotation as a solid continues out to a maximum speed ring whose radius varies from a few feet to a few yards as the tornado progresses, increasing with each new pulse of energy and dwindling as the whirl becomes eroded by friction. The strongest horizontal wind speeds may be as much as 200–300 knots, but are probably only attained over a width of a foot or so. With these dimensions the odds against any particular object ever experiencing tornado damage, even in the districts where the phenomenon is most liable to occur, must be many millions to one. Outside the ring of maximum wind strength speeds fall off fairly rapidly, and at distances of only a quarter of a mile from the path of the centre of the tornado there is usually little damage. At the centre a pressure reduction of several hundred millibars (up to a third of an atmosphere) is suggested by various phenomena in extreme cases. Tornado damage therefore takes several forms: besides lifting and twisting, objects may be battered down by the strength of the wind and buildings (especially windows) may burst open under the reduction of pressure.[1]

Tornadoes are most liable to develop near cold fronts or at places where the relief of the ground imparts a strong shear to the wind. Where considerable differences of horizontal wind speed (and sometimes direction) exist over distances of a mile or less, twisting can easily begin. The arrangement of surface winds needed to start feeding a rapid up-current from the ground can then organize itself. In many cases it is evident that the up-current develops first aloft within the cloud, and where a strong shear of wind exists near a front the twisting may develop within the cloud, which lowers towards the ground with the appearance of a funnel as the atmospheric pressure falls in the narrow core. The tornado may sweep the ground over stretches of a dozen miles or more, progressing in the direction of the upper wind. The heavy preponderance of trails from about south-

1. Two occurrences of tornadoes in England and Wales have been the subject of full scientific reports, which may be consulted for further details: 'The South Wales tornado of October 27, 1913' by H. Billett and 'Tornadoes in England May 21, 1950' by H. H. Lamb, both published in London by Her Majesty's Stationery Office as Meteorological Office *Geophysical Memoirs* (No. 11, 1916 and No. 99, 1957).

west to northeast (fig. 9) corresponds to the prevailing direction of the upper winds in the neighbourhood of cold fronts which are preceded by suitably moist unstable warm air.

Smaller tornadoes, whirlwinds and dust whirls may occur anywhere where there is a sufficiently strong local overheating at the ground. Heated pavements and asphalt favour them. Local eddies of the wind, due to buildings or other obstacles, may start the twisting; friction from other obstacles usually breaks them up. The dust devils of hot countries are of the same nature. A well-organized tornado, however, with a violently twisting column extending either vertically or at a slanting angle up through the heart of a storm cloud is liable to reorganize itself down to ground level again even after the funnel near the ground has been broken up once or more by friction. Severe tornadoes may therefore strike along a trail of several miles, then skip some distance before starting a fresh trail of damage farther along the same line. Rotating cloud pendants may be seen by observers even in the sections skipped over by the tornado without damage, and their tendency to re-form into a single funnel cloud and generate down to ground level again is a danger signal. The safest course for anyone who, despite its rarity, should find himself confronted by a tornado bearing down on him in the open would be to run away to the side, out of the track of the cloud funnel, or to lie flat (thereby offering least resistance to the horizontal wind and most resistance to the vertical lift), preferably in some hollow in the ground, and protect himself against flying debris.[1]

1. There is some interest in the precautions taken to provide tornado shelters in parts of the United States, especially Kansas, where the risk much more frequently presents itself than in England. The safest place is in the southwestern corner of a (specially dug) pit or cave open to the northeast, for there too tornadoes normally approach from the southwest. Modern reinforced concrete buildings appear to be proof against tornado damage, except, of course, for their glass windows. For further details see S. D. Flora, *Tornadoes of the United States*, Oklahoma Univ. Press, 1953.

4

Winds, Warmth and Weather Types

Temperatures near the surface

The favourable climate of these islands, the high average temperature for the latitude and the modest extremes, are largely due to the proximity of the ocean with prevailing southwest winds and warm water currents moving towards our shores. The overall average temperature (normal yearly mean), which reaches 10° C in Valentia, Co. Kerry and the Scilly Isles, is 5–6° C high for the latitude. Farther north on our Atlantic coasts, in the western isles of Scotland, where the average is still as high as 9° C in some places, the excess above the latitude average is 7–8° C; and the Lofoten Islands (68–69° N) off the coast of Norway, which are also in the path of the prevailing southwest winds and surface water of Gulf Stream origin, are nearly 14° C warm for their latitude. This is the greatest excess anywhere in the world. It registers the effect of the ocean integrated over the year. Nevertheless the extreme days of warmth come with light winds that have travelled far—or sojourned long—over sun-heated dry land on the continent, and have had only a short sea crossing to moderate their highest temperatures. This is because dry ground heats up in summer, and cools in winter, much more than the surface of the sea. The record figure in England, 38·1° C (100·5° F), at Tonbridge, Kent on 22 July 1868, was a clear case of this: it occurred in a southerly breeze a little before the cold front that interrupted a succession of heat waves. The temperature of the ground was all the more easily raised because it had become very dry over wide areas of Europe. Because of the more oceanic position the highest air temperatures ever recorded in Scotland and Ireland are lower (about 32–33° C, 90–91° F in both cases).

Combination of the same factors, and the long northern summer day, in southern Norway make Oslo's normal July temperatures (average 18·0° C) comparable with London's (average 17·8° C). The sheltered waters of Oslo fjord, supplied by the warm North Atlantic Drift and further heated by sunbaked rocks, in July and August reach the highest sea temperatures (average 18–19° C) in Europe north of the Mediterranean. The highest average sea temperatures on the British coast in August are nearly as high (about 17° C), occurring where similar factors come into play, on the Lancashire coast, parts of Cardigan Bay and the south-facing coasts of Sussex and Essex. Over more than half the year, however, land surfaces in these latitudes are colder than the sea.

The lowest water temperatures around our coasts are generally produced by winds off the land, which drag the warmer surface water away and cause upwelling of colder water from underneath. This affects the average temperatures off our northeast coasts (averages for February 3–4° C in Moray Firth and the Firths of Tay and Forth), owing to the prevalence of southwesterly winds. Other wind directions may bring unwelcome changes of water temperature on other stretches of coast, including the more usually favoured spots whether here in England or elsewhere. Such variations due to upwelling when the wind blows off the shore are most pronounced where there is a supply of cold water from the deeps or from cold rivers. Unlike the continental side of the North Sea, ice is virtually unknown on the coast of England, though it does occur in estuaries in the severest winters and small amounts have been reported on or near the coasts of Kent and East Anglia, where cold east winds have the shortest sea crossing.

The lowest air temperatures which we ever experience are attributable to radiation cooling of the ground under clear night skies in winter, affecting air that was already cold after pursuing a long track over snow-covered ground. For these reasons, the extreme lowest values ever recorded in light easterly windstreams from the continent reaching low-lying inland districts in central and southern England and the eastern valleys of Wales (about −25 to −27° C) are little different from the reported extremes in Scotland (−27 to −30° C), where the winter nights are longer but the likelihood of receiving continental cold air inappreciably modified by sea passage is far less. Temperatures below −20° C are commoner in Scotland than in England, but they are usually attributable to sharp local cooling of maritime Arctic cold air which has penetrated the sheltered glens and straths of the central and eastern Highlands and stagnated there.

The extra sea crossings ensure that the extreme air temperatures anywhere in Ireland are not quite so low, values below −15° C being exceedingly rare.

In the twelve-year period 1950–61 the numbers of years when the extreme air temperatures in England and Wales, Scotland and the six counties of Northern Ireland reached or surpassed certain levels are given in Table 1.

For most purposes a more practical view of the temperature distribution in different parts of the country is given by the frequencies of conditions beyond certain values that may be regarded as thresholds for this or that. Fig. 10 maps the average frequency of summer days when the air temperature gets above 25° C (77° F). This is an internationally adopted

TABLE 1

Frequencies of certain values for the highest and lowest air temperature
of the year, 1950–61

	≧35° C (95° F)	≧30° C (86° F)	≧25° C (77° F)	≦−10° C (14° F)	≦−15° C (5° F)	≦−20° C (−4° F)	≦−25° C (−13° F)
				Number of years out of twelve			
England and Wales	2	11	12	12	7	1	0
Scotland . .	0	3	12	12	10	4	1
Northern Ireland .	0	0	8	7	1	0	0

standard—perhaps in this latitude one might regard it as a continental standard—of a warm summer day, which is good for holidays and lazy outdoor pursuits. The number varies from 10 or 12 in an average year in the broad inland area of southeast England to one a year at the Atlantic coasts of the mainland and none in the western and northern isles. Fig. 11 gives the average yearly number of freezing days when the temperature never gets above 0° C (32° F): there are two or three in the average year in most inland districts and over five in upland Pennine dales and in the glens of central Scotland. Many more examples of useful maps of this kind may be found in climatic atlases. Of obvious importance to agriculture are such things as length of the growing season, commonly defined as the period with temperatures of $+6°$ C (42° F) or over, as well as the number of frosts and average dates of first and last frost. The latter vary very much with locality and could only be shown adequately on a large-scale map. One may say very broadly that the Home Counties are liable to occasional air frosts between about 10 October and the first days of May in an average year; but there are many variations from year to year and from site to site that will be indicated in the chapter on local climate and the historical appendix. The average frost-free period in the central Highlands from mid June to mid August is by no means guaranteeable in any particular year, and there are frosty spots even in the south of England where the temperature is not unknown to dip to the freezing point around dawn in any month of the year. At the other extreme, the numbers of warm nights, which are usually sultry with thick clouds and high humidity, for instance nights when the temperature never falls as low as 15° C (59° F)—see fig. 22 later—may be of interest in connexion with the hatching of insects and some human diseases and complaints. The frequencies are highest in the extreme south of Ireland and in England and Wales south of a line from Cardigan to the Wash and much lower in the northern half of Scotland, but the figure of 15° is arbitrarily chosen and does not represent any universal threshold.

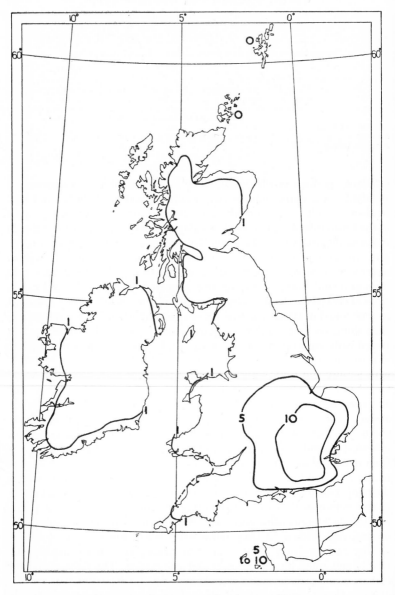

FIGURE 10. Frequency of Hot Summer Days.
(Average number of days a year between 1913 and 1940 when the air temperature at some time exceeded 25° C)

FIGURE 11. Frequency of Freezing Days.
(Average number of days a year between 1913 and 1940 when the temperature
failed to rise above 0° C)

Temperature changes with height, stability, convection and weather

The temperatures which characterize any windstream depend upon its previous history, and particularly on its duration of passage over heating or cooling surfaces. One may, in effect, read the significant parts of the air's recent history from any graph which plots the distribution of temperature with height. In air which has been heated from the ground or the sea, or which has been cooled aloft by loss of heat from cloud tops etc., temperature decreases with height. Since decreasing the pressure on a gas (including air and water vapour) lowers its temperature, the temperature of rising air decreases. This is a fixed lapse rate (or rate of change of temperature with height) of about 1° C per 100 metres (5·4° F per thousand feet), called the 'Adiabatic Lapse Rate'. Heating of the air from below or cooling aloft produces greater differences of temperature with height than this, unless and until rising and falling convection currents spread the heat change through a layer of some depth: the result of this stirring will be that the whole layer is heated or cooled but the lapse of temperature with height will be at the adiabatic rate.

Air which has been lately cooled from underneath has lower temperatures at, or near, the surface than higher up. This temperature distribution is called an 'Inversion', because it is inverse in sense to the usual lapse rate. When there is a wind and ground friction forces some stirring of the lowest air layers over a cold surface, the adiabatic lapse rate will be established in those layers and temperatures will be lowest at the top of the stirred layer. Immediately above that will be a strong inversion of temperature.

All the lower atmosphere contains moisture—i.e. water in the form of invisible vapour. The moisture is picked up from water surfaces, vegetation and even from the skin of animals and the housewife's washing on the line. The amount of water vapour which a unit of air can hold increases with its temperature. The temperature changes we have been discussing—cooling from the ground and the temperature-decrease which rising air undergoes—may therefore bring the air past its Dew Point, i.e. the temperature at which it is saturated by the moisture that is in it. Further lowering of the temperature produces condensation of minute water droplets or ice crystals. These processes release the latent heat of condensation, which partly offsets the fall of temperature. So the temperature decreases less rapidly with height in rising air when cloud is forming in it: this rate is about 0·5° C per 100 metres (2·7° F per thousand feet), called the 'Moist (or Saturated) Adiabatic Lapse Rate'.

The actual distribution of temperature with height observed in any airstream decides whether the up and down currents of convection are encouraged (i.e. accelerated) or damped—that is to say, it determines whether the air is (respectively) Unstable or Stable. Let us consider some actual cases. Suppose a small body of air—it may be pictured as a bubble or 'parcel' of air—rises a certain distance, either because it gets heated over a warm patch of ground or is forced up over a hill, then if the surrounding air at the height it has attained is warmer than the rising air, the latter will be denser than its surroundings and its ascent will slow down and ultimately stop; if the surrounding air were colder, the air moving upwards would be the less dense of the two and would be accelerated. Hence, lapse rates in the surrounding air greater than the adiabatic mean the air is unstable, i.e. vertical motion and exchanges of height are encouraged; lapse rates less than the adiabatic are 'stable', and vertical movements are resisted. If the air is unsaturated, it is the Dry Adiabatic Lapse Rate which applies; if condensation is occurring, the Moist Adiabatic Lapse Rate is the critical one for thermal stability or instability.

Unstable air is characterized by clouds with marked vertical growth, cumulus and cumulonimbus types (both illustrated in miniature in the drawing, fig. 6(e))[1]; clear sky appears in the spaces where the compensating down currents are, between the clouds. When there is great instability—i.e. a particularly big lapse of temperature with height—and enough moisture, the cumulonimbus clouds appearing in the violently accelerated vertical current, and fanning out at the top, quite commonly look like a picture of an explosion. Such clouds produce showers and gusty winds. The alternating sequence of showers and bright intervals known as 'April shower weather' is typical of cool, moist, unstable air which is being heated from below. Surface visibility is usually good in this kind of air, except in showers, because smoke, dust and moisture picked up from the ground are quickly carried up to great heights and so spread rather thinly through a deep layer.

Stable air concentrates the substances picked up from the surface in the lower layers, and haze collects. In light winds over cold ground or sea, fog is common. Stronger winds may stir the lowest layers and raise the position of minimum temperature above the surface, as already explained; fog is then lifted and commonly replaced by sheets of dull, uniform grey stratus, or rippled stratocumulus, clouds. Surface visibility is however seldom as good as in unstable air. The suppression of vertical motion means that the wind has difficulty in surmounting obstacles, and may be reduced to almost still air at the surface even when there is a moderate wind higher up. The wind is also inclined to pass round hills rather than

1. A photographic dictionary of cloud names is provided in a Meteorological Office pamphlet entitled *Cloud Forms*, London (Her Majesty's Stationery Office, M.O. 233), 6th edition, 1949.

over them, and local strengthening of the wind near hillsides and in straight valleys, as well as close to the crests of mountains and ridges, may be very marked: the strong wind, however, is not particularly gusty.

Cyclonic situations increase the activity of upcurrents in unstable air, owing to the general convergence of the surface airstreams, tending to make the cloud development heavy and congested. Anticyclonic situations usually limit the depth of unstable air, even when the ground is quite strongly heated, and thereby restrict the growth of cumulus and cumulus-type clouds, often drastically. Hence showers may be prevented or tend to die out when there is anticyclonic development. The temperature of the descending air in the middle levels of the anticyclone increases due to increasing pressure upon it, and this usually produces an inversion of temperature—a very stable condition—at the lower limit of the subsidence. The height of this 'Subsidence Inversion' is often critical for the weather in the anticyclone. If subsidence proceeds down to a low enough level, the surface air may never reach its dew point temperature in any vertical motion that is possible beneath the subsidence inversion: the sky then remains clear, except for haze accumulating in the layer between the ground and the inversion, especially when the wind is light. (At much greater heights above the maximum wind level the air accumulating when anti-cyclones are forming is usually rising, and this sometimes produces quite abundant white, feathery cirrus clouds at the top of the troposphere at heights of 10–15 km.) When, however, the air in the upper part of the ground turbulence layer beneath the subsidence inversion does become saturated, a persistent sheet of grey stratocumulus or stratus cloud commonly results. And this, with the murkiness due to gathering haze below the cloud, especially in winter, makes for gloom.

The average temperature differences with height through any consider-able range of altitudes over the British Isles amount to less than the dry adiabatic lapse rate. They approximate to the moist adiabatic rate of $0.5°$ C per 100 metres ($2.7°$ F per thousand feet), so that there is much greater frequency of instability and of vertical currents in saturated air than in dry air. In aeroplanes this fact is obvious because of the usual increase of bumpiness in cloud.

Air which has too small a lapse rate to allow vertical motion is sometimes unstable for upward motion at a gently sloping angle because of horizontal temperature contrasts. This situation is common in the frontal zones of these latitudes, where windstreams of widely different origins (and thermal histories) converge. Air rising vertically and undergoing a temperature fall of $10°$ C per km. (say, 3,000 feet) might find itself colder and denser than its surroundings aloft; but if, instead of rising vertically, it had moved several hundred miles (say, 100–500 km.) to the side, over a frontal surface, in the course of going up just one km., its 10° C temperature decrease might not be enough to make this air colder than its surroundings in the new position. The probability of such slantwise uplift is of course greatly increased if cloud forms in the rising air reducing the temperature decrease to about 5° C per km. Layers of stratus-type cloud (nimbostratus, alto-stratus and cirrostratus) produced by gently slanting ascent of air, at slopes between one in a hundred and one in a thousand, are extremely common, especially near fronts where convergence of the surface air impels the warmer airstream to override the cold.

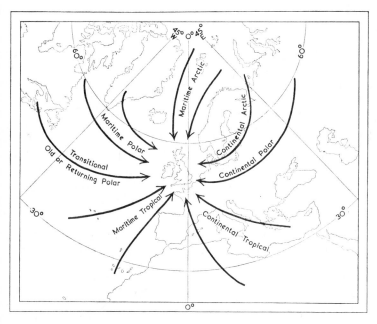

FIGURE 12. Airmasses commonly occurring in Britain.

Airstreams and airmasses

Fig. 12 shows the main paths by which winds come to the British Isles and therefore indicates the most usual airmasses experienced here. The vertical distribution of temperatures and moisture, which determine the weather prevailing in an airstream, are liable to differ from case to case.

If we consider only west winds of average strength over this country, sometimes the air at heights of a few kilometres has been moving at much the same speed and along the same track as the wind in the lower levels, and sometimes it has come twice or three times as fast from Canada, and undergone correspondingly less change of temperature etc. on the way; but sometimes the air aloft has come by quite a different path, maybe from warmer, maybe from colder regions. All these cases produce different results, which the weather forecaster tries to foresee from his charts of the winds at various levels. The following list (Table 2), however, indicates the commonest characteristics of the principal airmasses shown in fig. 12 when passing over this country[1]:

TABLE 2

Prevailing characteristics of principal airmasses in Britain
(Without cyclonic or anticyclonic influence)

Airmass name (and conventional abbreviation)	Characteristic surface temperature, as departure from the normal level for the season; thermal stability; distinctive clouds and weather
Maritime polar (mP)	Cold or rather cold at all seasons, especially on windward coasts and clear nights inland. Unstable. Cumulus and cumulonimbus clouds. Bright intervals and showers. Clouds and showers die out inland at night and in winter.
Returning maritime polar (rmP)	Temperature close to the seasonal normal. Instability decreasing. Cloud types various, but spreading out; stability characteristics increase the farther south the air has been before recurving northwards.
Maritime tropical (mT)	Mild or very mild in winter, rather warm and close in summer, warm in eastern districts. Stable. Dull skies and drizzle common on windward side, with low stratus cloud enveloping hills in fog, but clearing on lee side. Mists and fogs inland in winter and at night, when the wind is light and the sky clears. Some sea fog and coast fog in the Channel and Western Approaches in spring and summer.

1. Statistics have been published by Belasco, J. E., 'Characteristics of Air Masses over the British Isles', London (H.M.S.O.) Meteorological Office, *Geophysical Memoirs*, No. 87, 1952.

TABLE 2—*cont.*

Airmass name (and conventional abbreviation)	Characteristic surface temperature, as departure from the normal level for the season; thermal stability; distinctive clouds and weather
Continental tropical (cT)	Mild or very mild in winter, warm or very warm in summer. Unstable in the upper layers; stable below, especially in winter. Cloud amount seems to depend very much on details of the air's path, e.g. which mountains it has passed over or avoided, and length of the Mediterranean, Atlantic and North Sea crossings. Stratus cloud types in winter, but in summer cumulus and occasionally high level thunderstorm cloud. Commonly hazy.
Continental polar (cP)	Cold or very cold in winter, warm in summer. Unstable, especially in the lower layers, except near windward coasts in summer. Cloud cover depends greatly on details of the air's path, e.g. air from the Baltic and the north German plain is cloudier than air which has crossed the hills and mountains farther south; the northern air commonly brings skies overcast with stratocumulus cloud, especially in winter when it only clears west of the Welsh and English mountains and Scottish Highlands; cumulus or cumulonimbus cloud, with breaks, develop on the longer North Sea crossings to the Scottish east coast. All the cloud types concerned in winter are inclined to give occasional light sleet or snow. In summer all inland districts experience a good deal of clear sky and warm sunshine; eastern coastal districts get sea fogs (haars) and low temperatures with low overcast grey skies of stratus cloud, which sometimes clear completely in the afternoon. Often somewhat hazy at all seasons.
Continental arctic (cA)	Very cold or severe in winter, cold in spring and early summer. (This airmass is rare in high summer; when it does occur it is almost indistinguishable from cP and may be warm.) Unstable in the lower layers. Cloud and weather characteristics similar to cP at all seasons, though in winter and

TABLE 2—*cont.*

Airmass name (and conventional abbreviation)	Characteristic surface temperature, as departure from the normal level for the season; thermal stability; distinctive clouds and weather
Continental arctic (cA)—*cont.*	spring the precipitation is more likely to be snow. Visibility is clearer than with cP and sometimes extremely clear.
Maritime arctic (mA)	Cold at all seasons, very cold in winter when the weather may become severe if this air stagnates over the country. Unstable. Cloud types and behaviour resemble mP, but the showers are likely to be sleet, snow or hail in winter and spring. Leeward districts get long periods of clear sky. Extreme visibility and a beautiful blue opalescence of the distant view are distinctive characteristics.

A careful reading of the table reveals several points at which the character of the weather in this country is very sensitive to small changes in the path of the air. In winter, for instance, there is a very great change in the prevailing temperatures according to whether an easterly wind has passed just north or just south of the Alps. At that season, however, if the wind are light, even a breeze from due south may bring severe cold when France is snow-covered.

Prevailing weather—different outcome in different districts; continentality

The sharpest changes of prevailing weather character over short distance are those between the windward and leeward sides of the hills. Cloud amounts, the vertical extent of the clouds and the frequency and heaviness of precipitation from them are all increased on the windward side where the air is forced to rise over the hills. This affects all types of cloud. The rainfall near the windward coasts and the frequency of winter thunder (in cold air heated rapidly over the warm Gulf Stream water) appear to be greater than over the Atlantic.[1] Descent of the air on the lee side of hills 'dissolves

1. Problems of measuring rainfall over the ocean have not so far been solved owing to the motion of vessels floating on the waves and the disturbance of the free flow of the wind in passing over a ship. The comparison here made is based upon what appear to be the first trustworthy estimates, by G. B. Tucker, 'Precipitation over the North Atlantic Ocean', *Quarterly Journal of the Royal Meteorological Society*, Vol. 87, pp. 147–158, London, 1961.

the cloud in the same way as does subsidence in the free air in an anti-cyclone. Leeward districts therefore experience much more clear sky, and showers and rainfall become infrequent. Eastern districts of England and Scotland enjoy the 'rain shadow' of the Welsh hills, Pennines and High-lands to such an extent that annual rainfalls in many places are less than in the same latitude the other side of the North Sea, where the westerly winds have replenished their moisture. Nowhere west of 10° E on the German plain or north of Paris is the general rainfall so little as in parts of Sussex, Kent and Essex, East Anglia, the Fens and eastern Scotland between the Grampians and the sea. These are the districts where irrigation is useful to the farmer at some time nearly every year.

In most other respects as well, there is a change of climate across this country from oceanic in the west and north to a more continental character in the southeast. The change is sharpest across the first mountain ranges east of the Atlantic. It is noticeable in the distribution of extreme tem-peratures discussed earlier in this chapter and in the values shown in figs. 5, 10 and 11. The difference between the average temperature in January and in July, which is sometimes quoted as a measure of 'continentality', is almost twice as great in the area between the Sussex Weald and the Fens as it is in Barra, in the Outer Hebrides, and a third greater than in Corn-wall, Anglesey or the north and east coasts of Scotland between Cape Wrath and Dunbar. (In Berlin the figure is a third greater than in London, but it is four to five times as great as in Siberia.) The difference in this regard between north and south in Britain is due to lower summer temperatures in the north.

Differences in windiness are very marked. Northern and western dis-tricts of the British Isles experience more strong winds than the southeast because they are nearer the frequent paths of depressions over the Atlantic. The ocean exerts less friction upon the wind than a land surface, so that the surface winds over the sea and near the windward coasts move at a higher fraction of the speed of the wind in the free air overhead. These considerations combine to make a very great difference in the frequency of gales and strong winds between the oceanic fringe and inland southeastern districts of the British Isles (see fig. 13). In our northern and western districts one must learn to live with the wind: it is, perhaps, the most severe element of the climate of the Atlantic coast, limiting the growth of trees and plants and hindering human activity, though its power has been used to generate electricity for many an isolated farmhouse before the coming of the national supply. By contrast, in inland districts in southeast-ern England average wind speeds are less even than on the neighbouring parts of the continent: this seems to be partly due to the shape of the terrain, which except in the Fens is less open to the winds than the more

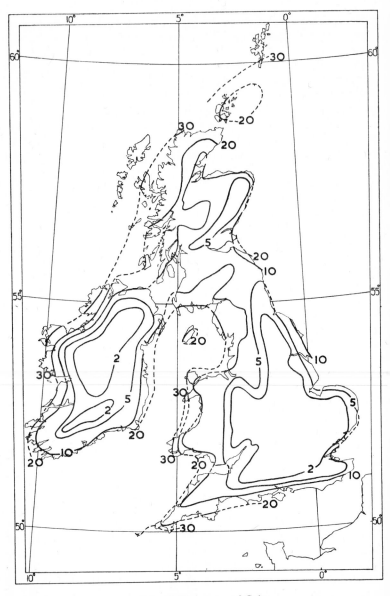

FIGURE 13. Frequency of Gales.
(Average number of days a year between 1918 and 1937 when the wind reached gale force, Beaufort Force 8 or more.)

maritime districts of northern and northwestern France, the Netherlands or northern Germany. The tendency for lack of wind (lack of ventilation) may be one reason why our heat waves are sometimes alleged to feel more oppressive than those on the nearer parts of the continent, even though the temperatures are no higher. Moisture differences are also probably involved.

There are sharp gradations of climate over short distances near the coasts. The frequency of high maximum temperatures falls within a few miles of the shore; but, for this reason, there is less convection cloud in the afternoon, more clear sky and sunshine. Frequencies of frost and lying snow decrease sharply near the sea, even in the north. The average number of days a year with snow lying on the links at Aberdeen, Montrose or Dundee differs little from that at Hampstead; but at the foot of the Grampians, twenty miles inland, the frequency is four times as great.

These differences of local climate occur within one and the same wind-stream. They illustrate the usefulness of local knowledge in interpreting the weather forecast. Besides those mentioned in this chapter there are many smaller scale intricacies, such as the effects of a particular hill, valley or lake. A curious example of the fine effects of relief over quite long distances occurs with northwest winds and polar air, which bring showers to Lancashire and North Wales but generally bright, dry weather in the southeast; it has often been noticed that showers succeed in passing through the gap between the Pennines and the Welsh mountains, and occasionally continue in the line of the wind through that gap as far as the Chilterns.

Weather types—classification

Since so much depends upon wind direction, there is obvious point in the attempts which have been made since ancient times to describe the weather types to be expected with each direction of the wind. Perhaps the earliest attempt that we know of was the eight-sided Tower of the Winds at Athens, built in the first century BC and still standing near the base of the Acropolis. The top of the tower bears a frieze, the eight sides of which are decorated with bas-relief plaques personifying the character of each wind at Athens. Naturally these characteristics differ from those in England, but the nature of this early approach is interesting. The essence of the plaques is as follows[1]:

---

1. This description of the Tower of the Winds is taken from notes and pictures given by Photios Karapiperis in *Weatherwise*, Vol. 4, pp. 112–113, Philadelphia, October 1951. Copies of the eight bas-reliefs are on the octagonal tower of Radcliffe Observatory, Oxford, and also on the library of Blue Hill Meteorological Observatory, Harvard.

BOREAS, the north wind, cold and stormy, is suggested by a bearded old man, warmly clad. He is holding a conch shell near his mouth, suggesting the noise made by the fierce wind.

KAIKIAS, the northeast wind, cloudy and cold, the bringer of snow, hail, and thunderstorms, is represented by a warrior tipping a shield full of hailstones ready to rattle down on the countryside.

APHELIOTES ('blowing from the sun'), the east wind, is regarded as a favourable one in Greece where it brings frequent light showers and is accordingly represented by a young man laden with fruits and grain.

EUROS, the southeast wind, brings much rain to Athens. In this case the picture is of an old man carrying nothing, but holding his mantle to protect himself and his face.

NOTOS, the south wind, brings warmth and rain to Athens and is pictured by a young man lightly clad, carrying a water jar which he has just emptied over the countryside below.

LIPS, the southwest wind, apparently represents the common sea breeze which favours ships' entry into the port of Piraeus. This is symbolized by a young man holding forward a model of the prow of a ship.

ZEPHYROS, the west wind, is pictured as a young man of beauty bringing many flowers carried in the skirt of his cloak.

SKIRON, the northwest wind, cold in winter, hot and dry in summer, though it also brings lightning and occasional thunderstorms, is portrayed by an old man as warmly clothed as Boreas, holding a brazen fire-basket, from which ashes and coals are scattered.

A modern meteorological description of the main types of weather in the British Isles is given below. It also follows the wind directions. It differs, however, from most earlier attempts at classification in envisaging a definable weather type as something which often lasts for some days, whilst the weather undergoes variations typical of the succession of airmasses and depression tracks etc. occurring with that prevailing wind direction and general type of weather sequence or spell. This conception implies that the prevailing wind direction over a period of days is the one closest to the main flow of the upper winds and hence related to the steering of depressions and anticyclones. The surface wind is likely to be closest to the direction of the main flow aloft during the passage of warm sectors—except in the case of the easterly type, when a well-marked windstream from the east aloft and warm sectors from the east at the surface only occur in some of the more extreme cases. With both easterly and northerly types the upper winds over this country are often light.

Such a classification is helpful in bringing out the occurrence of spells of weather and defining their meteorological nature.

The weather on almost any day can be described as belonging to one or other of the following types or as some hybrid between one of the wind direction types and either the cyclonic or the anticyclonic type:

ANTICYCLONIC TYPE (AC)

Anticyclones centred over, near, or extending over the British Isles. The type may include days with cols over the country between two anticyclones. Weather mainly dry, with light winds. Thunder, however, often occurs in the cols in summer. Usually warm in summer, cold or very cold in winter; mist and fog frequent in autumn.

CYCLONIC TYPE (C)

Depressions centred over, or frequently passing across, the British Isles. Mainly wet or disturbed weather, with very variable wind directions and strengths. Both gales and thunderstorms may occur. Usually mild in autumn and early winter; cool or cold in spring and summer; sometimes cold in late winter.

WESTERLY or SOUTHWESTERLY TYPE (W)

Pressure high to the south, sometimes also to the southeast and southwest, and low to the north of the British Isles. Sequences of depressions and ridges of high pressure travelling east across the Atlantic and farther east. Weather in the British Isles generally unsettled or changeable, usually with most rain in northern and western districts and brighter weather in the south and east. Winds shifting rapidly between south and northwest as each depression passes, sometimes even southeast or east for a short time. Cool in summer, mild in winter with frequent gales.

NORTHWESTERLY TYPE (NW)

Azores anticyclone displaced, or extending, northeast towards the British Isles or north over the Atlantic west of Ireland. Depressions, often forming near Iceland, travel southeast or east-southeast into the North Sea and reach their greatest intensity over Scandinavia or the Baltic. Unsettled or changeable weather, particularly in northern and eastern districts of the British Isles, sometimes with fresh or gale-force winds from between west and north. The warm sectors may contain unstable air—this and the selection of districts exposed to windward weather are the main differences from the westerly type. Cooler than westerly and milder than northerly type.

NORTHERLY TYPE (N)

Pressure high to the west and northwest of the British Isles, particularly over Greenland, and sometimes extending south from there as a continuous belt over the Atlantic to the Azores. Pressure low over the Baltic, Scandinavia

and the North Sea. Depressions move south or southeast from the Norwegian Sea, sometimes having formed in the Iceland–Jan Mayen–Northeast
Greenland region, sometimes having come through from still farther north,
and sometimes having entered the Iceland–Jan Mayen region by way of a
col near south Greenland. Cold, disturbed weather at all seasons, especially
in northern and eastern districts. Snow and sleet common in winter; also
associated with late spring and early autumn snow, especially on high
ground in the north, and with late spring frosts in all districts. The onset of
the northerly type is often accompanied by high winds.

EASTERLY TYPE (E)

Anticyclones over, or extending over, Scandinavia, from where ridges may
reach out to Iceland or to northern Britain. Depressions over the western
North Atlantic, sometimes passing on close to Greenland and thence far to
the northeast, depressions also in the Azores–Portugal–Biscay region. Cold
in autumn, winter and spring; sometimes intensely cold in southern districts
and in suitably exposed areas elsewhere, with occasional snow in the south
and snow or sleet showers in eastern and northeastern districts; fine in the
west and northwest. Warm in summer, though sometimes thundery. Very
dry weather in western districts, often fairly dry in many or most other
districts, though sometimes wet in the east and south.

SOUTHERLY TYPE (S)

High pressure covering central and northern Europe. Atlantic depressions
either blocked west of the British Isles or travelling north off our western
coasts. This type seems less persistent than the other types and occurs mainly
as an occasional variant within spells that are predominantly either westerly
or easterly. It is rare in summer from June onwards. A warm and thundery
type in spring and summer, mild in autumn. In winter it may be mild or cold
according to whether the air carried over the British Isles comes from the
ocean or the continent: for this reason it is usually mild in the west.

5

Rain, Snow, Hail, Lightning and Tempest

THE amount of moisture which air can hold in the invisible vapour form increases with the temperature. The increase is more like a geometric than an arithmetic progression; the amount of moisture which saturates the air at 20° C (68° F) is nearly four times that which saturates it at the freezing point. The corresponding quantities for different temperatures are given in Table 3. 16 to 17 grams per kilogram of dry air is about the greatest amount of water vapour ever carried by the air in the warmest parts of Britain: this corresponds to dew point of 21–22° C at sea-level pressures and is a rare extreme only approached in 'heavy', sultry, thundery weather. At temperatures below the freezing point the saturation amount of water vapour in the air differs according to whether there is liquid water or ice present, and for this reason two figures have to be quoted. This is important, as we shall see, in connexion with the growth of raindrops. For the present, be it noted that the amount of vapour required to saturate air which is in contact with ice is less than when only water is present.

TABLE 3

Dew point temperatures and saturation amounts of water vapour (at 1,000 mb.) in grams per kilogram.

Temperature* ° C	−40	−30	−20	−10	0	+10	+20	+30
Saturation amount in presence of								
(a) ice	0·08	0·24	0·65	1·63	3·84	—	—	—
(b) water . . .	0·12	0·32	0·78	1·79	3·84	7·76	14·95	27·69

* The Table is carried to temperatures far lower than occur at the surface in England in order to give some impression of the changed saturation values down to the temperatures occurring in the upper parts of the clouds. The effect of halving the atmospheric pressure, however, is very nearly to double the ratios of water vapour to a kilogram of air for saturation over ice and over water—i.e. double the figures given in the Table at heights of 5–6 km. (between 17,000 and 20,000 feet).

When air is cooled to its dew point (i.e. the temperature at which it is saturated), some of the moisture begins to appear in liquid or solid form by condensation either on water or ice surfaces or on microscopic particles of certain substances such as sea salt that may be present in the air and which by their shape act as the nucleus of a drop or ice crystal. In the absence of any water or ice surface, or of any suitable nucleus, supersaturation can occur. Normally, however, condensation begins when the dew point temperature is reached. (A small amount of condensation may even occur somewhat before true saturation if enough suitable hygroscopic nuclei are about in the air; sea salt acts in this way and very moist oceanic air is liable to be slightly misty even at temperatures slightly above the dew point and below the main cloud level.) Condensation occurs more readily on ice surfaces and ice crystals in the atmosphere than on water or water droplets, because it takes less moisture to saturate the air when ice is present.

Air may be cooled by contact with cold ground or sea, or through losing its heat by radiation to space—especially by radiation from clouds and water vapour present. These processes account for a greater prevalence of clouds and fogs in winter than in summer and in high latitudes than low. But at all times air is liable to have its temperature reduced to the dew point when it rises in convection currents, or by being uplifted at a front or over a hill, or when it moves to regions of lower pressure. Then cloud forms by the condensation of myriads of minute water droplets. In clean air in which ice is not already present condensation occurs mainly in the form of 'supercooled' liquid drops even at temperatures below the freezing point. The droplets in such supercooled clouds and fogs freeze immediately on impact with solid objects, whether these be ice crystals or snowflakes entering or falling through the cloud from higher levels or the stones and rocks and vegetation on ground enveloped in the cloud. In the latter cases they form white crystals of rime which slowly grow out to windward, producing thick encrustations after some days. They also freeze on aircraft flying through the cloud and on the windscreens of motor cars driving through the fog.

Descent of the air, as on the lee side of mountain ranges and hill ridges and in the general subsidence in anticyclones, usually raises its temperature above the dew point, causing clouds to evaporate.

The characteristic sizes of cloud droplets are only a twentieth of a millimetre or less in diameter. Such tiny droplets have an air resistance which is large in comparison with their weight, and accordingly are carried along in the air, rising and falling with it and having very little tendency to fall out. The maximum fall speed (relative to the air), called the terminal velocity, for drops of different sizes is shown in Table 4, which gives figures for drops up to the largest size (about a quarter of an inch across) at which raindrops get broken up into smaller units by the air resistance.

A very wet cloud is capable of producing drops up to the size of drizzle drops, 0·05–0·5 mm. in diameter, which fall gently. Growth to the size of raindrops, 0·5 to about 5·5 mm. in diameter, however, depends upon some speeding up process of which the most important in temperate

TABLE 4

Terminal velocities of water drops in a

Diameter of drop (millimetres) . . .	0·01	0·1	0·5	1·0	2·0	3·0	4·0	5·0	5·5
Terminal velocity									
m/sec.	0·0032	0·32	3·5	4·4	5·9	6·9	7·7	8·0	8·0
m.p.h.	0·007	0·71	7·9	9·8	13·2	15·4	17·2	17·9	17·9

and higher latitudes involves the presence of ice crystals. The further the temperature of rising air falls below the freezing point, the greater the likelihood of ice crystals occurring. At temperatures below − 10 or − 12° C condensation usually produces some ice crystals, and below − 40° C all condensation is believed to be in the solid form. When these ice crystals collide with cloud droplets, the latter immediately freeze onto them. But, because the air which contains supercooled water droplets is oversaturated for contact with ice, condensation proceeds rapidly onto the ice crystals and the liquid droplets tend to evaporate to maintain the supply of substance to the ice crystals, which grow further into snowflakes. These become big enough to fall, and at levels where the temperature is above the freezing point they melt into sleet and rain. Thus rain in this country usually falls only from clouds that have reached well above the freezing level and had their upper parts transformed into ice and snow. The characteristic streaky, feathery-edged appearance of clouds of ice crystals[1] can be recognized by the practised eye in the upper parts of rain clouds such as cumulonimbus and nimbostratus.

In air that is moving rapidly up and down in strong convection currents several further things may happen:

(i) the drops may be carried up again and grow bigger.
(ii) the largest drops may be split up. When this happens, they appear to acquire an electrical charge and the air which rushes up past them acquires an equal and opposite charge. The resulting accumulation of unlike electrical charges at different levels in the cloud produces thunder and lightning—the flash marks the discharge current, when the charges have become so big that the air's electrical resistance breaks down.
(iii) the rain drops may be carried up so far past the freezing level again that they freeze solid and become hailstones. These, too, grow further by collisions with liquid, or partly unfrozen, drops

1. The appearance of ice clouds is amongst the host of interesting matters illustrated by many good cloud photographs in *Cloud Study, a Pictorial Guide* by F. H. Ludlam and R. S. Scorer, London (John Murray), 1957.

and by direct condensation of moisture upon them. Moreover they are no longer liable to be broken up into smaller particles by the air resistance. The stronger the up-currents, the greater the chance of really large hailstones growing. The largest hailstones known to occur in this country, occasionally up to 5–10 cm. (2–4 inches) in diameter, require vertical currents moving up at speeds of 40–50 m./sec. (80–100 m.p.h.) to support them. Not surprisingly, other violent convection phenomena such as severe thunderstorms and tornadoes are also common in the conditions which produce large hail.[1]

Rainfall

Rainfall is important in questions of agriculture, water supply, health and comfort. Most parts of England are fortunate in having adequate rainfall without excess, well distributed through the year. It is only in the hill country in the west and north that there is rather too much rain.

The average annual rainfall varies from below 20 inches (500 mm.) on a small part of the coast of the Thames Estuary to nearly 200 inches (5,000 mm.) at a few points on the highest ground in northwest Scotland, Cumberland and North Wales. Over most of the country the amount is between 25 and 40 inches, the average being 33 inches in England and 50 inches in Wales and Scotland. To picture what this means, consider that an average really wet day of prolonged steady rain produces $\frac{1}{2}$ inch (10–15 mm.), and a rather severe thunderstorm 1 or 2 inches (25–50 mm.). Several extreme downpours in England have given 8–10 inches. The greatest measured falls since 1915 have been 11·0 inches (279 mm.) at Martinstown, Dorset on 18 July 1955, 9·6 inches at Bruton, Somerset in June 1917, 9·4 inches at Cannington, Somerset in August 1924 and 9·1 inches at Simonsbath on Exmoor, also in Somerset, in August 1952. Considering that so many of the record falls are from the southwest of England, it is evident that that part of the country is singularly liable to cloudbursts.

These downpours are very local, and many must have gone unrecorded. The record at Simonsbath was not from a proper rain-gauge, but from a cylindrical bucket graduated in quarts, which happened to have been left out in the middle of a field. In neighbouring places the fall may have reached 10 inches or more. A measure of the quantity of water which fell in the

1. The reader who wishes to pursue further the physical processes touched on in the foregoing paragraphs should consult works on the subject by Sir G. C. Simpson, B. J. Mason, F. H. Ludlam and R. S. Scorer. Amongst these, the textbook *The Physics of Clouds* by B. J. Mason (Oxford Univ. Press), 1957, and an article by F. H. Ludlam, 'The Hailstorm', in *Weather*, Vol. 16, pp. 152–162, 1961, are perhaps of most recent interest.

small basin of the Lyn rivers, only 39 square miles in area, is that the flow of water at Lynmouth on this occasion was nearly as great as the highest ever recorded in the Thames.

In the 38 years from 1915 to 1952 there were always 4,000–5,000 rain-gauges in operation in Britain. This might be considered equivalent to about 170,000 years of station record, and these include only eight falls of 8 inches (200 mm.) or more. This means that at any one place a fall of 8 inches might be expected once in something like 20,000 years, provided there were no change of climate in that time. Assuming that on occasions of violent rain a station represents a quarter of a square mile, and that a severe flood may be caused by a fall of 8 inches or more anywhere within a small river basin, a simple calculation shows that a basin of 39 square miles should expect a destructive flood once in about 125 years. The Editors of *Nature*, in the issue for 15 August 1953, commenting on the disaster, pointed out that with increasing population many potentially dangerous river sites are likely to be built on, unless responsible guidance is given.

Even downpours of 8 or 10 inches are modest compared with those in lower latitudes. Forty inches in a day has been exceeded in tropical hurricanes, in the mountains in Japan and the Philippine Islands and at Cherrapunji in India, where the warm, wet monsoon wind from the Indian Ocean enters a steep funnel-shaped valley which concentrates the flow of air and forces it to rise almost vertically, bringing much of the water which it contains down on one small area.

Annual rainfall alone is not a very good measure of the 'raininess' of a place. The Mediterranean coast of France gives the impression of being much drier and sunnier than the southeast coast of England, but it actually has more rain. Nice, for example, has an average of 32 inches compared with 28 inches at Dover. The difference lies in the nature of the rainfall; in Nice rain is heavy while it lasts, but comparatively infrequent, while in England rain is more often light and persistent. Thus during an average year Nice has only 102 'rain-days', compared with 178 at Dover.

The internationally agreed definition of a 'rain-day' is one with 0·1 mm. (about 0·004 inch) or more of rain. A fall of about a two-hundredth part of an inch of rain sounds very little; in fact, it may mean anything from a single short shower to some hours of drizzle. On this definition the average number of rain-days in Britain varies from less than 175 in the Thames Estuary to over 250 in the Western Isles of Scotland. The most complete map available for this country is that showing the average number of days a year with more than one-hundredth of an inch of rain (0·25 mm.); this is reproduced as fig. 14. The distribution pattern and gradients of frequency, though not the actual numbers, are identical to those of rain-days.

The Meteorological Office further defines a 'wet day' as one with a

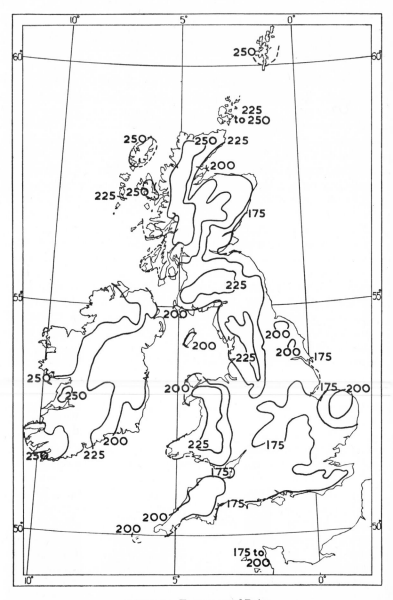

FIGURE 14. Frequency of Rain.
(Average number of days a year between 1901 and 1930 with over a hundredth
of an inch or ¼ millimetre of rain.)

millimetre (0·04 inch) or more of rain, and for many practical purposes the numbers of these are more significant than 'rain-days'. Complete statistics of the numbers of wet days are not available, but a good estimate can be made from the numbers of days with over 0·25 mm. of rain (fig. 12). In places like the Western Highlands and Islands of Scotland, the numbers of 'wet days' are 80–90% of the frequencies of the rainy days with over 0·25 mm., in central England only about 70%, and in eastern England rather less than that. The number varies from below 100 in Essex to above 200 in the wettest districts such as the Western Highlands, the Lake District and North Wales. The average for the whole country is about 130.

A useful criterion of heavy rain is a fall of 10 mm. (0·4 inch) or more in a day; on such a day outdoor work is generally impracticable, though in the English lowlands even these heavy falls may be concentrated in a thunderstorm downpour for a limited part of the day. The more one turns one's attention to the heavier falls, the more an erratic element enters, which is liable to make the particular day or even the particular month in question unrepresentative. This is because of the patchy incidence of the heavier thunderstorms. Thus the record heaviest rainfall in a day affected a rather small area in Dorset in the middle of one of the finest months (July 1955) in recent years. One must consider the average figures for a good many years before statistics of these falls can be expected to make sense. The average number of days with 'heavy' falls of 10 mm. or more appears to range from under 15 a year in the Thames Estuary and parts of East Anglia to over 100 in the wettest parts of the country, where even the heavier falls are more likely to be of the prolonged type. For days with over an inch of rain the disparity is even more striking, ranging from frequencies of about one a year in the southeast to over 40 in the wettest districts.

In an average year the wettest day in southeast England has about 1 inch of rain. In the hill country of Cornwall and Devon, Wales, Cumberland and Western Scotland the wettest day has about 2 inches, rising to 3 inches on the highest ground. Three inches of rain in a day is only seen in London once or twice in a lifetime.

Another measure of rain, especially important for holidaymakers and for all those whose occupation involves outdoor activity, is the number of hours with rain. Over nearly all southeast England, rain falls in measurable amounts for about 500 hours in the year, that is about one hour in seventeen. In the wettest parts of Britain in the west and northwest nearly ten times the amount of rain falls in something under three times as many hours—about 1,200–1,300 hours, or one hour in seven.

Brooks calculated an index of 'raininess' as a hindrance to outdoor activities by multiplying average yearly rainfall amount by the number of days on which it falls. This showed that, very roughly, 'raininess' in this country increases by about 8% of the sea-level value for every 100 feet of height above the sea. The figure varies with the orientation of the slope in relation to the prevailing winds, being greatest where the wind from the Atlantic meets a long high mountain ridge. Sea level values of 'raininess' were high in west Scotland, Cumberland, Wales, Devon and Cornwall and the coasts of west and southwest Ireland. Least rainy of the hill districts are the Cairngorms, eastern Grampians, and the hills of eastern England from Yorkshire to Sussex. Of course, here we have been speaking of the long-term averages: in a spell of northerly or easterly winds the distribution of raininess is very different.

Most rain in Britain falls with southwest or south winds. There are not many statistics; but a valuable series of 12 years' observations at the Building Research Station, Watford, was described by R. E. Lacy. These showed that if the amount of rain falling on a vertical aperture facing north (the driest direction) is taken as 1·0, apertures facing other directions receive, in order of magnitude in the course of a year, NE 1·13, E 1·25, NW 1·37, SE 2·25, W 2·8, S 3·5, SW 4·0. In winter the differences are greatly exaggerated, a SW aperture receiving seven times as much as a north aperture. In spring and summer the differences are small.

Over the British Isles as a whole December and January are the wettest months, especially in western districts nearest the Atlantic. October, November and August are generally runners up. In central and eastern districts, and on the Lancashire coast, there is not a great deal to choose between the various months. However, the time from February, March or April to June is generally the least rainy. July and August stand out as rainy in many districts because of their thunderstorms, and the period October to January also has higher monthly averages than the rest of the year. In all districts from central Scotland southwards September appears as a rather dry month sandwiched in between wetter seasons before and after. Closer examination of this shows a rather marked tendency for a dry period between about 10 and 17 September, when average rainfall in many districts is only about half the figures for periods of similar length two to four weeks earlier. As this example suggests, there is some interest in the incidence of various weather phenomena over periods of less than a month, which we shall discuss in a later chapter.

The 109 years 1841–1949 included in *A Century of London Weather*, by W. A. L. Marshall, published by the Meteorological Office in 1952, show

1. Lacy, R. E., 'Observations with a Directional Rain Gauge', *Quarterly Journal of the Royal Meteorological Society*, Vol. 77, pp. 283–292, London, 1951.

that in London the frequency with which each month was the wettest or driest of the year was as follows:

	Jan.	Feb.	Mar.	Apr.	May	June	July	Aug.	Sept.	Oct.	Nov.	Dec.
Wettest	5	4	2	0	7	5	17	9	8	26	15	11
Driest	7	21	13	13	8	7	7	5	9	3	9	7

Thus in the period covered, every month has been the driest of a year, and every month except April has been the wettest. In respect of dryness February derives advantage from its $28\frac{1}{4}$ days. Another way to show the difference in the character of the months is to tabulate the numbers of very wet and very dry months. A very wet month is defined in the table below as one with a total rainfall of 4 inches (100 mm.) or more, and a very dry month is one with a rainfall of less than four tenths of an inch (10 mm.), in London. These figures bring out the wetness of July and August and play down the dryness of February:

	Jan.	Feb.	Mar.	Apr.	May	June	July	Aug.	Sept.	Oct.	Nov.	Dec.
Very wet	4	2	4	1	4	3	18	15	8	18	11	7
Very dry	0	10	10	7	7	8	2	1	4	1	1	5

During this period two months were practically rainless in London—June 1925 and March 1929, and several others had less than a tenth of an inch.

If we want to consider frequency of rain rather than the amounts that fall, a fairer way to compare the character of different months is to consider the number of days with more than 0·1 or 0·25 mm. of rain. Using the latter criterion May, June, July and September come out best, each with under 11 days on parts of the coast of southeast England, and December worst with 17–20 days. In western Scotland and Ireland the best period is more narrowly confined to May and June, each with about 17 days; July and August each average about 20; in December and January the averages in these areas are as high as 23–26 days. The figures for Cornwall and Devon and west Wales, in most months, are about half-way between those for the Hebrides and those for Sussex and Essex.

Meteorologists distinguish three or four main types of rainfall: frontal and cyclonic, orographic and convection (or instability) rains. The rain produced by uplift of warm air at a front usually consists of a belt from 10 or 20 to 200 miles broad moving with (and mostly ahead of) the front: the belt of rain may extend 1,000 miles or more along the length of the front. The general convergence of surface winds in a depression, and in regions of strong cyclonic curvature of the isobars (as in troughs of low pressure), promotes uplift resulting in clouds and rainfall. This tendency increases the rainfall at fronts and mountain slopes, as well as instability rain, in depressions and troughs. Sawyer has studied the distribution of rainfall accompanying depressions on various tracks crossing the British Isles.[1] Places within a hundred miles of the path of the centre received on average nearly 15 mm. of rain; amounts fell off to only half as much at 200 miles; they were still appreciable at greater distances, though perhaps not much more than 300 miles north of the track. South of the centres 25% of depressions gave no rain at 350 miles. In eastern districts the peak rainfall was within 100 miles north of the depression path and the fall off to the south brought the figure down by a half within 100–150 miles of the track of the centre. Fast-moving depressions showed some tendency to give less rain than the slower ones.

Orographic rainfall results from moist winds blowing against mountains. Its amount depends on the strength and direction of the wind as well as on the height of the mountains. Most of the rainfall in the hilly west country is orographic. Since the winds are strongest in winter, and blow most from the southwest, winter is by far the rainiest season in these districts, having about twice the rainfall of summer.

Instability rain falls from unstable air in thunderstorms or thundery showers. Since these occur more in July and August than in other months, instability rain is heaviest in late summer and least in winter.

The annual variation of rainfall at any place depends on the relative importance of these factors. In flat areas in the west and north, where there are few thunderstorms, there is hardly any difference between the months. In the mountain areas in the northwest, winter, especially December and January, when the depressions are most vigorous and the winds strongest, is much the wettest and early summer (May, June and July) the driest period. Inland in the east, where thunder is most frequent, the wettest month is usually July or August.

Occasional droughts are also a feature of the climate of Britain. In parts of Essex and the Thames Estuary from 1906 to 1940 there were on average two to three periods a year when there was either no rain for at least 15 consecutive days or rainfall averaging less than 0·25 mm. a day for 29 days or longer. Such periods occurred only once in five years or more in the extreme northwest of Scotland.[2] The longest droughts with

1. Sawyer, J. S., 'Rainfall of depressions which pass eastward over or near the British Isles', *Meteorological Office, Professional Notes* No. 118 (M.O. 524r), London (H.M.S.O.), 1956.

2. Glasspoole, J., and Rowsell, H., 'Absolute droughts and partial droughts over the British Isles, 1906–40', *Meteorological Magazine*, **76**, 1947, pp. 201–205.

no day having as much as 0·25 mm. rain have lasted up to about 60 days in the southeast.[1]

Rain in moderation is a necessary blessing. Even the holiday-maker should not complain of a little rain, which cleans the air and refreshes the countryside. Snow is a more doubtful proposition. The dislocation of traffic by a severe snowstorm may represent a serious economic loss; and in the more lonely places lives may be endangered when people try to carry on, disregarding the weather. Losses of sheep are common in the hills in severe storms. These risks are particularly brought on by drifting of wind-blown snow into deep impassable banks in pockets of shelter, whether on the open moors or blocking a lonely road. At spots where the form of hedges or banks favours the piling of loose snow in windy weather, drifts may deepen swiftly enough to block the road ahead and close it somewhere behind the unlucky traveller. It is important to recognize the sort of road that is liable to drifting snow and to remember that, with the vast supply of moisture in the ocean to the west, the occasional falls of snow in our western districts include some of the heaviest in the world. Drifting snow is an occasional hazard in all districts of the British Isles except the most sheltered. But a blanket of snow may also benefit the farmer by protecting tender crops from severe frost. A period of snow may perhaps be regarded as a blessing in modern times, not only for the winter sports, but because it enforces a slower tempo of life while it lasts. Traffic afoot and awheel moves slowly, but also noiselessly. And the beauty of the winter scene, to which few can be altogether blind, doubtless affects our senses partly through the notable increase of light by reflection from the snow surface.

Snowfall

The frequency of snowfall is very much affected by elevation. On low ground the number of days a year on which any snow or sleet fell in 1912–38 (on the whole a period of mild winters) ranged from below 5 in Cornwall and below 10 on the south and west coasts generally to above 25 in the hill valleys of northeast England, and above 35 in northeast Scotland. Over the plains and east coast of England south of the Humber the number was between 15 and 20, London having about 15. South London has appreciably less snow than North London, because snow-bearing northerly winds are warmed up a degree or two during their passage across the great mass of heated buildings. The heating effect of our cities upon the air passing over them must be increasing as indoor heating standards are raised and heating plants become more powerful. The Chiltern Hills have

1. Brooks, C. E. P., and Glasspoole, J., *British Floods and Droughts*, London (Ernest Benn), 1928.

much more snow than any part of London; they shelter the whole London basin to some extent from snow with northerly winds, so that it is the least snowy area in eastern Britain apart from the Sussex coast, being fully exposed only to snowfall with easterly winds.

Over most of the country the snow season is generally from December to March, with occasional falls in November and April or May, but the farther northeast one goes, the longer is the period in which snow may fall. The effect of height can be allowed for by adding one day for every 50 feet above 200 feet. Thus with 15 days with snow in the lower Thames valley, at 800 feet on the North Downs the number has increased to about 27. In the Highlands of Scotland, which already have about 30 days in the valleys, at 3,000 feet snow can be expected on more than 80 days in the year, mostly, of course, in winter, but some in all seasons except the height of summer.

Lying snow

On most days, especially on low ground in the south, the snow melts either as it reaches the ground or within an hour or two, but sometimes it settles to form a snow cover which may persist for weeks in severe winters, though the average life of a carpet of snow on low ground in England is only about 6 days or less. The average number of days with snow lying (fig. 15) is under 5 a year all round the coast of Britain from western Scotland via Cornwall to the East Riding of Yorkshire, but conditions vary so greatly from year to year that the average has very little meaning. On the coasts of Cornwall and South Devon, Dorset, Hampshire and the Isle of Wight and Sussex, snow covers the ground only in exceptional years. On the streets of London it is also rare, partly for reasons already discussed; its chance of lying nowadays depends much upon whether it falls at the week-end. Inland the number of mornings with snow cover increases rapidly to more than 10 on the lowlands and 20 or so on the hills. In the mountain districts of Wales, Cumberland and Scotland snow lies much longer. It lasts longest not on the highest mountain tops, but in sheltered gullies into which it is blown by the wind, especially on the northeast face of the mountains. Two or three of the snowbeds in such positions on Ben Nevis and the Cairngorms are more or less permanent, lasting from year to year. They were thought to be permanent until they disappeared for a brief period in the late summer of 1933. They disappeared in three of the warm summers of the 1930s, and this has happened perhaps once a decade since. Warm rain in the latter half of the summer seems most conducive to melting of the lingering snowdrifts in such positions, especially after winters which did not produce much accumulation. But in the slightly cooler climate prevailing at the

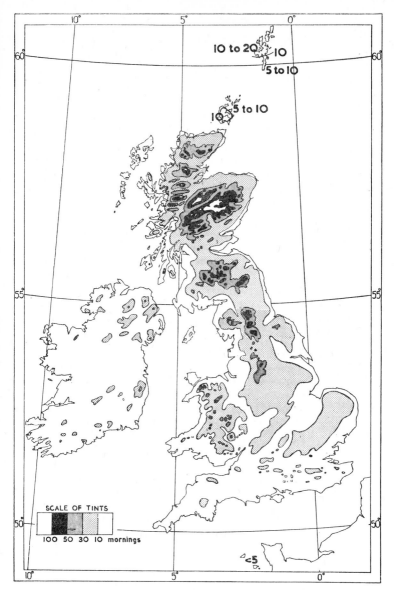

FIGURE 15. Frequency of Snow on the Ground. (Average number of mornings a year between 1912 and 1938 with the ground more than half covered by snow.) 1912–38 includes the mildest group of winters, but these are the only years for which a map is so far available. The figures on the map may therefore be a little too low to be representative on low ground. On high ground they are likely to be representative.

beginning of the century the condition of one Ben Nevis snowbed resembled an incipient glacier.

In the south and west snow rarely lies on low ground before December and in many winters is only an occasional visitor in December, January and February. Its rarity in comparison with most of northern, central and eastern Europe has more than once led to correspondents to *The Times* newspaper drawing unfavourable comparisons between the way English traffic is sometimes dislocated by conditions of snow and ice and that in which countries with more snow, but also more equipment, carry on regular traffic on their main routes. But late snows in March and April are not uncommon in this country and are occasionally heavy, leaving drifts in the banks and ditches long afterwards in cold seasons. The latest snows of any depth in southern England this century were as late as 16 and 17 May in 1935 and 1955. A deep fall in May is not unknown even in the west of Ireland in places where the winter may pass without as much as a snowflake being seen. Northerly winds, which are commoner in May than at any other time, are liable to bring fresh cold air direct from the Arctic ice. Such extremes of fickleness in spring are an aspect of our climate which some plants that thrive on the continent will not stand.

Christmas comes near the beginning of the season for snow in this country (except on the mountains) and snowy Christmases have never been the rule here. They were doubtless somewhat commoner than now in the rather colder winter climate of the period 1550–1850 and, perhaps, the Old Style calendar before 1752 which put Christmas Day on what is now 6 January increased the liability slightly. There has been snow on the ground near London over the Christmas holiday (including at some time on 25 December) 6 to 8 times in the last 60 years, sometimes only as patches of frozen snow left over from an earlier fall. Stripped of romance, it seems that the really predominant type of Christmas Day weather in southeast England is a rather calm day of pale winter sunshine. There was early morning frost inland in 18 to 20 years out of the past 60, and this lasted most of the day on 6 to 8 occasions. Mist or fog occurred 10 times. The weather generally became stormy soon after, and often milder. This is as near as we normally come to a 'white Christmas' in the present century, about 22 years out of 60 having some, usually slender, claim to the title in the countryside near London and a good deal fewer than this in the more maritime districts of England and Wales and Ireland.

On the mountains in the north the first snow cover comes much earlier. Snowstorms may be encountered on the highest summits in Scotland in any month, and much of the upper levels may be covered for a few days at any time from late September onwards. The snow sometimes melts away up to heights of 2,500 feet (800 metres) or more in mild periods during the winter, leaving only drifts in the furrows, but the loftiest summits and ridges commonly have a snow cover until April or May. Places at the foot of the Grampians, and in the glens, normally have from 30 to 70 days a year with snow lying (68 at Braemar); for the more extensive summit plateaux above 3,500–4,000 feet (i.e. above about 1,100-1,200 metres) the figures range from 150 to 250 days. The highest hills in England and Wales and in the Hebrides get about 80 days. At the opposite extremity of these islands in Kerry the frequency of days with snow lying even at heights of 3,000 feet and more (900–1,000 m.), 5–10 days a year, is only comparable with north London; and the heights of Dartmoor have it no oftener than the Chilterns (about 20 days).

Glazed frost

An unmitigated evil is glazed frost, or rain that freezes as it strikes the ground and solid objects. This happens when rain from warmer air overhead falls into air below the freezing point at the surface—a combination of circumstances that is not unusual along the Atlantic seaboard of the United States and sometimes occurs, though much more rarely, in or after bitter weather in this country. There have been about three serious cases of this, all in late January, in southern England in the last 40 years. The most widespread was on 27–28 January 1940, resulting from a day and a half of fine rain with temperature just below the freezing point over an area from Wales to Berkshire, Hampshire and southwest England. Everything in the rainy area became glazed with thick, shiny, slippery ice. Neither wheeled traffic nor people on foot could move without extreme danger. Birds had their wings frozen to their bodies and their feet frozen to the ground. Branches of some trees carried such a load of ice that they split and fell. Telephone wires carried up to 90 lb. of ice each between neighbouring posts, and many collapsed; high-tension electricity wires grew to 4 inches in diameter, and many were blown down in this condition. On this occasion, the overrunning mild southwesterly wind from the Atlantic, with a temperature about $+10°$ C (50° F), never reached the ground in England east of Dorset and by 29 January was ousted from the whole country by strengthening easterly surface winds. This halted the production of further glazed ice but strengthened the frost. A commoner sequel is for the mild air to arrive at the ground, and in America the name 'silver thaw' is used.

Hail

The formation of hail has been described in the first section of this chapter. Hail may occur in any month of the year, but the larger sizes of hailstone only grow when the temperatures near the ground are high enough to permit a particularly large moisture content in the air carried up in convection clouds. Small hail is therefore the characteristic form in winter and at temperatures near, or below, the freezing point: it is commonly angular in shape, having fallen through the cloud only once during growth with ice growing like rime mainly on the edges (where maximum impact and maximum fall-speed relative to the air and microscopic cloud droplets would occur). Large hail is more or less confined to the warmer part of the year, practically to situations with markedly unstable air (i.e. cold aloft) between May and October. The commonest size at this season is about that of a pea, and consists of a frozen raindrop surrounded by not more than one or two extra shells of ice resulting from being carried up in the cloud again before falling to the ground. But hailstones the size and shape of half grapefruit fell near Horsham, Sussex in September 1958. Hailstones of this size weigh several ounces and, as they probably strike the ground at speeds of 50–100 m.p.h., they are formidable missiles. They can do enormous damage to windows, glasshouses and crops, as well as to life and limb. Fortunately such storms are rare in England and their extent is only of the order of a mile across; but even the commoner pea-sized hail can damage crops. Storms which become major news items for the national press probably occur only about once in five years. Out of 31 such storms noted by Brooks, 27 were in England—6 in London, always first in the news—and only 3 were in Scotland and 1 in Wales.

Thunderstorms

The frequency of thunder is shown in fig. 16. The definition is a day with thunder heard; but, as in favourable conditions thunder is audible for 10 miles or so, this only means that there is a thunderstorm within that range. The frequencies run from about 5 or less at the most oceanic extremities of these islands to 15–20 in inland districts where the summer days are warmest. The distribution suggests that the great river basins (supply of moisture?) of Thames, Severn and especially Trent, and the nearby hills play a part in 'breeding' thunderstorms. Probably the number of storms which pass sufficiently nearly overhead to justify alarm even in the most nervous people is little more than a tenth of the frequencies given for thunder heard. In the most thundery places standing trees that have been killed by lightning, presumably at some time within the last fifty years or so, are a fairly common sight.

The frequency distribution of overhead thunderstorms is very local, and some areas seem to escape them almost altogether, a fact apparent from the 'thunderstorm survey' organized by Morris Bower. Even widespread thunderstorms seem to occur in a series of narrow streaks registering the life and passage of individual active cloud cells rather than in a

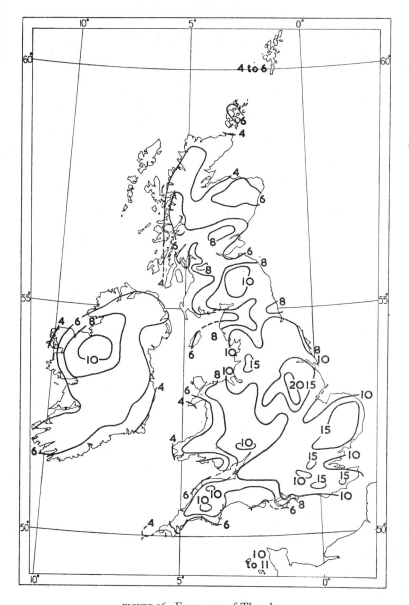

FIGURE 16. Frequency of Thunder.

(Average number of days a year between 1901 and 1930 when thunder was heard.)

broad massive area, as is well known to many country dwellers. These facts have lately been confirmed by radar observation of the cloud cells.

The most severe thunderstorms occur in summer (May to August, but especially in late July and early August) in the Midlands, east, southeast and southern England (fig. 16), where they often come after a few fine warm days. But although they are associated with warm, sultry weather, they do not always come in the heat of the afternoon; they often wait until evening. The greatest frequency in London, which is fairly typical of the inland districts of England, is between 1 and 2 p.m. G.M.T. (2–3 p.m. by summer time), closely followed by noon to 1 p.m. and 2–3 p.m., but frequency continues high until 11 p.m. Some of the worst storms in southeast England drift over from France, not arriving until after dark, which makes the lightning all the more impressive. A really severe thunderstorm needs plenty of very warm, moist air to feed it, and the limited area of Britain cannot often supply this air in sufficient quantity, so imports from the continent help out. According to a detailed study by Morris Bower,[1] these French storms strike the south coast oftenest around 8 p.m. (G.M.T.) and travel northwards to Norfolk, where they arrive about 2 or 3 a.m. the following morning.

Winter thunderstorms have some different characteristics. The intense convection in their case results from quick heating of very cold air from the Arctic or from Canada over the warm Atlantic waters. They are therefore commonest in districts nearest the Atlantic, in Shetland, Orkney, amongst the mountains and lochs of western Scotland and, especially, between the west coast and central Ireland—generally two to three times a winter, especially accompanying the violent upset of air at a cold front. The clouds are reported by airline pilots to be just as massive, and the vertical currents as violent, as with summer thunderstorms. But, because it is the fastest-moving cold airstreams that are heated most rapidly, these storms usually move fast with strong winds and each place is unlikely to hear more than one or two claps of thunder.

Lightning flashes are only dangerous when they strike downwards to the ground (or upwards from the ground). These include about half the total number of flashes in the year, but may be a larger proportion of the flashes in a particular storm; the others which go from one part of the cloud to another do no damage. The best estimate of the number of flashes to earth in London and central England is about 5 per square mile per year. The area of England (without Wales) is 51,356 square miles, which gives a total number of flashes to earth as about a quarter of a million a year. This sounds impressive, but a little consideration shows that

1. Bower, S. Morris, 'Diurnal Variation of Thunderstorms', *Meteorological Magazine*, **76**, 1947, pp. 255–258.

even in the open the risk of being killed by lightning is very small. From the point of view of a lightning flash, a wet man may be regarded as having an area of about 2 square yards, or less than one-millionth of a square mile, so the odds against death by lightning to a man out in the open country in every thunderstorm for a year are more than 200,000 to 1. Of course, people who take shelter under high trees, especially isolated trees, or who walk on bare hilltops and other exposed places during a storm, lessen the odds quite appreciably. However, only a small proportion of the population of Britain stays out in the country in a thunderstorm. In the streets of a town the risk is much less, because the buildings, especially those provided with lightning rods, act as an almost complete screen. Even indoors there is a slight risk, but only to those who stay close to high unearthed metal objects.

The official death-rate from lightning in England and Wales, 1921 to 1940, averaged a little more than 1 person per 4 millions per year. Among males the death-rate was 1 per 2 millions and among females, only 1 per 20 millions. This, of course, is because men, especially in the country, are more likely to be out in thunderstorms than are women. The number of deaths obviously depends on the frequency of thunderstorms as well as the number of people out in them, and is probably greatest in the agricultural districts of the Midlands and East Anglia.

Risk of damage to town buildings sufficient to warrant an insurance claim, based on some records from insurance offices in parts of Germany which have about as many thunderstorms as central England, is about 2 per square mile per annum. It is difficult to convert this into the risk to an individual building owing to complications of house height, areas of streets and gardens, etc. Possibly the chance of an average individual medium-sized house being struck in any one year is of the order of 1 in 10,000—and even then the damage is generally slight.

Besides these risks, the presence of abnormally high electrical charges in the air affects some people adversely, but these phenomena are very diverse and not well understood. They are probably mixed up with the nervous effects of the noise of thunder, and the only suggestion that can be made is that people who are nervous or on edge when thunder is about should as far as possible keep away from the districts where thunder is most frequent.

6

Mists, Fog and Soot

To continental peoples Britain is an island of mists and fogs. This was the opinion of Tacitus in AD 97 and seems to be a strong impression of those modern American visitors who take home tins of 'London fog' as a souvenir! Before the Industrial Revolution the fogs were chiefly feared as the embodiment of damp, causing rheumatism, agues and fevers. But latterly one meets increasing complaint of the sulphurous, tarry dirt of town fogs. Mist and fog, like clouds, are generally produced by the chilling of air until condensation begins as multitudes of minute droplets forming on microscopic nuclei, such as sea salt or other chemical particles floating in the air. *Radiation fog* forms when the temperature of the air next the ground drops below the saturation point on clear calm evenings. That it is the cooling of the ground under the clear sky that is effective can often be seen by the first symptoms being a low 'ground mist' forming just a foot or two over the grass. If one travels on such an evening, the mist is found first in those areas where the sky is clear. The coldest places are the dips and hollows and valley bottoms, and there the fog is found first of all— unless local moisture sources, such as a rain-soaked wood, a lake or a marsh, produce a higher dew point and corresponding early condensation of fog by the night cooling in their vicinity. *Advection fog* is formed when a warm moist air current advances over cold, especially snow-covered, ground. Condensation is copious with the arrival of mild maritime tropical air from the warm Atlantic after cold snaps in autumn, and cold walls inside our houses (and the cold metal of our cars) run with moisture. *Hill fog* is simply cloud so low that it envelops the high ground.

There is one other type of fog of quite different nature, occasionally seen in this country. *Steam fog*, or 'Arctic sea smoke' (from its occurrence over narrow leads of open water amongst the Arctic pack-ice), is formed in the same way as steam emerging from a kettle when the air is 20° C or more colder than water over which it is passing. Steam, usually in small amounts, is most commonly seen over estuaries and creeks in the first cold nights of autumn when the water is still warm. But the writer once saw a dense, turbulent steam fog covering miles of the Shannon estuary on a frosty morning in early October.

Radiation fog occurs oftenest in autumn and winter anticyclones, when the wind is light and the sky clear. In some anticyclones, however, there is a persistent layer of stratus cloud which prevents the ground from radiating away its heat, so that the nights are not frosty and the days are dull and cheerless. It is the other type of anticyclone, with clear skies above, which brings the frosty foggy nights; in towns the fog is smoky, peculiarly resistant to dissipation and often lasts through the day, to thicken again the following night.

The official definition of 'fog' is visibility less than 1,100 yards (1,000 metres), which is a serious handicap for aviation and somewhat less so for marine navigation but would pass almost unnoticed by the 'man-in-the-street'. For many practical purposes 'thick fog', visibility less than 220 yards, is more critical. This occurs on more than 10 days in the year, nearly all in winter in open country in the north Midlands and around London; elsewhere it is met on about 5 days a year, less on the coasts. Around London most fog is of the radiation type; hill fog becomes common only at heights above 500 feet. Advection fog is almost independent of height, but rarely causes thick fog near London. Hill fogs can be dense. They are also about twice as frequent on ground above 500 feet as fogs on the low ground. So there is a general slight tendency for dense fogs to be more frequent as one goes towards higher ground. The most frequently foggy place near London is Woldingham in Surrey, at a height of 797 feet, followed fairly closely by Elstree, Barnet and Mill Hill all around 400 feet or more. London itself gains from its own artificial warmth. It sometimes happens that visibility at street level is moderately good, but a thick pall over the roof-tops turns day into night. The heat from the buildings raises the air temperature enough to evaporate most of the fog droplets near them, but the air just above remains foggy and the smoke accumulates.

Modern factory chimneys have been designed to minimize pollution and inject it at a high level, but old-fashioned domestic fires put forth a lot of soot. Traffic also helps to thicken the fog with the moisture from steam engines and the exhaust pipes of diesel and petrol-driven vehicles. This can be serious when the air is very still and local concentrations of moisture linger: on a cross-country journey near London in December with visibility generally about 500 yards, and the rimy woods and meadows seen in a rather beautiful misty sunshine, one may sometimes find very dense fog reducing traffic to a crawl precisely and only on the busiest arterial roads. Only the electric railways are quite immune to this.

Clean white country fog consists mostly of nearly pure water drops with the merest trace of salt. In large towns the fog droplets tend to form around minute particles of soot, often chemically active. The resulting dirty yellow mixture, Dickens's 'London particular' or a 'pea souper', has long been a speciality of our capital city; it caused complaint in the days of Queen Elizabeth I, and long before that, of the unhealthy contagion and 'stench of burning sea-coal'.[1] In the *Annals of Philosophy* it is recorded that between 27 December 1813 and 2 January 1814 'a most extraordinary fog prevailed in London, and seems to have extended a great many miles round in every direction. It was frequently so thick that it was impossible to see across the street; candles were burnt in most of the shops and counting-houses all day long. . . . In London the thickness of the fog was still further increased by the smoke of the city; so much so, that it produced a very sensible effect on the eyes, and the coal-tar varnish might be distinctly perceived by the smell.'

The effect on health was brought home by the mortality statistics for 'Cattle Show' week, 7–13 December 1873, when a similar fog occurred. For the week in question these showed an increase in the Administrative County of London over the average death rate for the time of year by 243 per million of the population, an increase of 40%. Similar increases followed in the fogs of 1880, 1892, 1948 and 1952.

The London fog which developed in an anticyclone on 5 December 1952 illustrated the nature of the phenomenon. This was the first occasion on which the word 'smog' ($=$ smoke $+$ fog) was used to describe such an occurrence in this country, though the word had come into use in the United States to describe a similar disaster in Donora, Pennsylvania, in 1948.

The whole Thames valley was occupied by a pool of cold stagnant air to a depth of 200–500 feet, separated by a sharp boundary from the warmer air above. Thus London was sealed on either side by the chalk hills, and above by an impenetrable inversion. A natural fog of water drops formed in this enclosed space, but to this was added the smoke from London's innumerable chimneys, which accumulated from day to day. At County Hall, the weight of smoke in the air increased from 0·49 milligrams per cubic metre on 4 December to 4·46 on the 7th and 8th.[2] The cost of the necessary washing of curtains and clothes, and the damage to delicate fabrics, to say nothing of cleaning of walls and windows, probably ran into hundreds of thousands of pounds. Still worse, though less immediately obvious, are the chemicals in the air resulting largely from the burning of coal, but partly from industrial processes. The worst is sulphur dioxide, which is a very active chemical and reacts with the moisture and oxygen in the air to form sulphuric acid. It is this which gives a London fog its acrid taste; and besides its destructive effect on all sorts of materials, it is directly dangerous to health. The amount of sulphur dioxide in the London

1. See Trevelyan's *English Social History*, p. 31, Longmans, 1943.

2. 'The London Fog. A first survey of the December disaster', *Smokeless Air*, No. 85, Spring 1953, pp. 100–111, published by the National Smoke Abatement Society.

ir rose from 1 part in 7 millions to 1 part in about 1 million two days after he fog began. The soot in the air seems to have reached its peak on the second night of the fog, though it remained high thereafter. The sulphur dioxide which, being a gas, does not settle out reached its peak two days later. Visibility at London Airport was less than a dozen yards for almost 8 hours from the morning of the 6th. Deaths in Greater London increased from 2,062 in the week ended 6 December to 4,703 in the following week, and remained high until 20 December. The peak death-rate (900 a day) occurred on the 8th and 9th. Putting the normal weekly deaths at this season as 2,000, this fog cost altogether about 4,000 lives. The rise was especially great in deaths from bronchitis and pneumonia, which increased more than sevenfold.

Smoky fogs appear in every densely populated area. The cost is colossal. Taking into account damage to ironwork, buildings and fabrics, injury to crops and loss by death and sickness, *The Times* in an article on 21 April 1953 made a conservative estimate of the annual loss as £3 per head of population a year, or a total of £150 million a year.

The quantity of soot put into the air by the chimneys of Britain is measured in two ways. The pollution floating in the air is found by sucking a measured quantity of air through filter paper and comparing the resulting stain with a standard scale of tints. The pollution dropped from the air is collected in 'pollution gauges', like giant raingauges. There are not many of the filter type in use, but enough of the deposit gauges to enable a rough estimate to be made of the total deposit over the whole of England (without Wales). The figure just before the beginning of the attack on the problem by the Clean Air Act came out as about $4\frac{1}{2}$ million tons a year. This includes all kinds of 'pollution'—dust from the roads and fields, pollen from plants, etc., but it is estimated that rather more than half— 2,300,000 tons a year—comes from the burning of coal. This is an average of 47 tons per square mile, but it is very unequally distributed. Over the area within about 12 miles of the centre of London the deposit is very heavy, averaging nearly 220 tons to the square mile or about $2\frac{1}{2}$ ounces to the square yard. In 91 other large towns the deposit averages nearly 160 tons to the square mile. Over open country the rate is little more than 4 tons per square mile.

Fortunately for towns, but unfortunately for the countryside, in average windy weather about half the smoke is blown away. This applies especially to the chemical gases, such as sulphur dioxide, and the finest smoke particles. The smoke trails from London and the other great town areas, including those of the Low Countries and the Ruhr, may be followed sometimes for hundreds of miles over this country and the surrounding seas. Often the boundary is sharp, as when with westerly winds in autumn and winter one commonly finds visibility only 2–5 miles over eastern England between Lincoln and Tyneside, and in the Forth-Clyde Valley but visibility 50 miles or more in the intervening hill country of Northumberland and the Borders as well as everywhere north of the hills of Fife. In the Isle of Man winds from the southeast can quickly reduce visibility from 20 miles to a mere 3 miles.

Even the large soot particles are mostly blown some distance downwind from the chimney which produces them, and since the prevailing winds in this country blow from the west and southwest, the dirtiest parts of towns are usually those between the centre and one or two miles to the east northeast. Since the west and southwest parts of a town are the cleanest they tend to be the best residential districts. The densest population and the factories tend to congregate to the east of the city centre, and so increase the output of smoke in that district.

The relation between coal-burning and dirt is brought out in fig. 17 reproduced by permission of the National Smoke Abatement Society from work by Brooks in 1947. The three maps show: (a) an index of the consumption of coal, (b) the soot deposit, and (c) the frequency of poor visibility. Coal is used both in private houses and in factories, but as a rule factory furnaces are more efficient and have been taken to produce only half as much pollution per ton of coal as do house fires. The index used in fig. 17(a) is therefore the amount of coal burnt in house fires plus half that burnt in factories, in tons per square kilometre a year. The figures which were provided by the Ministries of Fuel and Power and of Town and Country Planning had to be smoothed before being plotted, and the value at any one point on the map represents the average figure for an area of 90 square kilometres (about 35 square miles). The black areas represent a consumption of over 4,000 tons a year per square kilometre, and the shaded areas over 1,000 tons. The densely populated manufacturing areas stand out very clearly.

The smokiness of the air in a town naturally increases with the population, but not proportionally. A rough rule worked out by Dr. A. R. Meetham is that smokiness is proportional to the square root of the population, so that quadrupling the size of a town doubles its smokiness. This rule does not apply to Cardiff, which is an unusually clean city because anthracite is a popular fuel there, or to London which, although the smokiest city in Britain, is less smoky than it ought to be for its size.

Fig. 17(b) shows the deposits in pollution gauges set up in open country or well to the west or southwest of large towns. The values are in tons per square kilometre per year, and show how even away from towns the areas of greatest coal consumption agree very closely with those of greatest pollution of the air. Finally, fig. 17(c) shows the effect on brightness of the

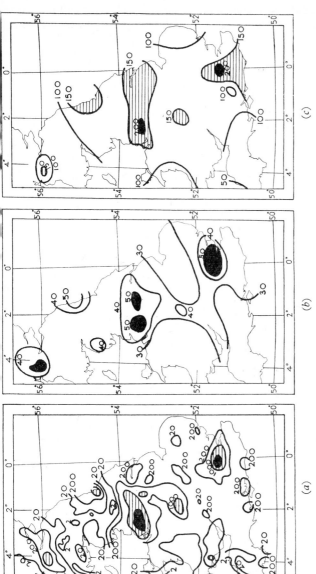

FIGURE 17.

(a) An index of Coal Burnt.
(b) Pollution measured at country sites.
(c) Average yearly number of Hazy Days—with visibility less than 10 km. (6¼ miles) at noon.

sky; it represents the annual number of hazy days (visibility less than 6 miles at midday). It can be taken as representing roughly the loss of light and heat from the sun, especially in winter, in the situation as it was before the Clean Air Act. In the three months December to February the number of hours of bright sunshine falls off from about 150 well away to the west of London to under 70 in the heart of the City, so that roughly speaking each additional day of poor visibility above 120 represents the loss of nearly an hour of bright sunshine.

One effect of atmospheric pollution on health was brought out in *Smokeless Air* for autumn 1953. A map showing the deaths from bronchitis of men aged 45–54 was found to resemble the map of air pollution reproduced in fig. 17(*b*). Superposed on a general decrease from northwest to southeast from 11 to 12 per 10,000 population in northern England to under 6 per 10,000 in the southeastern counties, were black spots of over 20 in the manufacturing area of Lancashire, 15–20 in the districts of Middlesbrough, West Riding of Yorkshire, and Birmingham, and 9–10 in London. The average annual death-rate from bronchitis for the whole country of 17·8 per 10,000 (in 1948) compared very badly with those for Scandinavia where the air is unpolluted—0·2 in Norway and 0·4 in Sweden!

As an illustration of the local effects in a large town, fig. 18 sketches the 'dirtiness' of London air in a manner comparable with fig. 17(*b*). This is

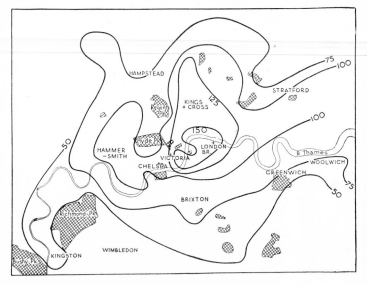

FIGURE 18. The 'Dirtiness' of London Air. (Before the Clean Air Act.)

based on data from pollution gauges, eked out by local figures of coal consumption and relative frequencies of fogs. It is necessarily generalized; for local conditions vary from street to street. A wide street running from west or southwest to east or northeast, giving free play to the prevailing winds, is cleaner than a narrow twisty street which obstructs the flow of air. London's parks are great cleaners, the trees and shrubs filtering out the smoke and soot particles, so that the soot deposit in the middle of Hyde Park is considerably less than that on its edges. This can be seen from the way the lines of equal dirtiness tend to curve round the parks (shown by shaded areas). The Thames appears to have little effect, partly because it has no trees to act as filters and partly because the factories and railways on its banks, and even the steamers on the river, are sources of pollution. The effect of the parks belt in the heart of west London—Hyde Park, Green Park and St. James's Park—is clearly shown by the pollution-gauge figures, making a comparatively clean strip, the influence of which seems to extend across the Thames. In the parks and open spaces, however, condensation of moisture in fog is commoner and thicker because of the lower night temperatures than in the built-up streets. For this reason, in foggy situations, particularly at night, the motorist often gets along best in the built-up streets of the city centre which constitutes a 'heat island'.

In the suburbs of London the smokiness of the air changes with the wind direction. For example, at Kew Observatory, near Richmond, to the west of London, the number of smoke particles per cubic metre of air in winter is about four times as great when the wind is from east or east-northeast as it is with winds from northwest, southwest, south or south-east. Winds from north-northwest are about half as smoky as those from east, because in that direction lie the populous suburbs of Brentford and Ealing. The pollution also depends on the season, time of day and lapse rate of temperature with height.

Amongst the massive building blocks of the city centres where the streets are like canyons between vertical walls, and air movement is reduced to a minimum, pollution is liable to become stratified in the vertical (as well as localized in patches that only slowly disperse whatever their level). At street level dust and the fumes of petrol and diesel oil are prominent, and concentrations of carbon monoxide 5 feet above the pavements during dense traffic in our big cities occasionally reach toxic levels for brief periods. Near roof level is the layer of greatest smokiness from the countless chimneys. The middle floors may get slightly cleaner air.

Winter is, of course, worse than summer, because more smoke is thrown into the air from house fires, and also because there is less vertical exchange of air by convection. At Kew Observatory smokiness in December is about three times as great as in June to August. There is a weekly cycle because in factory districts, where the fires are often damped down at week-ends, Sundays are relatively clean, but pollution increases rapidly on Monday mornings when the fires are stoked up again. Residential, especially working-class, districts also have a well-marked daily cycle. In the mornings, when the fires are lit for breakfast, there is a great outpouring causing a maximum of smokiness about 7–9 a.m. This smoke concentration drifts with the wind, and if the wind is light the smoke keeps together, bringing a haze (or fog) climax some time later at places away down wind. For instance, haze from Glasgow and the Lowland towns commonly thickens till midday or after in eastern Scotland. In the cities during the day the smoke clears to some extent, reaching a minimum between 2 and 3 p.m., both because the fires are allowed to settle down and because increasing convection clears a good deal of it away above the roof-tops. Then in the evening, fires are stoked up again and convection dies away, so that there is a second maximum of smokiness between 8 and 9 p.m. Finally, late at night the fires go out, the smoke gradually drifts away and, especially in windy weather, the cleanest part of the 24 hours comes between 3 and 4 a.m. On Sundays, of course, the cycle is different, the breakfast maximum comes about an hour later and is prolonged through the morning by preparations for the Sunday dinner in districts where cooking is done on coal fires. The fact that the daily pattern so closely follows the domestic round correctly indicates that domestic open fires are the main source of smoke.

The sulphur dioxide does not fall out of the air as do soot particles, but is rather more readily removed upwards by turbulence and possibly more easily washed out by rain. At any rate, the average 'life' of a smoke particle in the air is two or three days, that of a molecule of sulphur dioxide only half a day. The finest smoke particles are so small that in still air they fall only inches a day and can travel long distances, whereas the greatest concentrations of sulphur dioxide are close to the factory areas and districts where particularly sulphurous coal is burnt on domestic fires.

A detailed investigation was carried out in Leicester[1] in 1937–39 which threw much light on the problem of pollution. Three things were measured regularly: the weight of smoke particles in the air, the concentration of sulphur dioxide and the ultra-violet daylight. If we compare the values of these quantities in the centre of the city with the average at three points

1. Department of Scientific and Industrial Research, 'Atmospheric Pollution in Leicester. A Scientific Survey', *Atmospheric Pollution Research Technical Paper No.* 1, London (H.M.S.O.), 1945, 3s.

in open country, one $4\frac{3}{4}$ miles to the southeast, one $2\frac{3}{4}$ miles to the west, and the third 6 miles to the northwest, and call the values in the centre 100, we have as country values in winter: smoke 27; sulphur dioxide (volumetric measurements) 14; ultra-violet radiation 135. In summer the figures were: smoke 29; sulphur dioxide 20; ultra-violet 134. These figures show that sulphur dioxide is concentrated to a greater extent in the centre of the city than is the smoke, no doubt because of the factory chimneys there.

Smoke collects at times over any town. Old Edinburgh was affectionately known as the smoke producer, 'Auld Reekie'. But, in spite of smog disasters in London, Pennsylvania, the Belgian Meuse Valley (in 1930) and elsewhere, pollution is not insuperable. Pittsburgh, formerly one of the dirtiest towns in America, has set the example by achieving a reduction of 93% of the heavy smoke pollution after just six years of relentless legislation (as described in *Smokeless Air*, summer, 1953).

In this country the National Smoke Abatement Society (now renamed the National Society for Clean Air) waged a campaign for many years to limit by law the emission of smoke into the air. At last in 1956 the Clean Air Act was passed, though owing to the need for adaptation of much equipment it is still (1962) very far from fully effective. It began to take effect in certain places from 1958 onwards. Under the Act it became an offence to put out black smoke at any time, and local authorities are empowered to designate Smoke Control Areas within which it will not be permitted to put out any smoke at all. Time is allowed for the conversion of inefficient fireplaces and furnaces, so as to ensure proper combustion, and government grants are available towards the costs of conversion. Either electricity or smokeless fuels have to be used. The latter do not, however, reduce the production of sulphur compounds. By the end of June 1962, 1,026 orders had been made instituting Smoke Control Areas covering a total of 219,176 acres. About 87% of the acreage is in former centres of pollution ('black areas'). But they constitute only about 0·7% of the area of England and Wales, mostly in Greater London, Lancashire and Yorkshire. As the first places chosen have naturally been small areas which, for one reason or another, it was easy or important to convert to smokeless firing, it is too early yet for any convincing figures of reduced pollution due to the Act. All the Control Areas themselves are often subject to pollution blown in from neighbouring places where smoke is not yet controlled. There is evidence, however, of increased sunshine in central Manchester when the wind blows from the Smoke Control Area. Moreover London can be said to have lost its smoke when comparisons are made with the 1920s and 1930s. In the city of London pollution has been reduced by over 40%; although this is not a result of the Act, it is a result of conversion to central heating and smokeless fuels, coupled with better factory chimneys and furnaces than formerly outside the central area.[1]

1. For further study of the changes in air pollution the reader should refer to the yearly reports of the former Fuel Research Station, Greenwich and, since 1958, of the Warren Springs Laboratory, Stevenage, published by Her Majesty's Stationery Office.

7

Local Climates

SUPERIMPOSED on the general climate are local variations due to exposure and aspect, soil, the presence of water, trees and houses. We have already alluded to differences of climate over quite short distances in the occurrence of mists and fogs and noxious traffic fumes. Such local variations and others which we shall mention in this chapter require serious thought when choosing where to live, where to build a factory or where to site an orchard or merely pitch a tent. Their study is a special field known as Microclimatology, the subject of textbooks and treatises[1] whose applications range from the physiological reactions of the human body to the weather to the proper siting of crops. Moreover, a good knowledge of the characteristic climatic behaviour of one's own locality makes possible a more practical interpretation of any weather forecast.

Town climates

The disturbing effects of Man upon the free play of wind and weather are at their greatest in towns. One by-product of town-planning is a partial control of the climate that will be experienced in the streets and squares. It is well to know something of the factors involved so that this control can be exercised consciously and wisely. From the paragraphs that follow it will be seen that both the broad urban highways or boulevards of the twentieth century and the narrow cross-streets between high buildings favoured by an earlier age have their uses. Trees, as we have seen, make the parks oases of purer air; the presence of trees in the streets of a city centre is in most ways beneficial except in narrow streets where enough ventilation to clear the exhaust fumes of traffic is the major problem.

The city whose climate has been most exhaustively studied is Vienna, and the results have been published on behalf of the city council in a useful book[2] full of facts, figures and analysis, much of it applicable to our

1. E.g. Brunt, D., 'Some factors in micro-climatology', *Royal Meteorological Society* (Presidential Address 1945), *Quarterly Journal*, Vol. 71, pp. 1–10, London, 1945. and on a related subject:

Sutton, O. G., *Micrometeorology, a study of the physical processes in the lowest layers of the Earth's atmosphere*, New York, London and Toronto (McGraw-Hill), 1953.

2. Steinhauser, F., Eckel, O., and Sauberer, F., 'Klima und Bioklima von Wien', (parts) I, II and III, published 1955, 1957 and 1959 by the Gesellschaft für Meteorologie, Wien, Hohe Warte 38.

own towns. Many traverses right across the built-up area have been made by cars equipped with instruments measuring temperature and other items, starting in 1927. Lately Chandler,[1] with the support of the Department of Scientific and Industrial Research, has made some similar traverses across London. The results agree with the Vienna ones closely, apart from the obviously individual characteristics of terrain and town plan. Studies with a close network of observing stations have also been made in Bath.[2] Local differences due to complex environments are presumably greatest under clear skies and nearly still air in summer and winter, and such occasions have been picked by the investigators.

Height differences of up to 200 metres (600 feet) in the surroundings of Vienna as of London produced differences in the liability to fog, snow and frost. We shall here concentrate, however, on effects of the town and buildings.

In clear cold winter weather the city centres may be as much as 6 to 8° C warmer than the coldest spots on the outskirts at night and in the morning. Such values were measured in Vienna in February and on a frosty night in May and in London in October. On 1 January 1962 the minimum temperature in Westminster and Croydon was −5·6° C (22° F) against −13·4° C (8° F) at Gatwick Airport, Surrey. In the middle of a cold winter's day the temperature differences between town and country in Vienna were reduced to about 3° C, with sunny north–south streets 0·5° C warmer than shady east–west streets.

Daytime temperatures in spring and autumn appear to show only small differences of 1 to 2° C at most. Estates of small houses and broad roadways appear about this much warmer than either streets shut in amongst the big buildings of the city centre or squares with trees. At night these temperature differences are reversed.

Tests in Vienna on the hottest summer days with afternoon temperatures reaching 30–34° C (86–93° F) showed that places with trees and narrow shady streets with little traffic had air temperatures lower by 2–4° C, and in one case 7° C, than elsewhere. Broad streets in the city centre were 2–2·5° C warmer than leafy residential roads. The temperature differences between city and suburbs increase at night in summer too, with parks and gardens becoming notably cool.

In Vienna as in most British towns westerly winds are much commoner

1. Chandler, T. J., 'Temperature and humidity traverses across London', *Weather*, Vol. 17, pp. 235–241, 1962. See also 'London's urban climate', *Geographical Journal*, Vol. 128, pp. 279–302, 1962.

2. Balchin, W. G. V., and Pye, N., 'A microclimatological investigation of Bath and the surrounding district', *Quarterly Journal of the Royal Meteorological Society*, Vol. 73, pp. 297–319, London, 1947.

than north or south winds, so that streets running east and west are best ventilated. Eddies at corners and thermal currents due to differences of heating in sun and shadow (and between dark-coloured asphalt roadway and light-coloured pavements) may help materially in clearing petrol fumes up to roof level. Wind speeds are on average two to three times as strong at cross-roads as in the streets, and similar differences are found between the middle of the roadway and the side-walks. Trees reduce the prevailing wind-speeds on a street by 20 to 30%.

Humidity (dew-point) appears to be generally lowered in the city centres by the swift removal of surface moisture in drains and the lack of vegetation and porous soils. Relative humidities are also reduced by the higher temperatures prevailing.

Average frequencies of snow lying in the London area in the years 1920–29 were about 8 mornings a year on the outskirts at Hampstead Heath and Harpenden (Rothamsted), both over 400 feet above sea level, 4 mornings at Kew near the river and probably 2 or less in Westminster and Kensington. Averages for 1950–59 show rather greater frequencies on the outskirts (14 mornings at Harpenden and 6 at Kew) but not in the centre.

Let us now turn to factors creating local differences in natural climates.

Soil

Different soils have different heat capacities and conductivities, and these are subject to great changes according to whether the soil is dry or wet or holds much air. Sandy soils are poor conductors of heat; they also dry readily unless there is some impervious substratum of clay. Sandy areas tend to be a degree or so warmer by day than places on clay, but on the other hand night air temperatures tend to fall lower (by 3–4° C or more) over sand. This means that frosts may shorten the growing season by 6–8 weeks. The average period of immunity from damaging frosts at different types of site in the English Midlands is given by Manley[1] as:

Enclosed urban surroundings 5 April–5 November
Hillslope with favourable aspect 15 April–1 November
Low-lying ground generally 15 May–10 October
Frost hollows (cold air pools in valley bottoms) 5 June–12 September
Sandy lowlands (flat) 20 June–25 August.

Fig. 19 presents the general picture of frequency of night frosts in an average year over the British Isles, on which obviously strong local variations due to soil and relief must be superimposed. These dates and frequencies are also subject to wide variations in individual years. At

1. Manley, G., 'Topographical features and the climate of Britain', *Geographical Journal*, Vol. 103, pp. 243–258, London, 1944.

Rothamsted[1] in the years 1921–50 the date of the last frost in spring varied from 23 March to 29 May, the average being 29 April; the first autumn frost varied from 11 October to 15 November (a narrower range than in spring), average date 26 October. The length of the frost-free period ranged from 148 to 230 days, depending most on the spring date; the average was 180 days.

Light-coloured surfaces reflect away more of the heat and light of bright sunshine than dark surfaces do. Some of this falls on the passer-by. The effect is most clearly seen when the ground is covered with a layer of powdery new-fallen snow. This reflects 80% or so of the sun's rays falling upon it, so that the air seems full of sparkling light and the sunshine feels surprisingly warm. But this also means that the snow is absorbing very little heat, so fresh white snow is slow to melt. Light sandy soils and chalk produce similar effects only in much less degree, whereas dark soils absorb most of the radiation falling on them.

Air in the soil is a very good insulator: the more air there is in a soil (or in fresh snow), the more heat stays on the surface and the less penetrates to any depth. Loose sand on sand dunes becomes very hot in the summer sun, but one has only to scrape away an inch or two to find temperatures perhaps 20–25° C lower. The warmth and shelter to be found amongst the sand dunes has saved the day for many a would-be lazy holiday-maker in windy summer weather even in northern Scotland. (Picnic food and drink may need to be protected from the heat of the sand surface, preferably by a white cloth cover with plenty of air space underneath.) Hot ground warms the air above it, but the effect is large only up to a few inches to a foot above it.

	June		Highest Max.	November	
	Max.	Min.		Max.	Min.
Tarmac　.　.　.	42·5°	10·0°	53·3°	10·3°	0·0°
Bare earth　.　.　.	35·4°	10·4°	46·1°	8·4°	1·6°
Sand　.　.　.	35·1°	9·1°	44·4°	8·1°	0·4°
Brick rubble　.　.　.	31·1°	9·9°	—	7·8°	1·1°
Grass　.　.　.	29·3°	10·0°	38·3°	6·7°	3·4°
Shade air temperatures 4 feet above ground　.	21·8°	7·6°	29·5°	7·4°	1·2°

53·3° C is 128° F, and 42·5° C is nearly 109° F; it will be observed how dark surfaces undergo the greatest temperature variations, getting even hotter than loose sand. This table also illustrates the findings about differential heating in towns.

1. Smith, L. P., 'Length of a frost-free period', *Meteorological Magazine*, **83,** pp. 81–83, London, 1954.

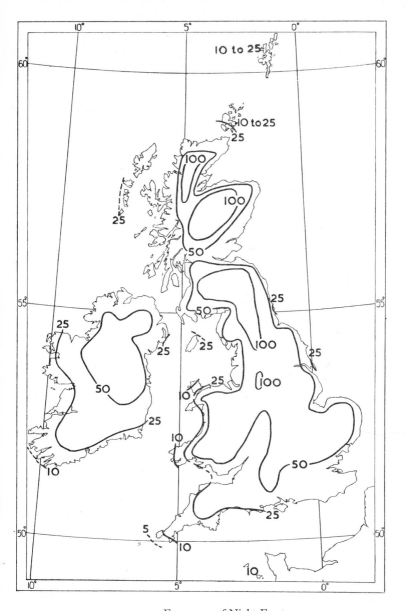

FIGURE 19. Frequency of Night Frosts.

(Average number of days a year between 1913 and 1940 when the air temperature fell to 0° C or below.)

Observations were made on Salisbury Plain in 1925 of temperatures just below various surfaces.[1] The table on p. 90 gives the averages of the highest and lowest temperatures (°C) each day in two sample months, a rather warm June and a notably cold November. It also gives the extreme highest values.

Wet soil behaves rather more like a water body. The heat capacity and conductivity of soil are increased in proportion to the amount of water it holds, and its temperature variations become small and sluggish. Evaporation also contributes to keeping the temperature of wet soil rather low. Permeable soils such as sand and chalk seldom become saturated right through. The moisture soaks away rapidly; these soils soon dry. Undrained soils and those that have impermeable clay beneath can dry only by evaporation; these soils tend to remain cold and damp for longer periods.

Brunt[2] has shown that the fall of temperature of the soil t hours after sunset can be reasonably represented by the expression

$$\frac{2}{\sqrt{\pi}} \cdot \frac{\sigma T^4 (1 - a - b\sqrt{e})}{\varrho_1 c_1 \sqrt{K_1}} \sqrt{t}$$

σ is the constant of Stefan's Law of radiation cooling such that σT^4 is the radiation from a perfect ('black body') radiating surface in gram calories per square centimetre per minute; e is the water vapour pressure in the air; and ϱ_1, c_1 and K_1 are the density, specific heat and specific conductivity of the soil. a and b depend on the level of absolute temperature T, i.e. $(273 + °C)$ prevailing; they can be assigned average values for each month. It will be seen that the cooling decreases as the water vapour content of the air increases. ϱ_1, c_1 and K_1 vary with the nature and condition of the soil. It appears, however, that the cooling rates they give for wet soil, dry soil and snow respectively are in the approximate ratios of 1 to 5 to 10. This confirms that the temperature of wet soils changes least from day to night, and that the cooling rate is greatly enhanced when snow covers the ground.

Vegetation

Grass traps a lot of air below the blades, particularly if it is long. This is why the day temperatures measured just within the surface under grass (see the table on p. 90) were lower than in bare ground, but the top of the grass gets hotter by day and colder by night than either bare soil or more open

1. Johnson, N. K., and Davies, E. L., 'Some measurements of temperatures near the surface in various kinds of soils', *Quarterly Journal of the Royal Meteorological Society*, Vol. 53, pp. 45–57, London, 1927.

2. Brunt, D., *Physical and Dynamical Meteorology* (2nd edition, p. 140), Cambridge, 1941.

egetation. Cornfields behave similarly. Paton[1] examined conditions in
ne summer weather within a field of ripening wheat. The highest tem-
)eratures attained in the afternoons were midway up the stems about the
evel where the leaves curl over and were 4° C higher than over neighbour-
ng fields of bare soil; these maximum temperatures were also 3° C higher
han at the level of the ears. Barley produced temperatures intermediate
)etween those of wheatfields and bare ground. These temperature differ-
:nces affect the location of convection and are potent sources of the ther-
nals that interest gliders. On clear nights the temperatures over cornfields
vere slightly (0·5° C) lower than over bare soil.

Forests produce rather larger scale effects. By day the upper surfaces
)f the leaves take up the sun's heat; the heated air spreads upwards or is
;wept away by the breeze so that the air beneath remains cool. At night
he crowns of the trees cool and the cooled air sinks, but as the whole layer
)f air beneath the leaves has to be cooled instead of a shallow surface layer,
:he fall of temperature is much less than over grassland.

A wood modifies the climate of the open country in several ways,
:hanging the temperature, humidity, sunshine, wind, evaporation and
:ven, to some extent, the composition of the air. On temperature the main
effect is to decrease the diurnal variation, but this differs considerably
according to the type of tree. Deciduous trees in summer cover the ground
with a high roof of leaves which forms a relatively light covering over a
comparatively clear space through which dappled sunshine finds its way,
while the wind makes a small but perceptible air motion; the difference
between day and night, though lessened, remains appreciable. In winter,
when the leaves have fallen, the bare branches offer little obstacle to the
processes of weather. Light conifers such as pine and larch offer less
resistance to the sun in summer than do well-grown deciduous trees, but
more in winter; consequently, the daily range of temperature in a plantation of light conifers is greater than in deciduous woods in summer, but
less in the other seasons. On the other hand, a dense stand of spruce forms
an almost impenetrable obstacle, shutting out sun, wind, snow and, to a
considerable degree, even rain. The ground beneath such a wood has,
practically speaking, no weather. The effect of this difference can be seen
by comparing the rich undergrowth of an open deciduous wood or natural
open forests of fir, pine and birch with the dead world inside an old spruce
plantation. The amount of the sun's warmth which reaches the ground in
a mixed forest, or an average pine wood, is about 3% of that in the open
country, but in a dense spruce forest it is less than 1%. The quantitative
effect naturally depends very much on local conditions. At any time of day

1. Paton, J., 'Temperatures and airflow within a wheatfield', *Weather*, Vol. 3,
pp. 22–26, London, 1948.

temperatures in a wood vary greatly from place to place, temperatures being generally higher under old high trees than among younger growth. On a typical summer day in high pine forest, without undergrowth, in Germany, H. G. Koch[1] found that at sunrise air temperature near the ground was 4° C higher than in a plantation of young trees 3 feet high. Two hours later the temperatures were alike, after which the more open situation was the warmer of the two until nearly sunset. The greatest difference, 2° C, was reached about 8 a.m.

The relative humidity near the ground in a wood is generally higher than in the open, partly because of the moisture transpired by the leaves and partly because the ground dries out less rapidly after rain than in the open. The difference is least during the night and early morning, when dew is deposited in the open and on the upper part of the tree crowns. A few hours later, when the dew on open ground has evaporated and the air there is warming up, with vertical convection developing, the difference of humidity becomes great. It is especially between about 4 p.m. and 6 p.m. on a hot summer afternoon that the forest appears most dank and cool.

Wind speeds in a wood are naturally much less than in the open. R. Geiger found that in a pine forest the wind below the crowns was almost uniformly about 40% of that above the crowns. In a dense beech wood the wind has been found to be weakest about half-way between the ground and the tree tops, at the level of densest foliage, where it is 40 to 50% of the speed above the trees.

In a forest clearing the climate is partly intermediate between that in the forest itself and in the open, but partly has a character of its own. The effects depend so much on the size, slope and aspect of the clearing and the height and species of the trees that it is almost impossible to generalize. Even a clearing may lose a good deal of sunshine, especially in the morning and evening. The loss can be estimated from fig. 20 (p. 102) in the same way as the loss from surrounding hills. As regards temperature, on sloping ground a moderate sized clearing may act as a frost pocket, since the trees below the clearing are a barrier against the outflow of cold night air. On radiation nights the ground in a clearing may be several degrees colder than under the adjoining trees. However, the protective effect of the trees extends for a distance about equal to their height beyond the edge of the woodland, partly because they intercept and return some of the outward radiation, and partly because there is some interchange of air between woodland and open. Hence a small clearing is likely to be warmer at night than the open fields.

1. Koch, H. G., 'Temperaturverhältnisse und Windsystem eines geschlossenen Waldgebietes', Leipzig, Geophysikalisches Institut, *Veröffentlichungen* 6, *Teil* 3, 1934.

In a large wood in level country this gentle interchange of air may act as a valuable protection on clear calm nights which bring the worst radiaion frosts. The mechanism is similar to that of land and sea breezes (p. 106), with the lowest temperatures near the ground in the open and the woodland as the warmer region from which the air rises and spreads back to subside over neighbouring open ground.

Wind speeds in a forest clearing are generally less than in the open but greater than in the wood, the sheltering effect of the trees extending downwind for some ten or more times their height. The air is also more turbulent in a clearing than in the wood.

For those who suffer from hay fever the pollen in the air from trees may be troublesome at times. The principal tree sources are ashes, oaks and elms within a quarter of a mile or so, but all these together fall far short of the ubiquitous grasses as pollen producers, especially in early summer. Unmown grass is probably the chief cause of hay fever, though the pollen of some flowers is also involved. Studies of the distribution of pollen in Great Britain[1] have shown that tree pollen makes up the greater part of the catch before June and is generally most abundant after a spell of warm weather. It does not always fall when the weather becomes cool again. The first windy cool days after heat may be particularly troublesome for the hay fever sufferer, especially if they are dry. The interior of a wood may be one of the best places in the hay fever season because of the shelter from the wind and from transport of grass pollen. The output of grass pollen in June and July responds to periods of bright sunshine. Wet days greatly decrease the catch of pollen, and this effect sometimes lasts till the next day. The best place of all for the hay fever sufferer is the sea or the seaside with an onshore wind.

Hill and dale

In hilly country exposure, aspect and slope are of great importance. We may begin by comparing hill top and valley floor. A hill top, if of moderate height and unwooded, enjoys unobstructed sunshine and is correspondingly warm on still, sunny days. Its average temperature, however, is slightly lower than in the valley, decreasing by about $1°$ F ($0.5°$ C) for each 300 feet; but against this the extremes of temperature are generally less. The heat of most summer afternoons is moderated by a breeze, while on winter nights the cold air drains away instead of accumulating in a frosty pool. From this point of view an isolated rounded hill top is better than the middle of a flat plateau. The amount of moisture in the air differs very little from that in valley air; the slightly lower

1. Hyde, Dr. H. A., 'Studies in atmospheric pollen. IV. Pollen deposition in Great Britain, 1943', *The New Phytologist*, **49**, pp. 398–420, 1950.

temperature makes the average relative humidity higher than in the valley, though at moderate heights the difference is too small to be significant. A higher hill top may be rather often enveloped in cloud, and moisture is deposited on walls and furniture. The rainfall may be slightly higher than in the valley, but again the difference is not significant at moderate heights. The effect is more noticeable in snow, which tends to lie in thicker drifts and to last longer on the hills. Hill roads, especially when sunk below the general level of the ground, are readily blocked by snow; and in severe winters, especially in the north and west and near the east coast from Caithness to Kent, hill villages may be isolated for days on end by deep drifts piled up by the wind.

Wind makes the greatest difference between hill and valley. A hill top is exposed to all the winds that blow, while a valley is generally sheltered. This is a mixed blessing; wind aids ventilation and reduces the frequency of radiation frost; in moderation it has a tonic effect, but a gale in an exposed situation may be too much of a good thing. Wind persistently moaning round a house in winter has an irritating effect on the nerves, which is increased by the banging of doors and rattling of windows, and their suggestions of damage. Exposed sites are not the places for nervy people to live. Moreover, stouter building is called for than in sheltered valleys. New houses on quite a low eminence exposed to the west wind at Hatfield, Herts, were unroofed by a severe gale on 4 November 1957.

Driving rain is also a problem at exposed sites. Rain blown at an angle to the vertical by strong winds penetrates porous surfaces and is driven into cracks between impervious stones and boards. Damage to buildings, to their interior decoration and contents commonly results. The rainwater absorbed also increases the thermal conductivity of the walls, lowering the temperature inside, increasing the risk of condensation on the inner face of the wall and increasing the fuel consumption required to keep the house warm. From a recent study of driving rain[1] it appears that the problem is about ten times as serious in hill districts in the west and north as it is in the most sheltered areas between Newbury, Berks., Nottingham and Ipswich. Measurements showed that the amount of rain penetrating vertical walls in the Glasgow area was proportional to the rainfall collected in an ordinary rain gauge with horizontal aperture multiplied by the average component of wind speed at right angles to the wall during the rain. An index was constructed, and mapped for the whole of the British Isles, of annual rainfall multiplied by the average wind speed (regardless of direction) during rain, which appears to be about 30% stronger than the average wind for the whole year. Values range from 10 to 20 generally in districts

1. Lacy, R. E., and Shellard, H. C., 'An index of driving rain', *Meteorological Magazine*, **91**, pp. 177–184, 1962.

nearest the Atlantic (but about 7 in Devon and Cornwall) to 2 in the sheltered lowlands of eastern England and 4 in other sheltered districts including parts of Angus and Aberdeenshire and smaller areas near Edinburgh and Dublin. There are certainly strong variations with local topography, and although southwest walls are most affected this is not so near the east coast and in other localities with an obviously different exposure.

Winds also help the cold to penetrate the house by draughts through doors and window frames and by cooling the fabric of walls and unlined roof spaces. To maintain an indoor temperature of 65° F (18° C) against fairly typical January temperatures of 35–40° F (2–4° C) outside a house on a windy hilltop may need 50% more fuel than in sheltered situations.

Farmers find the growing season, which is usually taken as the duration of temperatures above 6° C (42° F), shortened on the hills by the lower average temperature. Soil temperature is probably a better indicator of the prospects of germination and growth of plants than air temperature, but far more information about the latter is available so that for any reasonably full survey air temperatures have to be used. The length of the growing season is commonly estimated from the graph of air temperature obtained by joining the monthly means, taking the main period when the temperature is above 6° C and ignoring transient, out-of-season warm and cold intervals.[1] Accumulated temperatures in degree-days, obtained by adding up the number of degrees by which each day's (day and night) average temperature during the growing season exceeds 6° C or 42° F, are also of interest in comparing different places and different years. In countries like Britain and Ireland, where the seasonal range of temperature between summer and winter is small, increasing height above sea level greatly shortens the growing season at heights where the average temperature never rises very much above 6° and lengthens it to 365 days in the most maritime areas where the average temperatures of the coldest months keep just above 6°.

In Devon and Cornwall the growing season, defined in the manner described, is normally 365 days a year—a fact related to the successful growing of flowers for the London winter market—but the season shortens by about 9 days per 100 feet above sea level. The growing season is also 365 days in a normal year all the way along the actual coast from Portland Bill to Ilfracombe and most of the coast of Wales between Swansea and Llandudno as well as the south and west coasts of Ireland. In southeast England the coast itself gets 270–300 days. The following table shows how the figures go in other areas and how they change with height.

1. Gloyne, R. W., 'On the growing season', unpublished Agricultural Memorandum of the Meteorological Office, Edinburgh, 1958.

Area	Length of the growing season near sea level (days)	Decrease per 100 feet (days)	Standard deviation of the season's length (days)
Devon and Cornwall and W. Wales . .	365	9	
E. Wales, Hereford and Somerset . .	300	9	
Surrey and the Sussex Weald . . .	275	4	
East Anglia and SE. England north of the Thames	265	5	
N. Midland, Lancs. and southern Pennines .	265	5	±18
Northern Pennines, Durham and S. Scotland	245	4	±18
E. Scotland	245	6	
W. Scotland and Hebrides . . .	260–270	6	
Central Ireland	310	7	
Switzerland	(268)	2	

The average length of the growing season about 2,000 feet up on the northern Pennines is 150–160 days and it falls off to 0 at the top of Ben Nevis. The figures show how the decrease with height is most rapid in the most oceanic districts and least in the relatively continental.

The average spring starting date ranges from early March in most lowland areas in the south of England to end of March or early April in lowland places in the east and north of Scotland; the end of the season comes about end of November–early December in the south and early–mid November in the northern areas. Year to year variations in the starting date appear to be rather greater than those of the finishing date; at Eskdalemuir, Dumfriesshire where these variations were investigated over the period 1914–56 the standard deviations were respectively 15 days for the beginning, 11 days for the end and 20 days for the duration of the season of growth.

Forest trees generally require at least a mean temperature of 10° C (50° F) for the warmest month. But the upper limit of the region where trees grow in Britain is probably more often determined by wind than by temperature: at many places where the temperature of the warmest month is adequate trees are found only in sheltered ravines and gullies.

There is a strong resemblance between the most sheltered districts indicated on the map of driving rain referred to above, and the region of least frequent gales (fig. 13), and the growth of southern crops such as maize and special fruits such as the occasional peach and vine. Although Cornwall and parts of Devon are distinguished by mild winters in which growth of grass and flowers seldom ceases, it is clear that shelter plays a part in developing frequent genial summer warmth. Our forefathers who built their houses in positions sheltered from 'the unhealthy south wind and the violent west wind' were possibly wiser than the twentieth-century fashion for supposedly sunny hilltop sites open to the southwest.

The climate of a valley depends very much on whether its topography helps or hinders the flow of air. In clear weather with little or no general wind the ground cools in the evening by radiating its heat to the sky. The layer of air next the ground is cooled by contact with the ground. Cold air being denser than warm air, this cold layer begins to run downhill, just as water does, following whatever natural drainage channels it finds. In suitably shaped valleys these gentle streams of cold air off the slopes converge and run down the main glen like a mighty river, one or two hundred feet deep and moving fast as a strong cold wind in any narrows near the valley bottom. (Remember this when deciding where to camp in the Highlands! Even the sheep are reported to have discovered in some glens that it is less cold at night some way up the hillsides. Sometimes woods in the valley-bottom provide a wind-break.) These are 'katabatic' (Greek = down-flowing) winds, which normally reach their strongest development in the coldest hours of the night between midnight and dawn. Their turbulence and mixing with the overlying warmer air prevent extreme low temperatures being reached, but they feel very cold because of the air movement which increases the cooling power. In the broad flat-bottomed valleys in the south the cold air drainage commonly follows a rather different sequence. The cold air arrives at the valley bottom first along the foot of the slopes on either side. These two pools of cold air meet in the middle and pile up there, so that a small head of dense air is built up which forces a flow back towards the sides. This is only a passing phase, and soon the air acquires a general slow movement down the length of the valley. Some valleys are so broad in relation to the supply of cold air from the hills that this becomes exhausted, and flow down the valley ceases about midnight and a slight rise of temperature is sometimes observed about that time. The cold air drainage is usually renewed once more towards dawn.

After sunrise the ground warms up, and the supply of cold air ceases. The slopes which get most morning sun warm up first, and the warm air resting on them begins to rise up the slope. Finally, as the whole area becomes warm, the general tendency is for flow up the valley and up-slope ('anabatic') breezes.

In such broad valleys, or where the contours are gentle, these hill and valley winds are not entirely a disadvantage. It is true that on clear winter nights the cold misty air drifts down the valley, so that it is not desirable to have large windows facing uphill. In summer the cool night breeze after a long hot day may be a boon, providing relief from the heat and promoting sleep. In a valley opening southwards the front rooms of a house facing south have all the advantage of sunshine and a breeze by day, while the less important rear of the house bears the brunt of the night winds. A house facing down a valley opening to the east gets the morning sun and earlier relief from the cold night winds, but the sun goes behind the hills earlier in the evening and the night breezes set in sooner. In a valley opening to the west, the reverse holds. The most unfavourable site is a valley opening to the north.

If the main valley is narrow, tortuous or obstructed, conditions are different. Among the foothills of the Chiltern Hills between Rickmansworth and Chorleywood, Herts, is a residential district in a little valley 177 feet above sea level, with the surrounding hills a hundred feet higher. This is our best studied 'frost hollow'. The valley runs east-southeast, but turns at right angles towards south-southwest just below the point where E. L. Hawke[1] maintained a meteorological station from 1930 to 1942. About 300 yards below the bend it is partly blocked by a high railway embankment. On calm autumn evenings streams of cold air carrying smoke from garden bonfires can be seen converging at about 2 m.p.h. on the northern strip of the valley from all sides. These winds accumulate in a 'lake' of cold air 30–40 feet deep, and further smoke spreads out above this. Later in the evening a light westerly wind blowing at about 5 m.p.h. down the highest part of the valley arrives. This is the katabatic wind from the main ridge of the Chilterns, some 10 or 12 miles away, exceeding 800 feet in places. It flows over the pool of cold air, and sometimes mixes with it, causing a slight rise of temperature, but on very cold nights it fails to reach the valley floor.

The night climate of this enclosed valley is one of the most severe in Britain, even rivalling glens in Scotland. The air temperature at a height of 4 feet fell below freezing point in July, and reached $-17.9°$ C $(-0.3°$ F) in January. Temperatures on the grass fell below this figure in every month from December to March inclusive, and reached $-21.5°$ C three times in January. By contrast hot summer days produced temperatures above $30°$ C, the extreme being $35.3°$ C $(95.5°$ F). The climate of this valley is only an extreme case of what happens in many deep or shallow dells in this country. They thrust themselves upon the notice of motorists, and especially cyclists, making night runs across hilly country. Such sites are rightly termed frost hollows, and are as bad for farming as for house sites. These are the places where fruit blossom is lost in May, and grain, fruit and flowers may be damaged in any month. On one occasion a German meteorologist was able to map the lake of cold air during a spring frost by following the level along the valley sides up to which the crops were

1. Hawke, E. L., 'Extreme Diurnal Ranges of Air Temperature in the British Isles', *Quarterly Journal of the Royal Meteorological Society*, Vol. 59, pp. 261–265, 1933; 'Thermal Characteristics of a Hertfordshire Frost Hollow', *ibid.*, Vol. 70, pp. 23–48, London, 1944.

damaged by frost. This showed a sharp almost horizontal line all round the valley.

The most favourable sites are neither on the hilltops nor near the valley floor, but somewhere between, high enough to be above many frosts but sufficiently sheltered to avoid the gales. Even so, there is a good deal to be thought of. The first point is sunshine and the differences between slopes facing north, east, south and west.

Slope, aspect and sunshine

Aspect is important because ground that slopes towards the sun, especially towards the midday sun, receives more radiant heat per unit area than, say, level ground where the same bundle of rays from the sun is spread over a wider area of surface. This spread (and weakening of concentration) is greatest on northern slopes. The ground on a southern slope in Britain receives the midday sunshine appropriate to a lower latitude.

The elevation angles of surrounding hilltops, trees and buildings that may block the sunshine are also important. Here a large-scale map or plan is helpful. It may be useful to make a simple clinometer by hanging a small weight on a string through the zero of a semicircular protractor. One can then sight along the base of the protractor (held upside down) and read off the angle which the hanging (vertical) string makes on the degree scale.

The elevation of the sun at local noon depends on the latitude and the sun's 'declination', which is the angle between the vertical and the height of the sun at noon at the Equator. At the summer solstice, on 21–22 June, when the sun is farthest north of the Equator, the declination is almost $+23\frac{1}{2}°$. At the equinoxes, 21 March and 22 September, the noon sun is overhead at the Equator. At the winter solstice, on 21–22 December, when the sun is farthest south of the Equator, the declination is almost $-23\frac{1}{2}°$. The declination on any other day of the year can be found in *Whitaker's Almanack*, the *Nautical Almanac* and other yearbooks. The elevation of the sun at local noon can be found by adding 90° to the declination and subtracting the latitude. Thus in latitude 55° N on 21 June the sun's elevation is $(90 + 23\frac{1}{2} - 55)$ or $58\frac{1}{2}°$. At the equinoxes it is simply $(90 - 55)$ or 35°, and on 22 December it is $(90 - 23\frac{1}{2} - 55)$ or $11\frac{1}{2}°$. Consequently, any site in latitude 55° N from which the ground slopes upwards to the south by $11\frac{1}{2}°$ (a gradient of one in eight) will have no sun on the shortest day. Sites on steep northern slopes are not good to live in in winter and places at the foot of the northern face of even small hills are liable to be depressing.

Fig. 20 shows the altitude and azimuth (direction) of the sun in latitude 55° N on the shortest and longest days and the equinoxes. The concentric circles represent solar elevations of 0, 20, 40 and 60°. The broken lines show the direction of the sun at different local mean times and the full lines the sun's elevation at those times. It will be observed that in summer the sun changes its position very quickly between 9 a.m. and 2 p.m., so that it is southeast at 10 a.m. and southwest at 2 p.m., and due east and west at 7 a.m. and 5 p.m. instead of 6 a.m. and 6 p.m. as might be expected.

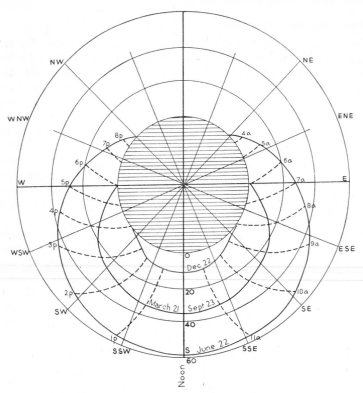

FIGURE 20. Altitude and Azimuth of the Sun at 55° N.

The diagram can be roughly modified to suit any other latitude in Britain by (a) adding to each full curve 1° to the elevation at noon for every degree of latitude south of 55° N and subtracting 1° for every degree north of 55° N, and (b) marking on the innermost circle the local mean times of sunrise and sunset on the dates in question. However, the diagram as it stands is probably near enough for most practical purposes in any part of Britain. The amount of sunshine which will be lost on clear days by the intervention of hills and other obstacles can then be found by sketching in the contours surrounding the site, as suggested above.

Apart from tops of high buildings, which are favourite sites for sunshine recorders at health resorts, the maximum possible sunshine can be obtained only on the tops of isolated hills or on extensive level ground without trees, completely open between northeast through south to northwest. Such sites are not very desirable for other reasons. As not many people rise before 6 a.m., obstacles to the north of east do not matter and may provide valuable shelter from cold winds. Spring and summer evenings are the times to be out in the garden, so an exposure open between, say, west-southwest and northwest may be welcome except from the point of view of winter gales. There is one other point to remember, namely, that a free exposure may not always remain free. Trees have a habit of growing, especially the favourite evergreens such as Cupressus, and other houses may be built to steal the sunshine, especially in winter when it is most needed.

The slope of the site governs the warmth and dryness of the soil as has been explained. Observations by Professor R. Schulze[1] at Hamburg showed that between 11 October 1951 and 9 January 1952 a vertical wall facing south received 1·5 times as much warmth from the sun and sky together as a horizontal surface, while a slope of 45° to the south received 1·6 times as much as a horizontal surface. For vertical and 45° slopes facing north the corresponding figures were 0·4 and 0·56. These figures show that radiation received from the sky (especially from cloudy skies) is of some value though much less than direct sunshine. On very clear days the differences were greater, a vertical wall or inclined surface facing south receiving more than twice the warmth on a horizontal surface, while a vertical wall facing north received only a quarter, and a 45° slope a third, of the horizontal surface. Those who choose the sunniest aspects must weigh the advantages of early fruit, flowers and vegetables against accentuated effects of drought in fine weather.

The would-be houseowner should also consider the track usually followed by the cold winds flowing down the sides of the valley. Cold air, like water, tends to follow the natural drainage lines. A nook or dell in a hillside is liable to be occupied on clear nights by a stream of cold air, unless the flow is blocked or diverted by some barrier—a wall, a tall thick hedge or a thicket of trees. A spur between dells may be a better proposition from this point of view, though more exposed to the wind. The soil in a hollow is, however, often deeper and richer.

1. Schulze, R., 'Licht und Wohnung—Strahlungsgenuss geneigter Flächen', Hamburg, *Annalen der Meteorologie, Medizin-Meteorologisches Heft*, Nr. 8, 1953 pp. 126–140.

On the lee side of a ridge there is usually an eddy in windy weather that causes a downdraught about a quarter to half a mile from the crest, which is liable to reverse the draught of chimneys and fill the rooms with smoke. Cowls or special chimney pots are a remedy in most cases.

The possibility of flood water after heavy rain should not be forgotten. It may be unwise to build a house across an apparently dry valley.

Inland waters: lakes and rivers

The effect of surface water near a house depends on the depth and movement of the water. Owing to the high specific heat, a good-sized sheet of deep water, such as a lake or estuary, acts as a moderating influence on temperature; on a hot summer day it cools the air over it and on calm days may give rise to a gentle lake breeze blowing off it like a miniature sea breeze. On cold nights the opposite effect is found; the water warms the air over it and may set up a gentle circulation with the surface air running out over the water, rising and returning aloft. Such a sheet of water is quite a useful protection from frost. Shallow water is much less effective, as it rapidly warms up in hot sunshine. Moreover, the cooling effect of the presence of water in warm weather is always partly offset by the increased humidity due to evaporation and to transpiration from the reeds and other vegetation growing in the water. Also it encourages flies.

The extra humidity in the air near lakes and rivers affects the frequency of mists and fogs in their vicinity. Because the temperature of the water fails to rise as high as that of the surrounding dry land on warm summer days several things happen. On lakes and estuaries several miles wide miniature sea breezes blowing towards either shore may be enough to ripple the water surface near the shores (though hardly enough to move a boat with sail). These breezes are supplied by subsiding air over the water, so that convection cloud is often absent over and near broad sheets of water, especially in spring and early summer when the water temperature is lagging. Nevertheless the humidity put into the air may feed all the bigger clouds not far away. All through the autumn and winter the thermal effects described are reversed and cloudiness tends to be greater over and near water bodies than elsewhere.

One obvious point about rivers, yet one which is often forgotten, is that their level varies. Many Thames-side dwellers acquiring an up-river house or bungalow in summer, thinking how pleasant it is to have the river at the bottom of the garden, must have regretted their choice in a rainy winter, when the garden was at the bottom of the river. Before committing oneself to such a site, it is desirable to find how high the river has risen in the past. Flood levels are often marked on bridge posts or buildings; failing this, the office of the local surveyor or newspaper, or the 'oldest inhabitant', can probably produce the information. Unfortunately, with improved drainage and tarring of roads, rivers nowadays tend to flood more quickly and to somewhat higher levels than formerly, but in the Thames above Richmond the well-documented floods of November 1894 provide a reasonable guide as to the limits of what is to be expected once in a generation. The highest flood levels in 1894 exceeded 'normal' (summer) level by the following amounts: Oxford 3·7 feet, Abingdon 7 feet, Goring 11 feet, Reading 6·8 feet, Henley 6·25 feet, Maidenhead 7·9 feet, Windsor 8·9 feet, Kingston 11·5 feet. Below Teddington the river becomes 'tidal', and the height of the flood above normal fell off rapidly. Another very deep flood occurred in the spring thaw, which was accompanied by rains, after an exceptionally snowy winter in 1947. People living in the Severn valley and near other rivers in the English lowlands are similarly acquainted with occasional widespread flooding. Such floods are a great disaster to the riverside towns and villages in damage to fabric and furnishings of houses, loss of time, etc. That this warning is not an idle one may be inferred from the fact, recorded in the account[1] of the 1894 flood, that dozens of noticeboards protruded from the water offering 'Eligible building land to let'.

In the lower Thames and parts of the Fens and East Anglian rivers the danger is not so much from rainwater floods as from the winds and abnormal sea tides. The southern part of the North Sea is especially liable to tidal floods, when strong northerly or northwesterly winds come at or near a 'spring' tide. The flood of the Thames in London on 6–7 January 1928 was due to a 'storm surge' caused by a northerly gale of about 70 knots (80 m.p.h.). The surge coincided with a spring tide which, though high, would not, in normal conditions have been the highest of the season; the 'predicted' level given in the Admiralty Tide Tables was 21 feet above mean sea level at London Bridge, compared with a maximum spring tide of 25 feet. However, the water actually rose nearly 6 feet above the predicted level, and reached the highest-known level in London. At several points in the City, Southwark, Westminster and Hammersmith the water overtopped the embankments and flooded low-lying riverside districts, pouring into the basements of houses; 14 people were trapped and drowned.

The coast and coastal waters

To be near the sea has advantages and disadvantages. The fresh breezes, clean air and more abundant sunshine than inland are healthful factors. But the wind is sometimes excessive, and near the most exposed parts of

1. Symons, G. J., and Chatterton, G., 'The November Floods of 1894 in the Thames Valley', *Quarterly Journal of the Royal Meteorological Society*, Vol. 21, pp. 189–206, London, 1895.

the western and northern coasts where trees cannot grow the sound of the wind is an almost constant background to life. Low-lying parts of the east coast of England and Holland were inundated by a sea flood on 1 February 1953 like that which occurred in the lower Thames in 1928. The level of the North Sea was raised as a depression passed over it preceded by a westerly gale and followed by a northerly storm with maximum windspeeds over 100 m.p.h. that also destroyed forests in Scotland. Another such storm surge flooded northwest German lowlands near Hamburg in February 1962.

The meteorological effects of a storm on the level of the North Sea are of two kinds.[1] Reduction of atmospheric pressure within a depression causes the sea to rise, behaving like an inverted barometer. If a steady state were reached, the rise would be about 1 cm. for 1 millibar (13 inches for an inch of mercury). But also southwesterly gales on the Atlantic fan more water into the North Sea, and when these are followed by northwesterly or northerly gales in the North Sea the surge travels southwards, and builds up in the shallow constricted waters at the southern end, like a tidal wave. Nevertheless danger only arises when the surge happens to arrive with the tide.

The gentle sea breezes of summer, which spring up somewhat before noon on a warm day and die away again in the evening, are one of the attractions of the sea-side. They are due to the heating of the land surface during the day. At night when the ground becomes cooler than the sea a light drift of air from land to sea takes their place. These 'diurnal' breezes are often explained crudely by saying that the air over the warmer surface rises and is replaced by cooler air blowing in from the sea (or off the land at night). The actual motions are more complex and depend upon the development of the sort of convection cells that form cumulus clouds over the heated ground inland. A net upward transport of air then takes place (rather more going up than comes down in the clear spaces between the clouds) and the loss is replaced by a cool current of air drawn in horizontally over the coastline. A new transfer of air from land to sea compensates this at much higher levels. If the air is too stable (cf. Ch. 4) for vertical currents, as in air of tropical origin or in very anticyclonic weather in Britain, no sea breeze may develop. Consequently, some hot days pass without the relief of a sea breeze.

The most favourable days for sea breezes are when the vertical decrease of temperature with height is already great in the morning before the sun's rays begin to take effect. And the most favourable situation is where

1. Bowden, K. F., 'Storm surges in the North Sea', *Weather*, Vol. 8, pp. 82–84, 1953. See also Jensen, A. P., 'Tidal inundations past and present', *Weather*, Vol. 8, pp. 85–89.

a coastal plain is backed by hilly country; here the air readily finds its way up the sun-warmed flanks of the hills and upwards from the crests, which often serve as developing points for cumulus clouds above them. Then the daytime anabatic breezes of the hill slopes become linked into a single system with the coastal sea breeze. This effect has the possibly surprising result that the sea breezes of the Scottish east coast are the strongest in Britain, in spite of the rather high latitude, reaching 15 knots or so on the most favourable days. The geography is suitable down much of the length of the east coast and the coolness of the upwelling waters

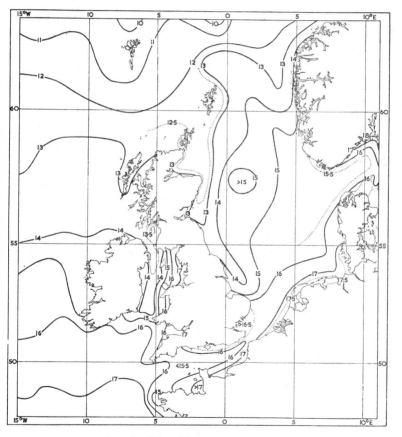

FIGURE 21. Sea Water Temperatures ° C in August.
(Average temperature of the surface water from observations chiefly in the 1920s and 1930s.)

off-shore increases the thermal contrast between land and sea, so the east coast sea breezes are rather fresh as far south as East Anglia and contribute to the bracing quality of the climate.

In suitable spells of weather when there is a general on-shore wind prevailing the diurnal sea breeze effect is felt just as a strengthening of the wind at the coast. This often happens on our western and southwestern coasts because of the frequency of windstreams from that quarter. The wind may become strong enough in the afternoon to be awkward for some pursuits near the sea-shore, but it does not bring so much fall of temperature because of the relative warmth of the water.

Average sea temperatures in August are shown in fig. 21. This map, prepared by the International Council for the Exploration of the Sea, is one of the first to cover the inshore waters. Its implications are of undoubted interest to bathers and thick-jerseyed or open-shirted yachtsmen. The deep sea is warmest on the top, though generally a layer up to several metres deep is stirred by the waves: for this reason coasts where the water is deep are unlikely to attain as high temperatures as the shallower places. This probably accounts for the difference between Brittany and the warmer Dutch coast. The prevailing west and southwest winds blow the warm surface water towards our western and southern coasts, and it is then further heated in the extensive sandy shallows near the Lancashire coast, Cardigan Bay and in the Bristol Channel. In fine weather the return of the tide over sun-heated sand contributes to the warming. Almost as high average temperatures are attained in the less disturbed coastal waters between Hampshire and Suffolk. The prevailing winds blow the surface water away from most of the east and northeast coasts, and upwelling of colder water accounts for the low temperatures there.

Still shallow waters take in more radiation from the sun and sky than escapes by re-radiation—a sort of greenhouse effect. The result is that they are able to maintain a higher average temperature than that of the air above or the neighbouring dry land. Experiments with a shaded thermometer in water 1 to $1\frac{1}{2}$ metres (3–5 feet) deep in shallow tideless bays in the warmest region in southeast Norway in the cold unsettled summer of 1962 showed that the surface water temperature fell 2 to 3° C (3–5° F) on disturbed days of wind and rain but regained its former level of about 17° C after one to two calm days of sunshine, although the air temperature did not exceed this level for more than a few hours. The human body is very sensitive to small variations of water temperature, especially near the limit of what is acceptable. The noticeable warm and cool patches in shallow water with which every bather is familiar were generally found to represent temperature differences of rather less than 1° C. Average temperatures of the water coming in from the Atlantic vary by a degree or

wo from one summer to another. Average values in coastal waters around
hese islands appear to differ by two to three degrees between the warmest
and coldest recent summers.

All through the spring and early summer the seasonal warming of the
sea lags behind that of the land. At this time of the year therefore the sea
is colder than the warmest airmasses that pass over it, particularly along
the east coast. This produces sea fogs. Sea frets in Cornwall, over the
Goodwin Sands and the cliffs of Kent and Sussex, and haars in eastern
Scotland, occur in maritime tropical air or warm air from the continent.
These fogs are primarily an early summer phenomenon (though not unknown at other times). They become involved in the sea breeze circulation
on some days that are warm inland, and muffle the coast with their chill
grey world; later in the day, if enough interchange of air between land
and sea takes place in the coastal circulation, the fog may clear over the
coast and over the offshore waters as far out as the coastal sea breeze is
blowing—up to 10 or 20 miles out.

The question of ozone is an interesting one. It used to be a popular
belief that sea breezes were scented by this powerful oxidizing agent.
When the ozone layer was discovered at a height of some 15 miles, the sea
breeze ozone was dismissed as a myth, compounded of decaying seaweed.
Now it appears that though ozone is mostly formed 15 or 20 miles up
by the sun's ultra-violet radiation, a tiny portion is brought down by
descending air currents to the Earth's surface. There is often a marked
decrease in the ozone content during the onset of a depression, followed
by a rapid rise when the warm front passes.[1] The amount of ozone near
the surface seems to be greatest in May, when surface heating makes the
atmosphere to great heights least stable, so that vertical movements are
facilitated, and least in November, when the lower atmosphere is cooling
rapidly and thermal stability develops. The annual variation, however, is
somewhat masked by the variations from day to day. Some ozone is produced at lower levels by lightning discharges, especially flashes from cloud
to cloud, and also even in fair weather at metal points such as tips of
lightning conductors. Near the ground ozone is rapidly destroyed, partly
by oxidizing organic refuse and in the lungs of animals, and partly by
chemicals in the air, such as ammonia and methane. This process of destruction takes place more rapidly on land than on sea surfaces, hence sea
air actually does contain more ozone than land air; and though the
quantity is minute, it may add to the tonic effect of the stronger breezes.
Unfortunately, measurements of surface ozone are few and not all com-

1. Gluckauf, E., 'The Ozone Content of Surface Air and its Relation to Some
Meteorological Conditions', *Quarterly Journal of the Royal Meteorological Society*,
Vol. 70, pp. 13–19, London, 1944.

parable, owing to differences of technique, but those available from different parts of Europe may be grouped roughly as follows:

	Ozone, micrograms per cubic metre	
	Average	Range
Inland, below 1,500 feet . . .	15	0–100
,, above 1,500 feet . . .	20	0·3–102
Nordeney, North Sea . . .	25	5·5–73

Coal smoke is especially destructive of ozone, so that town air has less ozone than country air. Woodland air is generally poorer in ozone than air over open country.

A detailed study of the variations of ozone was carried out at a hospital near Breslau (Wrocław).[1] In settled weather there was a clear diurnal variation, amounts increasing rapidly from 6 a.m. to noon, then more slowly until 8 p.m. At night from 10 p.m. to 6 a.m. there was a steady fall, attributed to the stagnation of the air. In disturbed weather this diurnal variation almost disappeared. In the only thunderstorm that occurred during the investigation period there was a marked increase. Amount of ozone was always high in dry air, low in moist air. Fog, drizzle and dead calm brought an especially rapid decrease of ozone. There was a slight tendency for ozone to increase with rising, and decrease with falling, temperature. The closest relations were found with the local air circulation —increase with subsiding airmasses (which are normally dry) and decrease with air flow up the hillsides. No definite relation was found between ozone and the place of origin of the airmass.

Iodine, also, has some importance for health. Iodine is present in sea water and is collected by seaweed, being liberated into the air when the weed is burnt as it is, or used to be, for the iodine, on the coasts of Brittany, Ireland, Orkney, Shetland and Norway. If seaweed were the only source, inland districts would be rather poor in iodine, but another source is the burning of coal. The amounts actually found vary from about 0·4 to 0·6 mg. per cubic metre in the northwest coastal regions to about 0·1 in inland parts of Europe.

1. Renger, F., and Lücke, O., 'Über die meteorologischen Bedingungen der Ozondichte in bodennaher Luft', Berlin, *Meteorologischer und Hydrologischer Dienst der Dt. Demokratischen Republik*, 1953.

8

Climate and Health

IT is when one comes to consider the connexions between climate, health and vigour that one appreciates most of all the virtues of the climate of these islands. The only necessary reservation is where the effects of over-crowding, and the atmospheric pollution that results therefrom unless strenuously controlled, thrust themselves upon us. Too often when people dream of emigrating to some warmer land of everlasting summer they are thinking only of averages. Climate is more than averages, it comprises everything the weather can do. The variations are important. The extreme ranges of solar radiation, temperature, humidity and wind should be considerable though not too great. A place with no weather is very dull to live in. And there is plenty of evidence that being accustomed to alternations of warmth and cold that are not too extreme, and of storm and sun, is beneficial to health, gives zest to life and affects character.

Psychological attributes such as character are hard to study scientifically because of difficulties of definition and measurement. The work of Ellsworth Huntington[1] has drawn many critics but it did focus attention on some climatic influences that are undoubtedly real. He prepared graphs and maps of various aspects of human vigour—health and longevity, productivity of workers and, finally, the level of 'civilization' in each country. The last of these is, of course, a matter of opinion, but, 'in the multitude of counsellors there is much wisdom', so he sought the co-operation of 213 men of the world—geographers, historians, diplomats and others who had travelled widely. To each he sent a list of 185 countries or provinces, and asked him to arrange them into ten groups in order of the level of civilization according to certain standards. Most of the recipients replied, and though many were highly critical of the method, 50 of the replies, from all over the world, were sufficiently definite to be used as part of a numerical estimate. In spite of the natural bias of inhabitants of different continents, there was essential agreement among *all* the contributors. Every contributor put England and Wales in the first group, and in the result this country headed the list with a score of 100 only equalled by the Atlantic seaboard states of U.S.A.—New York, Pennsylvania and New Jersey, closely followed by western and northern Germany and northern France with 99. Scotland, along with Holland and Denmark, scored 98, and most other

1. Huntington, E., *Civilization and Climate*, New Haven, Conn., 1924.

areas between northern Italy and Norway and Sweden 94 to 97. Ireland got 82—no doubt an expression of the gradient between Dublin or Belfast and the remote districts in the West where 'time stands still'. Countries in the tropical zone scored 10 to 50, and in the Mediterranean most areas scored from 50 to 75. The world distribution of civilization mapped on this basis agrees quite closely with another world map, also drawn by Huntington, of the average output per head in factories. The great centres of industrial output are (or were then) in the British Isles, western and central Europe, the eastern U.S.A., southeast Australia and New Zealand. If the work were repeated today, output in the Pacific states of U.S.A. and in parts of the Soviet Union would have to be rated much higher than it was in Huntington's day—probably also in Japan and China and perhaps parts of northern India. Farm productivity might also appropriately be used.

All the main centres of high civilization and vigour are in regions of moderate temperature and humidity with high agricultural potential. They are also all near the principal storm tracks, a situation which gives them plenty of weather. From his data on factory output Huntington worked out a formula for climatic energy, which takes account of both climate and weather, in terms of optimum temperature, changeability of temperature and so on. As regards average temperature, on his scale which regards 100 as climatic perfection, London scores 99·7 but is actually surpassed by Quito, Ecuador with 99·9. Quito, at a height of 9,350 feet in the tropics, has been termed the city of eternal spring. But the people of Quito do not show the vigour of Londoners, and the reason is possibly to be found in the word 'eternal'; eternal spring becomes an eternal bore. Changes of temperature from day to day depend on the alternation of winds from different directions—in other words, on the passage of storms. Storms also bring changes of humidity, which are as important for health and vigour as are changes of temperature. Polar air is appreciably drier as well as cooler than tropical air, and the change from tropical to polar after the passage of a storm centre is especially bracing. Storms also bring wind and rain, both of which in moderation have a tonic effect.

The great majority of people react to these changes of weather, even those in good health; on some days they feel brisk and energetic, on other days slack and slothful. In America some far-seeing business men recognize that these ups and downs are factors in business; the brisk days are 'sellers' weather'. Statistics compiled at different times by the police in Paris and Hamburg suggest a general tendency for car drivers to drive rashly on the same days, producing significant peaks in the accident rate which do not appear to be due to the condition of the roads but to some subtler effect on the condition of the drivers. The causes are obscure and have been insufficiently investigated.[1] The writer's own observation suggests one such class of occurrences may be attributed to excessive zest affecting some drivers on the first really spring-like days, and when the weather clears after a depressingly dark cloudy period, especially when these changes coincide with the time of release from work.

Sunspots have been blamed for this as for many things. This suggestion may not be entirely absurd because of their known effects on the electrical state of the Earth's atmosphere, though these are most apparent at very high levels. Brooks,[2] actually found that the total number of thunderstorms over the world in a year appears to go up and down with the sunspot number. Changes in the ionosphere from day to day and hour to hour at times of solar disturbances cause short-wave radio fade-outs and thereby interrupt communications. The Earth's surface and the ionosphere act like the negative and positive plates of an electrical condenser. The field strength of this condenser, or gradient of electrical potential, in the neighbourhood of the ground averages about 120 volts per metre height. It is subject to great variations in time and space: convection currents of air affect it, it is generally less in moist or polluted air (presumably owing to the greater conductivity) than in clean dry air, it is reduced under trees and vanishes altogether inside buildings where the structure acts as an electrical conductor. Registering instruments which record minute-to-minute disturbances of the gradient of electrical potential over small differences of height near the ground effectively indicate the activity of vertical exchanges of air as well as changes in the amount of impurity present. Both thunderstorm electricity and these invisible changes in the static electrical field are believed to act upon the human nervous system. Weather changes are also suspected of affecting the blood serum. Probably the best way of looking at physiological reactions to the weather is that human beings are, or readily become, attuned to a certain regular variation of weather in the course of the day, and also in the course of the year, and that interruptions of this regular rhythm cause unrest and nervous disturbance. It has been suggested that amongst the critically sick, for instance after surgical operations, such disturbances may cause relapse and even death.

Studies in this field are difficult—theories used in diagnosis are bound to

1. See, however, Werner Köhn, 'Hamburger Verkehrsunfälle und Wetter', *Medizinmeteorologische Hefte, Band II, Heft Nr. 11*, Hamburg (*Annalen der Meteorologie*), 1956.
2. Brooks, C. E. P., 'The variation of the annual frequency of thunderstorms in relation to sunspots', *Quarterly Journal of the Royal Meteorological Society*, Vol. 60 pp. 153–164, London, 1934.

affect the statistics—and have been most actively pursued in Germany and Austria. There is a journal and an international society for bio-meteorology and bioclimatology (founded in 1956, with its headquarters in Leiden (Oegstgeest), Holland). These are the sciences of the influences of weather and climate on all forms of life. A number of empirical relation-ships have been found, some of them supported by enough firm statistical evidence to justify at least provisional acceptance, though the mechanism of the relation can usually only be guessed at. It is a field where one must beware of premature conclusions based upon insufficient or selected evi-dence: enthusiasm and special pleading are liable to fog the scene. Never-theless a promising liaison has been established between weather forecasters and doctors and hospitals in Hamburg, Munich–Bad Tolz and elsewhere which is believed to have had beneficial practical results—e.g. through the timing of surgical operations so as to avoid meteorological situations that might have disturbing effects.

Ailments in which weather and climate enter in can be considered in various classes according to the manner of the connexion. For instance:

(i) Cases where there is an obvious physical connexion with atmo-spheric conditions—e.g. asthma and bronchitis.

(ii) Cases where atmospheric conditions have a distinct bearing upon the abundance of the virus, or on the organisms and insects that carry the disease germs ('disease vectors')—this probably affects poliomyelitis through the chances of flies picking up the virus in sewage in dry summers. The climatic limits of the malarial mos-quito are an example of the effects upon the vector.

(iii) Cases where there may be a psychical connexion—e.g. suicides, epileptic fits, mental unrest.

(iv) Cases where atmospheric conditions or events may act as the trigger for troubles which threaten fundamentally because of the constitutional condition of the patient—heart attacks, strokes, etc.

This has led in recent years to the recognition of about fourteen patho-genic weather situations, primarily connected with the passage of fronts and strong vertical motion in the lower atmosphere.[1] The effect of these situations upon normal healthy people is generally stimulating. American doctors, however, believe that the notably sharp changes which frequently accompany the passage of fronts across the U.S.A. are dangerously over-stimulating. Taking a less pessimistic view, there is clearly a case for the climate contributing to the zest that strikes Europeans as a common trait of American character.

1. *Klima, Wetter, Mensch* by L. Weickmann, H. Ungeheuer, B. de Rudder and others, Heidelberg (Quelle und Meyer), 2nd edition, 1952.

Spells of weather doubtless affect the incidence of the common cold, hay fever (see p. 95), asthma, bronchitis, influenza, tuberculosis, poliomyelitis and rheumatism. In some cases the effect is directly upon the condition and powers of resistance of the human body, in others it is upon the organisms that carry the disease and upon social habits—such as crowding in trains and buses—that influence the chances of infection being spread. It has recently been suggested that some virus diseases, such as influenza and the common cold, may be transmitted more readily in a dry atmosphere such as prevails indoors in winter because the outside air which we take in and warm necessarily has a low moisture content. There are some grounds for thinking that the slight, but appreciable, climatic changes of the last thousand years (see Ch. 11) may have caused important differences in the liability of temperate Europe, including this country, to plague, malaria, poliomyelitis, tuberculous and bronchial diseases.[1,2] Shortage of ultra-violet radiation is, or used to be, responsible for the occurrence of rickets in children in large nineteenth- and early twentieth-century industrial towns with their shut-in streets and smoke-laden air and skies. (Vitamin D, taken in with animal fats in the diet (as in milk and butter), is an equally effective protection against rickets, since the value of ultra-violet radiation is that it produces Vitamin D in the fats in the skin.) The anti-rachitic part of the sun's radiation is of wavelengths 297 to 313 $\times$ $10^{-3}\mu$, near the short-wave end of the spectrum below which the radiation is entirely cut off by the atmosphere. None of this ultra-violet reaches the lowlands of England in winter even in open country, but it is plentiful in summer. In modest doses it is beneficial, aids growth and protects against rickets. Overdoses cause skin disease. Sun-tan is Nature's protection against overdoses. That is why *sudden* exposure of unaccustomed skin to strong sun causes unpleasant burns and blisters. Some delicate skins never develop this protection.

Sleeplessness, though doubtless mainly due to the nervous strains and excitement that we impose upon ourselves in our overcrowded, over-organized modern life, may be an example of a condition that is aggravated by a long-continued, somewhat oppressive weather situation. It seems to be connected with pre-frontal weather conditions rather than with the passage of a front—a cold front clearance tends to bring relief.

Sensitivity to aches and pains (in old wounds or damaged joints and so on) increases as cold fronts approach, and this is attributed to electrical disturbances propagated some distance ahead from their place of origin.

1. *Klima, Wetter, Mensch*, 1952 (*loc. cit.*).
2. Russell, Professor J. C., 'Late Ancient and Medieval Population', *Transactions of the American Philosophical Society*, New Series, Vol. 48, Part III, pp. 1–152, Philadelphia, 1958.

This relation has been tested by an instrument called an 'algimeter', in which a gradually increasing stimulus is applied until a change of blood pressure shows that the subject feels pain. Measurements on 16 patients at Munich showed that a smaller stimulus is needed to call forth a response before the arrival of fronts than in undisturbed weather. So corns and rheumatism as weather prophets may have some scientific basis. In some cases, however, the effect is simply due to increasing humidity of the air. The well-known fact that dried seaweed goes limp before rain is due to this.

The oppressive effect of the warm, moist south wind in the Mediterranean, the Scirocco with its overcast skies, low mists, and 'sticky' nights when dew may be deposited even on wooden furniture indoors, is recognized in all the countries affected. It is even taken into account in legal hearings after murders, suicides and other desperate affairs. This country happily knows only milder versions, represented by the similar, but less humid, maritime tropical air sometimes brought by southwest winds from the Atlantic and occasional sultry summer nights with a light southerly wind (or no wind at all)—the sky is overcast with threatened thunder that fails to come or to produce a clearance, and the temperature refuses to drop below $15°$, occasionally even $20°$ C ($68°$ F). Night minimum temperatures quite so high as this are rare apart from the London basin, the south coast of England and the Channel Isles. Fig. 22 shows the average frequency of minimum temperatures above $15°$ C (i.e. $60°$ F or over), ranging from 5–10 a year in the south to frequencies less than one in 5 years in northern Scotland. In the Channel Islands the frequency is higher, 25 to 30 a year; such small islands do not cool off much below sea temperature at night. The temperature probably fails to fall below $20°$ C on about one night a year in central London and little less often in Jersey. Frequencies of muggy maritime tropical air, which can occur in any season, would show a gradation from highest values in the southwest of England and Ireland to very low values in eastern Scotland and northeast England.

Damp air has the characteristic that only a narrow range of temperatures divides conditions that feel unpleasantly warm (or 'muggy') from those that feel uncomfortably cold (or 'raw'). When it is warm and there is little or no wind, muggy moist conditions are generally called 'close' or 'sultry'. Different criteria for sultriness have been suggested, but they all boil down to meaning warm or warmish weather with particularly high humidity. Brooks suggested that a day would feel sultry if the following conditions (see Table on p. 118) were reached or exceeded in well-ventilated places in the shade.

Whether we accept this definition or incline towards a slightly lower threshold of sultriness, it is probably correct in implying that wet bulb temperature around 20–22° C (68–72° F) or higher will strike most people

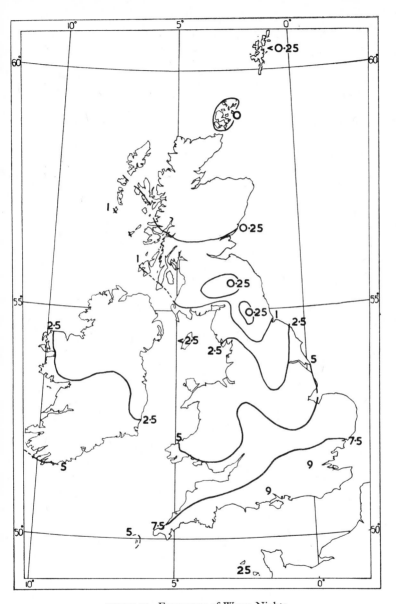

FIGURE 22. Frequency of Warm Nights.
(Average number of nights a year between 1913 and 1940 when the lowest air
temperature was above 15° C)

as sultry if there is no wind, and as very muggy and 'lifeless' (i.e. stifling energy) even with a wind. There are very few really sultry days in Scotland, but noticeable approaches to this condition occur at times of stagnant muggy air amongst the deep glens and sea lochs of the west and southwest.

Relative Humidity	Accompanying Dry Bulb Temperature	Wet Bulb Temperature	Dew Point
100%	22° C	22° C	22° C
90%	23° C	22° C	21° C
80%	24½° C	22° C	21° C
70%	25½° C	21½° C	20° C
60%	27° C	21½° C	19° C
50%	28½° C	21° C	17° C
40%	30° C	21° C	15½° C

Average frequencies of sultry days, on approximately Brooks's criterion, rise to 3 to 5 a year in the warmest inland districts of England, especially in the Severn, Thames and Trent valleys. Sultry days are fewer on the coast owing to the breezes; on the east coast sultry conditions are rare, on the south coast they may be felt on two or three days in an average year between Devon and the Solent.

The feeling of oppressive warmth in sultry or near-sultry conditions is, of course, an individual matter depending amongst other things on what one is doing and what one is wearing. It is felt sooner hurrying about one's business in office clothes than lazing in a 'bikini' on the sands. It is also brought on, however, by exposure to sunshine and even to the diffuse radiation which comes through haze or light cloud, raising the body temperature without changing the humidity of the air. Indoor 'climate' in a room with several occupants and insufficient ventilation can often induce the same sensation, especially if modern windows with large areas of glass let in too much radiation from the sun and sky. A draught may be needed to sweep away the heat and moisture produced by the human bodies. Many people in a room themselves produce some, usually slight, effect on the temperature, 7 or 8 people being roughly equivalent to a 1 kw. electric heater; but the effect upon humidity may be considerable. The increased humidity retards evaporation of sweat, and so makes the maintenance of normal body temperature more difficult, causing a feeling of discomfort. In and near woods sultry conditions occur oftener than elsewhere because of the humidity produced by transpiration of the vegetation and moisture from the ground. In sultry weather the best place to be is where there is most air movement, such as the open coast or heaths and hill tops—though the latter are not so desirable if thunderstorms are liable to develop. Enclosed bays can be stuffy places on sultry days, particularly when the sun shines on a wide stretch of moist sand.

Sultry days are not common in Britain partly because when the temperature is high the relative humidity is usually low; also 'heat-wave' temperatures are not common. In the 44 years 1900–43 30° C (86° F) was only reached on average on rather less than 2 days a year at Kew. The relative humidity averaged 39% at the time. Nearly half the years (17) had no day as warm as this, whereas 1911 had as many as 13 such days. The beautiful summer of 1959 only had 2 days as warm as this at Kew (3 at London Airport). The frequencies at Kew over the 44 years were 3 cases in May, 9 in June, 40 in July (25 between 11 and 22 July), 20 in August and 4 in early September. The longest spells of very high temperatures lasted four days with maxima 30° C, in one spell 32° C (90° F), or over, on four successive days.

Sir David Brunt has devoted a good deal of attention to the problem of the effect of weather on comfort and efficiency. In a memoir[1] he has given two sets of curves. The first gives the limits of tolerable air conditions (temperature and humidity) for various degrees of activity. A short study of these curves shows how fortunate we are in our summer weather, for conditions here never become 'intolerable' for anyone resting indoors. For resting, clothed, in sunshine, the limit varies from an air temperature of 76° F (24·5° C), with relative humidity 100%, to 90° F (32·2° C), with relative humidity 40%. The limits for walking at 4 miles an hour without sun are nearly the same. These conditions are very rarely approached in England even at midday inland, and never on the coast. For a person walking at 4 miles an hour in sunshine, the air temperature limit is about 8° F (4·5° C) lower, i.e. from 68° F (20° C) at 100% humidity to 82° F (27·8° C) at 40%; these conditions agree closely with the figures given on p. 118 for the onset of a feeling of 'sultriness'.

Brunt's other diagram analysed the popular usage of words to describe various combinations of temperature and humidity. Brooks tried this diagram on average midday values in January and July at Plymouth and Birmingham. At Plymouth, January had 8 'raw' days, 13 'cold' and 10 'cool'. In 10 years there was only 1 'keen' day. July had 12 'oppressive' and 19 'warm' days. For Birmingham the figures were: January, 15 'raw', 13 'cold' and 3 'cool' days; July, 6 'oppressive', 23 'warm' and 2 'cool' days with 1 day in 10 years classed as 'stimulating'. Low relative humidities make cold days feel more keenly cold; at higher temperatures the effect of very dry air is stimulating, sometimes to the point of irritation inducing restlessness, though this extreme is rarely met in these islands. High

1. Brunt, D., 'The Reactions of the Human Body to its Physical Environment', *Quarterly Journal of the Royal Meteorological Society*, Vol. 69, pp. 77–114, London, 1943.

relative humidities make warmth oppressive, and above the figures quoted from Brunt as the limit of the human body's toleration the risk of heat stroke presents itself.

R. Reiter,[1] of the Bioclimatological Institute of Munich, has classified the physiological effects of weather at great length. He finds dangers in regions of stagnant air—such as enclosed valleys at night or forest clearings—in which the freshness of the air is not renewed by vertical exchange. As regards weather situations, he states according to a summary by Brooks:

'*Inversions and static situations.*—No convection; static electrical charges, atmospheric pollution and large nuclei. The effects, which are greatest on low ground, include aches in amputated limbs and scars, headaches and brain troubles, influenza and troubles with the blood circulation.

'*Unstable air, charged clouds, showers.*—The suggested effects include local nervous trouble in amputated limbs, spasms, colic, cramp, breathlessness, heart trouble, rheumatism, slow reactions. In thundery zones with lightning discharges within a few hundred miles these troubles are especially developed; slowness of reactions leads to an increase in the number of accidents. Reiter also alleges that births are most frequent at such times. Nervous troubles are especially frequent when the atmosphere is becoming electrically charged before a thunderstorm.

'*Warm fronts, warm front rain, stationary weather situations.*—The common feature is warm air flowing gently upwards over a sloping surface of colder air. The rain is usually steady but not heavy. Aches and pains are little felt, but there is a tendency to mental depression and, according to Reiter, to embolism.'

Probably most people think of climate and health in terms of 'bracing' and 'relaxing' weather. Some places seem to fill one with energy, so that the days pass in a whirl of activity—these are 'bracing' or 'tonic'. In other places one feels lazy and restful, inclined to take things easily; these are 'relaxing' or 'sedative.'

The quality which makes a climate 'bracing' is not well understood, and is probably complex. The frequency of weather changes is one element. The 'cooling power' of the air is certainly important; this depends on temperature, humidity and wind speed. A moderate cooling power calls for the use of sufficient energy to tone up the body, and hence is stimulating, but a great cooling power makes too heavy demands and may require energy to be used up in carrying heavy clothing which impedes movement. The mechanical impact of the wind on exposed parts of the

1. Reiter, Reinhold, 'Neuere Untersuchungen zum Problem der Wetterabhängigkeit des Menschen', *Archiv für Meteorologie, Geophysik und Bioklimatologie*, Ser. B, **4**, pp. 327–377, Vienna, 1953.

body is also a factor. Finally, the stimulating quality of the air is believed to depend partly on its oxidizing power, which is increased by the presence of ozone. But there are other factors; the aesthetic quality of the scenery and surroundings plays a part, which varies from person to person but is doubtless present in all, and it would be impossible to evaluate the 'bracing' quality of a place from meteorological statistics alone. On the other hand, there is a good deal of medical experience as to which places are tonic and which sedative. Fig. 23 has been prepared from assessments given by Dr. E. Hawkins,[1] and fits in well with expectations from climatology. It is divided into five degrees: *Very Bracing*, mainly limited to the northeast coast, with a small outlier on the Peak District of Derbyshire; *Bracing*, including the rest of the east coast, shorter sections of other coasts, and hill districts generally; *Average* (unshaded); *Relaxing*, including the south coast of Devon, Cornwall and Wales and most of the lower ground in the western half of England and parts of the Thames Valley; and small *Very Relaxing* areas on the western part of the south coast. The map is, of course, generalized; in any hilly district there are appreciable differences between the bracing hills and more relaxing lowlands. This was noticeable in the difference between the summits and northern slopes of the North Downs and the London suburbs in the valleys at the foot of the slopes. Woodlands, being more humid and less windy than open country, are relatively relaxing, and so are bays facing south and partially enclosed by high cliffs. Doubtless any mountain-girt inlet, loch or firth tends to be relaxing, especially if narrow.

A similar assessment was carried out by Tyler[2] in 1934, who obtained independent opinions from four persons, one a doctor, with extensive experiences of spas. They divided 25 watering places or seaside resorts into Bracing, Intermediate and Relaxing. The result showed that all the east coast and Brighton, Newquay, Harrogate (Spa) and Buxton were regarded as Bracing (but Margate, curiously, as Intermediate), the south coast from Ventnor westwards, Cheltenham, Bath and Tunbridge Wells as Relaxing, others as Intermediate. 'The effect of wind, temperature, humidity and sunshine on the loss of heat from a body at a temperature of 98° F' was the subject of a study by E. Gold,[3] but neither this study nor any of the participants in a discussion of these papers at the Royal Meteorological Society provided a clear definition of what makes the difference between a bracing and a relaxing climate.

1. Hawkins, E., *Medical Climatology of England and Wales*, London (Lewis), 1923.

2. Tyler, W. F., 'Bracing and Relaxing Climates', *Quarterly Journal of the Royal Meteorological Society*, Vol. 61, pp. 309–315, London, 1935.

3. *Quarterly Journal of the Royal Meteorological Society*, Vol. 61, pp. 316–331, London, 1935.

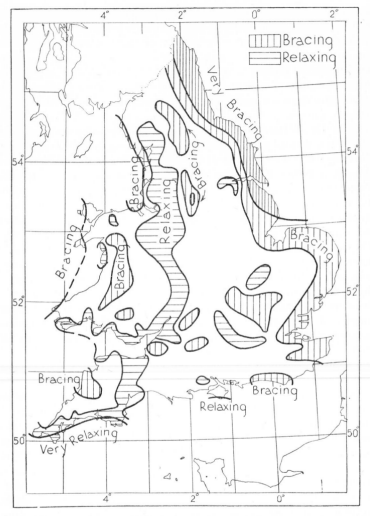

FIGURE 23. 'Bracing' and 'Relaxing' climates.

Cooling power of the air, which is essentially a function of temperature, humidity and wind speed was the favourite candidate, and of these wind is probably the most important. For a climate to be bracing there must also be plenty of sunshine, rather low humidity and average temperature, with a good range of temperature between day and night.

Bracing climates may be chosen for convalescence after operations or severe illness, for people with a tendency to tuberculosis and for recovery from moderate overwork. Very bracing climates, however, are not good for some maladies, notably nervous upsets. Relaxing climates, marked by greater cloudiness and humidity and more equable temperatures, may be chosen for their sedative effect—valuable, for instance, in cases of severe strain from overwork. Medical advice should be sought whenever special questions are involved. And it may also be useful to check up on the actual climatic records of places for which great virtues are claimed. Care and discretion should be exercised before deciding upon convalescence in climates that are foreign to the patient. This applies particularly to the old. The familiar changeableness of the weather in this country with its modest extremes may be safer than the climates of lower latitudes with their occasionally sharp changes of local wind, temperature and humidity from day to night and their buildings that often have no provision for heating (or cooling).

Since the main factor in a sedative climate in Britain is the moist equable west or southwest wind from the Atlantic, the bracing quality increases from west to east, and with shelter from west winds and exposure to east winds. Coasts facing west or south tend to be relaxing, those facing east or north bracing. Hill climates have livelier winds and slightly lower temperatures than the neighbouring lowlands, and for that reason are bracing, especially on the chalk downs and sandy soils of southeast England, where the porous rock keeps the soil dry and the open grassland allows full play to the winds. In the west, high hills, though admirable as play-grounds, tend to be damp and cloudy, especially in winter.

Fig. 24 shows the average distribution of bright sunshine for the year. The units chosen are percentages of the possible duration of sunshine since this varies with latitude, being greatest in the north in summer and in the south in winter. Subtracting these percentages from 100 gives a reasonable indication of the average cloudiness in per cent of the sky covered. Average sunshine totals range from about 1,750 hours a year on the southern coasts from S. Devon to Suffolk ($4\frac{1}{2}$ to 5 hours a day), and almost 1,900 hours/year in the Channel Islands, to 900–1,000 hours/year (about $2\frac{1}{2}$ hours/day) in the cloudiest parts of the northwest Highlands in and near the Great Glen and 1,000 in the northern isles. The percentage of possible sunshine is materially greater in the Highlands in May and June, about 30%, than in the other months. The highest sunshine figures in the world, in the desert zone, range from about 3,000 to 3,750 hours a year or from nearly 70 to 86% of the possible sunshine.

There is little doubt that the climates of the far west and north of Scotland are relaxing in spite of their windiness and cooling power. Brooks

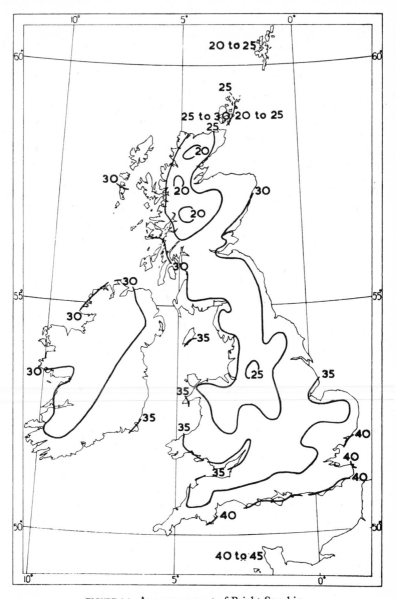

FIGURE 24. Average amount of Bright Sunshine.
(Percentage of the possible duration of sunshine received during the course of the year between 1901 and 1930.)

was of the opinion that this was because the temperature was too low, though rather colder climates in the east of Scotland and in eastern Norway are clearly bracing. It seems more likely that excessive wind, rain frequency and cloudiness are the real defects in the Western Highland climate and that this applies to parts of Ireland and Wales also. Part of the success of the Scotsman 'coming south' is certainly due to the fact that since time beyond memory in Scotland it has been necessary to work hard in order to live, and the habit of working hard continues after leaving the country where it was born.

9

Where to Live; Where to Holiday

WE are now in a position to point to some practical conclusions from the foregoing chapters. The first consideration for those who have any choice in the matter is where to live. And for those that cannot choose, the skill of the town and country planner in using sites in the best way may make life easier and pleasanter. This involves attention to the things that determine local climate, including the climate of the town. Very local effects over distances of yards rather than miles enter in and can be important.

Choice of home

It may be that the future for many in our heavily populated island lies in living in high blocks of flats in compact towns, so that the maximum area of open country can be preserved. Already there is too little unspoilt countryside, but with modern techniques country can be reclaimed from derelict areas. It is true that in America the trend is still the other way, towards ever more sprawling towns, but in this country there is far less land to waste, much of it is fertile and some of it is very beautiful quite close to our biggest cities. Life in the town centre is again becoming—at least potentially—more attractive than it was in the recent past for both office and factory workers, as buildings are built high allowing room for the return of trees, grass and flowers where formerly were only dismal streets. The main reasons for wanting to live outside the town are to get away from the smoke and fog and traffic roar. But smokeless zones and increasing application of the Clean Air Act, as well as careful routing of traffic arteries, are likely to take care of these objections: already an increase of sunshine has been achieved even in central Manchester. But when considering flats in a high 'tower', the prospective tenant should inquire about any peculiarities of the indoor heating climate on different floors, and which other buildings cast their shadow over his flat and for how long in the day; and he may be wise to prefer structures which do not have so much glass as to make the indoor temperature uncontrollable in strong sunshine or cold winds. Positions of the main sources of smoke and smells in relation to the prevailing winds are important wherever one lives, but particularly to the town-dweller. Winds from southwest and west are the most frequent everywhere in these islands; hence the western quarter of most towns usually has the freshest air. But elevation may affect this, and the light breeze during smog conditions in quiet autumn and winter weather in southern Britain is often from the east; it also tends to follow the valleys.

A commuter's daily journeys are expensive and exhausting. They give many occasions for accidents and for the passing of infections—particularly when standing huddled in suburban trains and buses. And they cut down time for relaxation. There are more varied amenities close at hand for the town-dweller, and if the town has been built to a compact plan open country need not be far away. Interesting beginnings of this trend have been made in the plans of some new town communities of limited size and in remodelling the centres of one or two of our old towns. Some, however, prefer to live away from their work and others find their work in the country. For these, for farmers and gardeners, especially, and for those who just find commuting forced upon them, their choice of a site is likely to be influenced by soil and landscape and climate.

Apart from the obvious questions of sunniness and warmth, a site should be judged for its shelter from strong winds (mostly from the south and west except near the east coast) and driving rain. Winds from between SE and N are generally the coldest in winter. Other things to think of are liability to flooding and to local mists, fogs and frosts (frost hollows). In some places, particularly near dry pinewoods on sandy soil or heaths and gorse thickets, the record of forest and heath fires in dry springs and summers may be worth looking into. The day to day problems of farmers and gardeners are beyond the scope of this book. They are catered for by the National Agricultural Advisory Service, working in conjunction with the Agricultural Branch of the Meteorological Office. Amongst the services available are special forecasts and warnings, notifications when dry spells of at least 3 days' duration are imminent and so on. Much useful information about things ranging from frost protection to wind and snow shelter screens, from weather conditions for pest control to situations that make for potato blight, is given in works by L. P. Smith.[1, 2] In the case of pests and diseases, he remarks that the leading villain seems to be humidity. Since this applies also to conditions favouring the breeding of insects and microbes that carry the germs of human diseases, enough wind for ventilation and well drained land are desirable points. The length of the growing season is affected strongly by latitude and altitude in these islands, the changes about 53° N and 500 feet above sea level roughly marking a natural frontier for success with a number of warmth-loving

1. Smith, L. P., *Farming Weather*, London (Nelson), 1958.
2. Smith, L. P., and Searle, S. A., *Weatherwise Gardening*, London (Blandford Press), 1958.

plants. 53° N is however also the effective northern limit of large hail and tornadoes.

The choice of where to live is always a compromise. The afternoon and evening sunshine come from the same direction as the heaviest winds and rain. Moreover the best choice will differ for different people. From most points of view, however, a hillside is to be preferred to either valley floor or hilltop as a place to live. Some thrive best on bracing conditions, whereas others need a somewhat relaxing haunt to rest their nerves. Perhaps the latter consideration is important for all who use up a lot of nervous energy in their jobs in town and in travelling to and fro. Living in a very bracing place is a temptation to spend evenings and weekends in constant strenuous activity.

Holiday places and holiday seasons

Everybody's guiding principle on holidays is that 'a little bit of what you fancy does you good'. Where and when to go depends on what one wants to do and the facilities for doing it. In few cases is the choice entirely independent of the weather.

Walkers and climbers will choose the hills in the west and north and accept the chances of rain and low cloud that are undoubtedly more frequent there than in the south and east: navigation by compass and cairn in hill mist may be regarded as an interesting challenge to be undertaken with a cool head and awareness of the risks. From 1883 to 1904 the weather was observed hour by hour at an observatory on the top of Ben Nevis, 4,406 feet (1,343 m.) above sea level in the Northwest Highlands, one of the first 'permanent' mountain top weather stations in Europe.[1] The summit was enveloped in cloud 69% of the time and sunshine averaged only 758 hours a year. However, when the weather is clear it is very clear and the Highland scenery is unsurpassed anywhere in the world. The extremity of the change is vouched for by the figures: for, in spite of the prevalence of driving mist and rain, the driest air ever observed in the British Isles has also been reported from the upper levels of Ben Nevis. Relative humidities as low as 6 to 15% have been measured in the subsiding air in anticyclones. The exhilaration of experiencing the transparency of such pure air, the unlimited distant view and the clear colours of the landscape are worth a lot of waiting. The chances of wet weather are actually by no means equal in all seasons; and there is much to be said for a visit to the hills in April, May or early June when the tops are still tinged with snow. Moreover, it is at the end of the winter, or just after, that a

1. The station on the Puy de Dôme (1,468 metres) in central France was opened in August 1876. Interesting accounts of the Ben Nevis venture by J. Paton and C. T. R. Wilson are to be found in *Weather*, Vol. 9, pp. 291–308, 309–311, October, 1954.

short open-air holiday may do most good in swiftly restoring the condition
of body and mind.

Other hill-tops at heights of 2,300 to 3,400 feet (about 700 to 1,000 m.)
with western exposures in Cumberland, Galloway and the Western Highlands appear to be cloud-covered 50 to 55% of the time over the year as a
whole—the frequencies being least in spring and in the afternoons. Of
more interest to many are some facts brought to light in special investigations by Shellard, Gloyne and Holgate of the Meteorological Office in
connexion with the planning of motorways: visibility on the present A6
road summit at Shap (1,375 feet) is below 300 yards for 15 to 20% of
the winter and at a bad point about the same height on the moors west of
Huddersfield for 25% of the time. The frequency of visibility under
300 yards appears to be less than 5% everywhere along an existing road
that takes an eastern route over the Pennines, avoiding exposure to the
moist southwest winds. Even high ranges of hills, such as the Cairngorms,
east of the main watershed probably have appreciably lower frequencies
of cloud cover than hills in the west.

Uplift of moist air over the windward slopes of hills has the effect of
extracting so much of the moisture—in fog drops, drizzle and rain—
that the air descending on the lee side has notably less water content, less
cloud and higher cloud base. Visibility is often excellent, because the air
has been washed clean in its passage over the hills. The dry air descending,
with its temperature rising at the dry adiabatic rate (see p. 44, first para.),
attains higher temperatures than existed at the same levels on the windward
side, where uplift and condensation were accompanied by temperature
decrease with height at the smaller, moist adiabatic rate (see p. 44, foot). This
is the Foehn effect, called after the similarly warmed, dry south wind in the
northern Alpine valleys. The long-term operation of this warming effect
upon the prevailing southwest and west winds may be sensed in the rich
farmlands and forests of Morayshire, Aberdeen and Angus and the evidence still visible of medieval prosperity in these counties in east and
northeast Scotland. The sharp contrasts between the weather of the windward and leeward sides were clearly illustrated in the Scottish Highlands
during the persistent west winds of March 1938: a raingauge at Loch
Quoich, Inverness-shire amongst the hills near the west coast had 50
inches of rain in that month, whereas Balmoral, in Deeside amongst the
high hills on the eastern side of the main watershed, and under 80 miles
in a straight line from Loch Quoich, had 0·5 inch—and, of course, prolonged sunshine. The skilful holiday-maker, equipped with car, caravan
and transistor radio (to listen to the weather situation reports), can take
advantage of this most regular of meteorological effects to ensure that,
whichever way the wind blows, he himself is always on the lee side of the

hills. By this technique he can ensure maximum sunshine and may even find some breaks in the cloud on the worst of days.

The devotee of other types of specialist holiday may be much more dependent on the weather, most of all the sunbather and the skier. Those who want boating, swimming and sunbathing will generally be attracted by places with warm water and not too much wind (or tide), though sailing and surf-riding demand some wind and 'sea' (i.e. waves). The usual season of light winds is from May to September, though more narrowly limited to late May, June and July in the north. If warmth is the chief requirement, shallow inland waters and pools may, however, please the swimmer best. The sea is warmest in August and coldest in February, its temperature changes being smaller than, and lagging behind, those of the land.

Skiing holidays have become increasingly organized in Scotland in recent years, with bus transport supplied from hotel to ski grounds and chair-lifts on Cairn Gorm and in Glencoe. This means that the visitor can be nearly sure of getting to the snow between mid winter and Easter, though he may have to be taken far above the tree-line. There might be room for the profitable organization of ski runs on ideal cold snow much nearer the big population centres, and in surroundings having the aesthetics of trees and shelter associated with skiing in the Alps and Norway, if hotels in likely areas in the Pennines and Lake District combined with the railways and local bus firms to lay on complete arrangements for people to be conveyed from the north of England towns at short notice whenever the right weather came. Meteorological forecasts and outlooks for a few days ahead would have to play a part, and the facilities offered for weekends (and long weekends) would have to be well known beforehand and then promptly announced. There are places near Manchester, Leeds and Bradford with 30 to over 50 days with snow lying in an average winter (see fig. 15). Snow frequencies are higher and attractive hillsides with forest and clearing abound near Aberdeen, Dundee and Perth, but the distances from the major population centres are greater. It seems, nevertheless, that more ways could be found along these lines of enjoying our climate instead of grumbling at it.

In the Cambridge and Lincolnshire Fens skating championships have long been arranged at fairly short notice whenever the weather is suitable, and some towns in the eastern English lowlands have arrangements for flooding and lighting meadows for skating in times of frost.

Those who need a holiday purely for their health, for convalescence after illness or rest from overwork, will be guided by the prescribed requirements of bracing or relaxing climate, warmth, comfort and only moderate exposure. Figs. 10, 11, 13–19, 21–24 may all be helpful in making the choice, though local factors should also be considered where known.

Adequate knowledge of local climate, and of facilities offered, is especially important in choosing for frail patients. The longest duration of summer conditions for sitting out of doors and most sunshine are to be found in the south between Kerry, South Devon, Sussex and the Channel Islands.

For sunshine the early summer months have the advantage. The bright early mornings and late evenings of May are also the time of bird-song. And the vegetation is freshest in that month. By the end of April the sun is already above the horizon longer than it is in mid August. But this is not the only reason why May, June and July have the longest duration of sunshine. Because the seas are still cooler than the land, and because of the types of weather situation that occur in those months, average relative humidities and cloud amounts are least just then. The percentage of possible sunshine normally received has its highest values in May, ranging from just over 50% on the southeast coast and in the Channel Islands to 30–35% in the Pennines and Lake District, parts of the Welsh mountains, most of the Highlands and central Ireland. Coastal values reach 40–45% as far north as Tiree and Barra in the Hebrides. Because of the longer days in the northern summer there is actually little to choose between the southern Hebrides and Kent for hours of sunshine in May and early June (7–7½ hours a day on average in both places), but there is an abrupt decrease in the sunshine figures in western Scotland after mid June, associated with changes of prevailing wind and weather pattern that will be described in the next chapter. The average sunshine in the Hebrides in July and August is 4–5 hours a day. In the south and east the figures remain high in July and do not fall greatly even in August, but west Wales and western Ireland experience something of the decline that affects the Hebrides so markedly about the longest day.

The period between sunrise and sunset does not, of course, coincide with the holiday-maker's day. Few people in Britain on holiday rise before 7 a.m., by which time the sun (even with daylight saving time) is well up in the sky. So the time of sunrise matters little; it is the time of sunset that counts. In all Britain clocks take their time from London, but the sun does not. The sun rises, and sets, 4 minutes later for every degree of longitude (about 43 miles) west of Greenwich. Thus, according to the clock, the sun sets 20 minutes later in the longitude of Cornwall, Pembroke and the Western Highlands than it does in the same latitudes on the Greenwich meridian; at the western extremities of Ireland in Kerry and Connemara the difference is 40 minutes. The total effect of the long day, the western longitude and the statutory change of clock means that at 58° N 7° W in Harris the sun does not set on 21 June until 10.30 p.m. B.S.T. compared with 9·21 p.m. in London.

Twilight[1] is also longest at midsummer. Even around London the northern sky does not become completely dark at midnight for a week or two in June. In Shetland it is light enough to read in the open at midnight. For grown-ups the long light evenings of late May, June and early July are perhaps the best part of the summer, especially in fine weather when the days are rather too hot. For children, however, the light nights disturb the daily rhythm by delaying sleep.

Where to retire

Where to go to live when one has cast off the cares and ties of a regular job is largely a question of tastes and hobbies; but climate and health may also affect the decision.

For those who require above all dry climates, or to whom watching the course of Nature in the round of the seasons adds drama and zest to life, the most continental climates are found between the counties of Huntingdon, Northants, Buckingham and quite near the East Anglian coast, together with parts of Surrey, Kent and Sussex. The driest sites are on the limestone, chalk and sandy ridges in this area, but the clayey valleys are often damp and misty. For those who prefer the most equable climates, these are found in the west and southwest, in Cornwall, Wales, the Hebrides and the west of Ireland. The frequency of rain is greater than in the southeast, but the winters are milder and frosts are few.

For the active healthy man who is looking forward to retirement to do all the things he has never had time to do before, a moderately bracing climate may be best. The man who wants to potter, and laze in the sunshine, will choose a more relaxing place, the south coast of England being most favoured. Extremes, either of bracing or relaxing climate, are best avoided. So are damp, misty places where catarrh and rheumatism flourish. Access to a town for entertainment, shopping, library and medical services is important and this may become difficult at times in districts liable to much snow or flooding. But so many men, so many views, and everyone must please himself. The best advice is not to choose a place only on its summer looks but to see it if possible on a drab wet day in winter. If it looks all right then, it will probably do.

1. By definition Civil Twilight ends when the sun is 6° below the horizon (lighting-up time for vehicles is intended to correspond to this); Nautical Twilight ends when the sun is 12° below the horizon (this is when it becomes for practical purposes dark); Astronomical Twilight ends when the sun is 18° below the horizon (and then the twilight glow is normally gone from the sky). Astronomical twilight lasts all night in 50° N from about 3 June till 10 July, and in 60° N from 25 April till 20 August. Nautical twilight just lasts all night in 54–55° N (the latitude of the Lake District) on the longest day; in 60° N it lasts all night from 12 May till 31 July. Civil twilight just lasts all night in 61° N on the longest day: in the latitude of London ($51\frac{1}{2}$° N) it lasts 48 minutes after sunset at the June solstice (till 10.9 p.m. B.S.T.), 33 minutes after sunset about the equinoxes and 41 minutes at the December solstice.

10

Seasons and Saints' Days

Ancient knowledge: Weather lore

THE old saying about St. Swithin's day, which is still well known, that if it rains on that day (15 July) it will rain for 40 days thereafter (till 24 August), is but one example of many pieces of folk weather lore that have come down to us from the past—about long spells of weather in different seasons, alleged indicator dates and turning points around which time such spells are liable to start or finish, as well as briefer weather episodes that tend to occur around a particular time of the year. The dates were mostly identified, as was natural, by the saints of the Christian calendar. Our forebears lived closer to the weather than we do, constantly observing it and exposed to its vagaries; and, though much nonsense was doubtless talked upon the basis of inconsequential reminiscence and faulty memory, some of the observers were shrewd and some of their wisdom has stood the test of time.[1]

The St. Swithin legend probably began as a superstition, started by the memorable events of the year AD 971, but survived because in some shadowy way it corresponded with something real and important in our climate. It is alleged that Swithin, who was bishop of Winchester, expressed a wish before he died in 862 to be buried in the churchyard where the rain from the church eaves might fall upon his grave. He was buried there, but a century later a splendid tomb was built inside the cathedral and 15 July 971 was the day appointed for his removal to it. When the day came, there was such a storm of rain, and 40 wet days thereafter, that the pious people remembering the saint's humble wish abandoned the idea of his removal.

Now it is a fact, verified as we shall see by recent research, that most English summers settle down by about mid July into some persistent character—either mostly wet or mostly fine or repetitive alternations. Indeed this is one of the most noticeable bits of seasonal behaviour in the whole year and is bound up with the behaviour of the atmospheric cir-

1. A remarkable collection of this material is contained in *Weather Lore*, compiled by R. Inwards, first published 1869; 4th edition, London (Rider & Co. for Royal Meteorological Society), 1950. An older collection in German in a work called *Bauern-Praktik*, originally circulating in manuscript and first printed in 1508, ran through sixty editions and became the most widely circulated meteorological book.

culation over most of the northern hemisphere. Moreover, the circulation normally undergoes great changes during June (already referred to in the last chapter in connexion with sunshine in the Highlands and Hebrides), so that the type of weather that is going to settle in for the height of summer often does not become apparent until nearly 15 July. The next pronounced shake-up of the general pattern of winds and storm tracks over the hemisphere is normally around 24 August, so that there is indeed a tendency for our spells of high summer weather to end about that time.

It reflects no discredit on the medieval observers that the adage somewhat imperfectly expressed what we now know from hemisphere-wide weather maps and many years of reliable records. In this case, as in others, the chief fault with the old saying is that it expects too much accurate repetition from the performance of the atmospheric circulation and attaches far too much significance to the exact day. The margin of variability of date that should be allowed in these cases does not, however, appear to be very wide—in some cases not more than a few days. This was probably appreciated by some observers, and was perhaps why the shrewdest formulated rules from ancient times were remembered over centuries when the old Julian calendar was gradually getting further wrong—3 days every 400 years until the improved modern or Gregorian calendar was adopted (in 1752 in England, but between 1582 and 1700 in the neighbouring continental countries with which England had most contact). A remarkable, and at first sight very surprising, aspect of the roughly calendar-dated events in the seasonal development of atmospheric circulation and weather is the evidence that some of them persisted in their occurrence throughout the quite noteworthy changes of climate in recent centuries. The climatic changes were perhaps primarily a question of temperature level, but also affected the proximity of frequently cyclonic and anticyclonic areas to the British Isles: hence total annual rainfall and the over-all frequency of different wind directions did also undergo changes.

Nature's seasons: a modern approach to understanding

Current scientific investigation of these matters is based partly on a register of the classification of each day's weather type over the British Isles since 1873 according to the definitions given in Ch. 4 (pp. 55–56) and partly on daily values of the measurements of meteorological instruments at places all over the hemisphere. A somewhat similar register of each day's atmospheric circulation pattern over the wider area of Europe and the eastern Atlantic, but inevitably based on a much larger number of different pattern types, has been used in Germany.[1]

1. Hess, P., and Brezowsky, H., 'Katalog der Grosswetterlagen Europas', *Berichte des Deutschen Wetterdienstes in der US-Zone*, Nr. 33, Bad Kissingen, 1952.

One of the simplest and earliest results[1] of these studies confirmed the observation of former ages that long spells of set weather character are by no means equally common at all times of the year. They have their seasons—times of the year, evidently, when the large-scale features of the wind flow over the hemisphere are liable to favour a long-continued run of this or that type of weather near the British Isles. These long spells may be looked upon as defining natural seasons, as explained in the next paragraphs.

Long spells lasting over 25 days of one or other of the weather types defined on pp. 55–56, or of groups of related types, were considered. Several combinations of types were common, such as westerly and cyclonic (a westerly spell in which the depression centres passed close to, and often over, the British Isles), westerly and anticyclonic, and anticyclonic combined with easterly and either northerly or southerly types (anticyclones affecting Britain, Scandinavia and Greenland or Britain and the continent respectively). Minor interruptions, such as might be caused by a ridge of high pressure passing across the British Isles during a cyclonic sequence, were ignored so long as they did not last more than 3 days. 158 long spells were identified in the 50 years 1898–1947, about three a year on average. In the list were many famous spells, remembered for their drought or warmth, wetness or severe cold. (Some of the most outstanding spells of this and of earlier times appear in App. 2.) Moreover, more fleeting occurrences of weather of somewhat similar type are often noticed in the less settled periods before and after the main spell. In most cases, therefore, the occurrence of a spell of this length gives a distinctive stamp to that particular season.

Fig. 25 shows the frequency of occurrence of these long spells on each day of the calendar year—the percentages are just double the number of occurrences in the 50 years (1898–1947) examined. A division of the year into five natural seasons, with some useful subdivision into shorter periods as described later in this chapter, suggests itself from this curve and from other more detailed studies. It turns out that our weather settles down into a long spell of one kind or another at some time during July–August in about 70% of the years studied, and this frequency is reached again in the autumn. Perhaps it is not surprising, however, that the natural seasons marked out by these habits of the atmospheric circulation awkwardly fail to agree with any of the neat conventions for dividing the year up into four seasons of equal length adopted in diaries or even in standard climatological statistics—where summer is taken as June, July, August; autumn

1. Lamb, H. H., 'Types and spells of weather around the year in the British Isles: annual trends, seasonal structure of the year, singularities,' *Quarterly Journal of the Royal Meteorological Society*, Vol. 76, pp. 393–438, London, 1950.

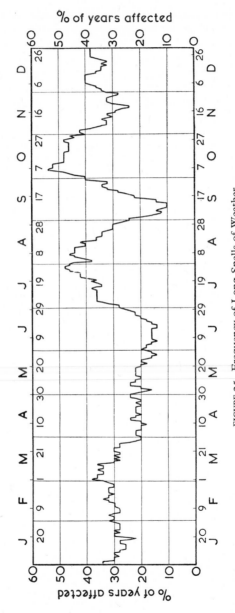

FIGURE 25. Frequency of Long Spells of Weather.

(Percentage of the years between 1898 and 1947 in which each day of the year fell within a long spell of any set weather type lasting over 25 days.)

as September, October, November; and so on! The natural seasons and suitable names for them appear to be as follows. Since brevity makes for clarity, the dates of the year are given in the remainder of this chapter according to the notation 18/6 for 18 June.

HIGH SUMMER: from about 18/6 till 9/9.

Sequences usually of westerly and northwesterly types, combined with cyclonic or anticyclonic weather types in different years, coming to notice in late June or early July develop a marked tendency to persist. Long spells within our definition become established for 25 days or longer in about seven years per decade. Years affected by wet cyclonic sequences are about twice as numerous as persistently anticyclonic ones, but more years than either of these are characterized by the westerly and north-westerly types with their alternations of bright and disturbed days. This is the weather that keeps the grass of the English village fresh for cricket, fair-ground and the village dance, often fresher than it was in May and early June when drought is more liable to parch the green. Interruptions of the spells once established seem to be commonest around end July–first days of August. The anticyclonic spells show rather more tendency to continue into September than the cyclonic ones which are very prone to change in the last week of August.

AUTUMN: from about 10/9 till 19/11.

Long spells within the definition again become established for 25 days or longer in over two years out of three. Types which give fine, and in the South mostly calm, weather are more characteristic of the spells occurring in September and early October—Keats' 'season of mists and mellow fruitfulness'—and they usually break down soon after that. About equally numerous are the spells which give persistently wet, stormy autumns, though these are seldom established before late September–early October and go on later, usually into November. The period between 23/10 and 13/11 nearly always contains some wet, stormy weather. These late autumn rains usually make up any soil moisture deficit developed by excess of evaporation over rainfall during the summer, and by about this date the topsoil in grassy fields in the south of England becomes usually saturated.

EARLY WINTER: from about 20/11 till 19/1.

Long spells are distinctly less common than in high summer or autumn but nevertheless affect about half the years during this period. These are mostly cases when the westerly, mild winter types become firmly estab-lished, the sequences being often stormy and wet but in just a few cases rather anticyclonic and dry. Any frosts occurring at this time in recent decades have seldom lasted much over a week, though some longer frosts in early winter were recorded in the past, notably in the seventeenth and eighteenth centuries. Except in 1962–63, none of the long spells established in this part of the winter, during the last 150 years, seem to have carried on without a break into the later part of the winter after mid January. The period is, however, occasionally affected by brief foretastes of severe weather which does not become firmly established until February.

LATE WINTER and EARLY SPRING: from about 20/1 till 31/3.

Long spells affected about half the years studied during this period, but they were of such widely differing types that this was sometimes the main period of winter and in other years firmly developed the character of an early spring from some time in February onwards. The increasing tendency towards anticyclonic and easterly types, and declining frequency of westerly winds from late January on, was apparently correctly spotted in an old legend about Candlemas Day (2 February), that if that day were fine and bright (anticyclonic) more frosty weather was likely to follow. Very persistent mild, westerly weather is probably slightly less common than the sum of long spells of the various cold types, though these affect only a minority of winters. Most of the remaining less cold Februarys are rather changeable. This section of the year is not one that would suggest itself as a single season from a study of the temperatures prevailing in Britain— apart, perhaps, from the Highlands. The increasing power of the sun becomes very noticeable from late February onwards (and average daytime temperatures begin to rise abruptly from their rather flat seasonal minimum maintained through the winter since late November) unless defeated by cold winds, cloudiness or deep snow. Nevertheless the barometric pressure and wind patterns of February and March in this part of the hemisphere show more tendency to similarity (persistence) than those of any other pair of months except July and August. The effect of this is that one and the same anticyclonic spell may give severe frost in February which gradually passes into warm, dry, sunny weather in March (as happened in 1929). But cold weather produced by persistent easterly and northerly winds seems more inclined to stay cold at this time. The dwindling frequency of the westerly weather type drops more sharply after about 9/3; westerly weather in Britain then becomes more uncommon than it is at any other time except late April–early June. The circulation pattern types that between them dominate most years from about mid February–mid March onwards account for the greater frequency of droughts in spring and early summer than at other seasons. By some time in March the topsoil in grassy fields in the south of England is often dried out, though the date varies over 5 to 10 weeks either way from year to year. By the end of April there is on average a moisture deficit in the top 2–3 feet (*c.* 75 cm.).

SPRING and EARLY SUMMER: from about 1/4 till 17/6.

During the first half of April there is a temporary recovery of frequency of westerly and northwesterly types in Britain, one or other of these types occurring in 50% of the years on most dates. This marks the period off from March, but it is a situation that does not last. The long spells of the previous season are over, and this is the time of year least given to long continued runs of similar weather, though chiefly because westerly type sequences fail to persist. From mid to late April onwards anticyclonic and easterly spells return to some prominence, but still more noticeable is the year's most pronounced peak of northerly weather: northerly type long spells occur in 10–20% of the years during this season. In the majority of years the weather is changeable, with some warm anticyclonic days alternating with cold northerly outbreaks. The very clear Arctic air brought by these winds from the northern seas and ice contributes to the fresh beauty of the May scene but is also liable to give late frosts on still nights, especially when the ground is dry and cools readily. By the end of May the long spells of this season are generally over, unless they be anticyclonic ones—these are liable to continue into June. Changes are under way in the hemispheric patterns which very frequently give Britain anticyclonic weather. Anticyclones affect this country in 30–45% of the years on most dates between 20/5 and 12/6, and though these are mostly in short spells they help to make this usually the loveliest time of the year.

May is often a dry month, particularly after the period of somewhat heightened liability to cyclonic type in the first 7 to 9 days (see later, fig. 26 and App. 1 and 2) is over. Dry Mays may be followed by either wet or dry high summers. But even in the finest summers, which are remembered as *long* fine summers because of a lovely May, there is normally a radical change of circulation pattern in June to early July. This means that the extent of the area of prevailing fine weather to the north and northwest of the British Isles, e.g. as regards Iceland and north Norway, and sometimes even Scotland and the Hebrides—becomes more restricted. By contrast, the wettest high summers in England are liable to give good weather in places far enough north of the belt of travelling depressions—e.g. in north Norway, and sometimes even in west Scotland and the Hebrides, which from time to time in such summers enjoy lee-side weather.

Singularities

The rapidity, and marked preference for dates between 2 and 20 June in most years, of the hemispheric circulation changes that bring back the westerlies as the prevailing wind in Britain by 20/6, after three months in which they have been rather less frequent than east and north winds, brings us to a consideration of the evidence for some more or less sharply dated episodes in the normal round of the seasons. This particular change, as we have seen, produces an abrupt and lasting increase of cloudiness in western districts. On the continent it has been widely called the onset of the European monsoon. Many are the summers recorded in England and neighbouring continental countries in the same latitude which, after early promise, broke down at midsummer or soon afterwards, to be followed by weeks of disappointing, or frankly wet, weather. Seemingly endless successions of fronts coming across from the west, or sequences in which the depression centres passed over or quite near, brought the rains. 'Before St. John's day (24/6) we pray for rain, after that we get it without praying' —as an old English saying has it.

The earliest scientific attempts to study an episode of some practical importance which was thought to be tied to particular dates of the calendar concerned May frosts and their occurrence over a large area of Europe.[1, 2] This phenomenon was an unfortunate choice and led to disappointment in ways that illustrate several characteristic difficulties and the need (however hard) to get our ideas clear. There were countrymen's sayings in different parts of central Europe connecting frosts particularly with the period 11–14 May, and the saints whose names (Mamertus, Pankratius, Servatius and Bonifatius) graced these dates of the calendar had acquired the name of the 'Ice Saints'. In fact, there was a peak frequency of cold spells in central Europe between 1766 and 1845 occurring in just 53% of the years (the maximum frequency) on 10 and 11 May. This was often enough to be important, but not a high enough frequency to amount to a forecast for any particular year; it did not exactly coincide with the saying nor did it indicate any really fixed dates. Over the next hundred years after 1846 the pattern changed and shifted somewhat, giving maximum incidence affecting just 39% of the years on 8–9/5 and 20–21/5. (It may turn out to be interesting that the frequency round about the dates of the original Ice Saints was again high during the 30 years 1881–1910 which were on the whole another cold climatic epoch in some ways resembling times before 1845.) Dove rightly concluded as early as 1856 that the cold outbreaks were due to the transport of air from higher latitudes, but that the dates in May affected have such a scatter over a period of years that one cannot connect them with three particular days as the old sayings do.

1. Pilgram, A., *Untersuchungen über das Wahrscheinliche in der Witterungskunde durch vieljährige Beobachtungen*, Vienna, 1788.

2. Dove, H. W., 'Über die Rückfälle der Kälte in Mai', *Abhandlungen des kgl. preuss. Akad. der Wissenschaften zu Berlin*, 1856.

The farmers' concern seems to be connected with the vulnerability of the fruit-blossom to frost just about the dates mentioned, coupled with the fact that outbreaks of cold air flooding over much of Europe from the north are particularly frequent in the first three weeks of May. The entry of the returning west and northwest winds into the continent in June (the so-called European summer monsoon), which exhibits more strongly preferred dates and affects the seasonal trend of average temperature more than the Ice Saints in May, had not achieved such ill renown, presumably because there is normally no question of frost damage in June—though, to be sure, there were folk traditions in Germany about the *Schafskälte* ('sheep cold') coming around 10–15/6 and the weather of the *Siebenschläfer* (Seven Sleepers of Ephesus) day (27/6). All over Germany farmers will tell you that, if it rains on the *Siebenschläfertag*, it will rain for 7 weeks thereafter (i.e. till about 15/8).

The first serious attempt to draw up a calendar of these peculiar seasonal episodes in the British Isles was by Alexander Buchan,[1] a leading spirit in the vigorous old Scottish Meteorological Society throughout most of its existence. However, Buchan's periods, having been picked out from the observations in Scotland for just 10 years (1857–66), were insufficiently firmly based. They are printed below chiefly for their historic interest:

Cold periods	Warm periods
7–14/2	12–15/7
11–14/4	12–15/8
9–14/5	3–14/12
29/6–4/7	
6–11/8	
6–13/11	

Statistical investigations[2, 3] of the incidence over longer periods of years of warm and cold departures from the ideal smooth annual temperature curve with its maximum in July and minimum in January have not supported the dates identified by Buchan as of any lasting significance in Scotland. However, these same studies have left suggestions that *some* more or less regular interruptions of the smooth course of the seasons do occur, that they persist from century to century and that they are most readily identified in an area which may extend from Italy to the Baltic

1. Buchan, A., 'Interruptions in the regular rise and fall of temperature in the course of the year', *Journal of the Scottish Meteorological Society*, New Series, No. 13, pp. 3–15, Edinburgh (Blackwood), 1867.

2. McIntosh, D. H., 'Annual recurrences in Edinburgh temperature', *Quarterly Journal of the Royal Meteorological Society*, Vol. 79, pp. 262–271, London, 1953.

3. Craddock, J. M., 'The representation of the annual temperature variation over central and northern Europe by a two-term harmonic form', *Quarterly Journal of the Royal Meteorological Society*, Vol. 82, pp. 275–288, London, 1956.

and from the borders of Russia to southeast England though hardly to Scotland.

Buchan's days suddenly became a news item in the 1920s when the proposal for a fixed date for Easter was being discussed. E. L. Hawke, some time Secretary of the Royal Meteorological Society, noticed that the date proposed, the Sunday between 9 and 15 April, usually fell in one of Buchan's cold spells. When the matter was looked into, however, it was found that the actual Easter weather in London over a long period had been better than could have been obtained on any fixed date! Despite these difficulties, we may catch glimpses in what follows of a physical interpretation of the events observed by Buchan. Of his periods, 12–15/7 may simply be the dates of the summit of the annual temperature curve in Scotland; 7–14/2 and 3–14/12 correspond to circulation developments which appear to show a significant degree of regularity in the central European winter high pressure region and the Atlantic depression belt respectively, but are less regular in their significance for the temperature in Scotland; and 29/6–4/7 doubtless came out as a cold period because of the effect in Scotland in the years Buchan studied of the late June break-through of the westerly and northwesterly winds into Europe.

First among those who have attempted in the present century to draw up calendars of fairly regularly recurring seasonal events in European weather was Schmauss,[1] who coined the name *Singularity* because the curves of meteorological elements show singular points in the mathematical sense ($dy/dx = 0$, sharp turns, etc.) at the dates concerned. The name quickly came into general use, perhaps because it also implied something which claimed attention but was not yet understood. Schmauss based his studies on the average temperature, pressure, frequencies over many years of rainfall and of different wind directions, and so on, for each day of the calendar year. He favoured an explanation in terms of exchanges of polar and tropical, oceanic and continental air. Unfortunately he attached importance to just about every jag on the curves and counted 66 singularities in the course of the year. Clearly, the rigour of statistical tests of significance had to be brought to bear upon the problem, to distinguish between variations whose magnitude might be important and those random fluctuations that must be expected to show up in any limited sample of years. Another possible test is that one would not expect persistence of date in different sample periods; if this occurs, a fluctuation might be significant even though its magnitude were small.

Space does not permit further review here of the development of this

1. Schmauss, A., 'Synoptische Singularitäten', *Meteorologische Zeitschrift*, **55,** pp. 385–403, Berlin, 1938.

difficult debate.[1] The most successful definitions of singularities have been in terms of atmospheric circulation patterns. Calendars of singularities affecting Britain and Europe, mostly with some claim to be regarded as statistically significant, have been put forward by various authors, the best known probably being those of Baur,[2] Flohn and Hess,[3] Brooks[4] and Lamb.[5]

Flohn and Hess's list is made up of 10- to 12-day periods of the year within which some particular type of large-scale circulation pattern occurred on at least 3 consecutive days in more than 66% of the years 1881–1947. This definition allows no greater variation of date than 5 days earlier or later than the middle date for each singularity. Most of the 14 singularities which satisfied this criterion fall in autumn and winter (September–March). The others are connected with the onset of the so-called summer monsoon in Europe and subsequent pulses of oceanic air invading the continent in summer. The average duration of the specified type of weather situation was in each case 6 to 8 days. All the lists mentioned are in general agreement so that it has been possible to combine them into one in the table in App. I, to show the salient points as regards what may affect the weather in Britain. It is noticeable that over much of the year, particularly in the winter months, singularities of more or less opposite character alternate at roughly half-month intervals. This suggests the possibility of an underlying time-wave phenomenon affecting the Atlantic depressions and European anticyclones. Some attention has been paid to this by Flohn[6] and Scherhag,[7] particularly to a roughly 30-day oscillation of pressure values over central Europe.

None of the lists indicate firm dates for the northerly outbreaks in spring, except for the peak occurrence of the northerly type in Britain and the Norwegian Sea affecting 30% of the years on and around 15 May (cf. the Ice Saints) in three different 25- to 40-year epochs since 1873.

1. A very useful review of the subject from its beginnings to the most recent approaches in many parts of the world has lately been published in German by Karel Bayer in 'Witterungssingularitäten und allgemeine Zirkulation der Erd-atmosphäre', *Geofysikalni Sbornik*, pp. 521–634 (Works of the Geophysical Institute of the Czechoslovak Academy of Sciences, No. 125), Prague, 1959.

2. Baur, F., *Musterbeispiele europäischer Grosswetterlagen*, Wiesbaden (Dieterich), 1947; and in *Physikalisch-statistische Regeln als Grundlagen für Wetter- und Witterungsvorhersagen*, II, pp. 76–78, Frankfurt/Main (Akad. Verlag), 1958.

3. Flohn, H., and Hess, P., 'Grosswettersingularitäten im jährlichen Witterungsverlauf Mitteleuropas', *Meteorologische Rundschau*, 2, p. 262, 1949.

4. Brooks, C. E. P., 'Annual recurrences of weather: singularities', *Weather*, I, p. 110, 1946.

5. Lamb, H. H., 'Types and spells . . .' (*loc. cit.*), 1950.

6. Flohn, H., *Witterung und Klima in Mitteleuropa*, p. 182, Zürich (Hirzel), 1954.

7. Scherhag, R., *Neue Methoden der Wetteranalyse und Wetterprognose*, Berlin (Springer), 1948.

The difficulty over this may be connected with the fact that long-sustained changes in the over-all frequency of (blocking) anticyclones over Greenland (and over Scandinavia) are a marked feature of the climatic variations of recent centuries. Between about 1893 and 1950 northerly outbreaks in this sector were notably less frequent over the year as a whole than before or since. There is a noticeable tendency, in any case, for the singularities listed in the table to become less definite, or less precise as regards preferred dates, from about mid winter onwards. In some cases—for instance, differences in the penetration of Europe by westerly winds from the Atlantic in early January—this is clearly related to variations in the maximum vigour attained by the winter circulation and corresponding differences in the extent and pattern of snow cover in different winters. The effects of such differences presumably reach their maximum at the end of the winter and in spring.

Fig. 26 displays in black dots the frequencies in the 50 years 1898–1947 on each day of the year of the three commonest weather types over the British Isles—Westerly, Cyclonic and Anticyclonic. It also indicates the grounding of the estimates of statistical significance referred to in the table of singularities (App. 1). The line through the middle of the dots marks the course of the 29-day average frequency around each date. Within each 29-day period the scatter of frequencies for different days was considered: the two outer fine lines mark the limit of variations up to twice the standard deviation from the mean. About 5% of the daily values could be expected to go beyond these limits if only random (chance) fluctuations (attributable to using a limited sample of years) were present. Bigger deviations than this from the mean may be significant, especially if still greater departures from the 3-month mean (not shown in the figure) are involved. In the case of all three types the number of big deviations is greater than might be expected to occur by chance, though in the case of the Westerly type this margin is small. Other statistical tests have been applied to establish the degree of significance (percentage probability of occurrence by chance) of the bigger and more rapid changes of frequency level of various types seen at certain times of the year. Such statistical tests are not, however, a final arbiter so much as an assessment of the magnitude of particular features in relation to the general variability of frequency from day to day. One or two sharp frequency peaks have been found, such as that of the cyclonic type at the end of February between 1898 and 1947, which appear to pass the severest statistical tests (approximately 0·1% probability of occurring as a purely random fluctuation), yet this feature is either not to be found in the earlier and later decades examined or only by admitting shifts of 10 days in either direction which appear to make the feature meaningless. By contrast, the tendency for high pressure over the continent

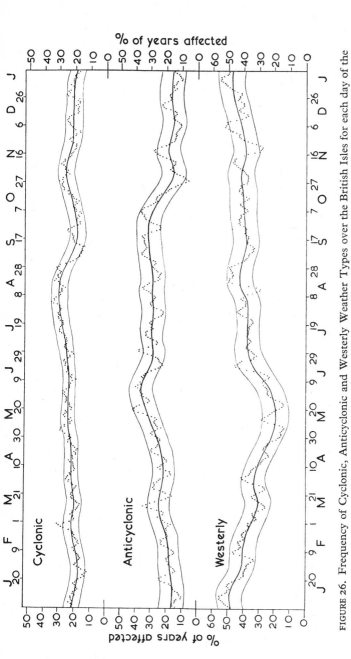

FIGURE 26. Frequency of Cyclonic, Anticyclonic and Westerly Weather Types over the British Isles for each day of the year between 1898 and 1954.

(The date scale is continued at the right-hand side of the diagram as far as 15 January, to make it easier to appreciate frequency levels about New Year.)

(especially the Alpine region) in the middle of each of the winter months, which appears so persistent that it can be recognized in the observations made in Zürich from 1550 to 1576 by the pastor W. Haller,[1] and must therefore claim attention, produces only modest peaks and troughs in the frequencies of the British Isles weather types. Attention has therefore been paid to the occurrence of the singularities listed in the table in different spans of years—1873–97, 1898–1938 and 1938–61 with some additional references to 1550–76 and 1763–1896.

The dates which show an anticyclonic tendency seem (cf. App. 1) to be more regular in central Europe than most of the cyclonic ones. In the districts of the British Isles nearest the Atlantic it is some of the cyclonic episodes, associated with the development of storms on the ocean, that show most suggestion of regularity. An interesting aspect of the climatic difference between the 16th and 20th centuries is, however, that the Zürich observations of 1550–76 show more evidence of the (still) preferred dates for depressions pushing east from the Atlantic than do the more recent observations from central Europe.

The question may be asked what happens to the singularity calendar during long spells of set weather character dominating the greater part of a natural season. Such questions can only be answered on the basis of a fuller understanding of the physical nature of the singularity phenomenon. In some ways, however, it may be legitimate to regard the singularity calendar as a sort of steeplechase: if a particular long spell succeeds in getting over a hurdle—i.e. in surviving dates which the singularity calendar indicates as unfavourable for it—the spell may be firmly enough established to continue a good while longer. This point has been verified by investigation in certain instances: it seems to apply in particular to anticyclones over Europe which survive to the end of September and to the end of January. About the end of October, November and December European anticyclones almost invariably do break down or cease to influence this country: at these dates it is rather a question of any cyclonic or westerly spells which may be already established being likely to continue for a while.

Some of the singularities in our list (App. 1) clearly play a part in determining the limiting dates of the natural seasons defined at the beginning of this chapter. This applies to the Return of the Westerlies in June, the End of Summer Turning Point in August, the Mid-November Anticyclones and Winter Return of the Westerlies in December, as well as to the Mid-winter Mildening and the Late-winter Decline of the Westerlies in different years.

1. A digest of these observations, with frequency diagrams, has been published by H. Flohn in 'Klima und Witterungsablauf in Zürich im 16. Jahrhundert', *Vierteljahrsschrift der Naturforschungsgesellschaft in Zürich*, **95**, pp. 28–41, 1949.

There is fragmentary evidence pointing to very long continued operation of this seasonal calendar in the historical records of the years of Roman and Norman invasions of Britain. Julius Caesar was held up for weeks by persistent adverse W to NW winds on the Channel coast of France in summer 54 BC, while it was very droughty (anticyclonic) in France: these winds ceased about the end of August and were followed by much more variable winds in September. The events of the preceding year, 55 BC, followed a somewhat similar course. In AD 1066, after a long dry summer, W–NW winds prevailed in the Channel all through September and it was a break-down of this anticyclonic northwesterly spell that gave William of Normandy his chance to cross on 7 October (New Style) 1066.

The anomalies of the wind circulation which produce long spells of weather may be understood as either shifts of position of the main wind-streams or excessive strength or weakness of their development. In a season when the Atlantic westerlies are (for reasons which may or may not be physically identifiable) persistently displaced or diverted to the north, well away from the British Isles, it becomes unlikely that this country will feel much of the effects of any bouts of intensification of the Atlantic depressions even if they do occur about the usually preferred dates. This was the situation in the fine summer and autumn of 1959, and may have been associated with the pattern of persistent anomalies of the temperature of the North Atlantic sea water (cold in the west and warm in the east) that existed from early in that year. Intensification of the Atlantic depressions did occur about the normal dates in early autumn, but only very minor effects were felt in the form of light rainfall in Scotland and northern England: it was not until late October that the main depression sequences came near enough to break the fine weather in Britain completely. Similarly, in seasons when the westerlies are strong and close to our own latitude, as in mild winters in this country, no effect may reach here from any variations of pressure level in anticyclones over central Europe or farther east. Careful reading of the calendar (App. 1) will show that there is also a tendency for the dates of some singularity features to wander, though this is chiefly a characteristic of those singularities which merely correspond to the broad (and obviously imprecisely dated) climax of some long-continued seasonal trend—e.g. the greatest strength of the westerlies in mid winter.

Interpretation of singularities and the seasonal progress of the wind circulation

The origins and mechanism of the singularity phenomenon have remained until now among the most difficult and elusive points in meteorology. For the benefit of the curious, however, we can carry this analysis of seasonal advance and retreat and singularities a stage or two further and indicate those current lines of thought on the matter which appear most promising. Those readers whose interest is satisfied by knowledge of the statistical results given earlier in this chapter and in App. 1, and who are not concerned to probe into the mechanisms at work, will skip this section and pick up the threads on p. 156.

As has already been implied, we may distinguish three kinds of events in the singularity table (App. 1):

(1) broad, imprecisely dated climaxes of various seasonal trends—the year's greatest and least developments of various weather types.

(2) short periods of heightened tendency for various phenomena within a week or so of particular dates—the sharper peaks and troughs of various types. The roughly 30-day pressure oscillation over central Europe in winter, producing anticyclonic singularities around or just after the middle of each month, shows up clearly in the waves on the frequency curve for Anticyclonic type in the British Isles (fig. 26).

(3) Abrupt, almost step-like changes in the frequency level of particular weather types about particular dates—e.g. the return of the Westerly type to prominence in June and the decline of the Anticyclonic type in October or of the Cyclonic type in early September (fig. 26).

If we examine the barometric pressure values observed anywhere in the northern hemisphere over a long period of years, we find features corresponding to all three types of singularity. Moreover, it is not only the *average* pressure that is affected: although there is a considerable scatter of the pressure values occurring on any particular date in different years, especially in the zone of travelling depressions in 50–70° N, the whole cluster of most frequently observed values moves up and down appropriately about the dates of the best attested singularities. It is therefore useful to consider the fine structure of the seasonal development of the atmospheric circulation in terms of maps of average pressure for suitably short periods of the year. Average maps for each individual day of the year would not be much good unless averaged over 100 years or so because of the distortions produced wherever a particularly deep depression happened to be in one year or another. But if we take averages for 5-day periods ('pentads'), the depressions move enough to smooth this out and their tracks appear as troughs of low average pressure. Average pressure maps for two different 20-year periods 1890–1909 and 1919–38 have been studied by the author for every pentad of the year and the corresponding maps in either series compared.

The course of the seasonal changes in 1890–1909 and 1919–38 agreed in many important details despite the known warming of the Arctic and increase of general strength of the atmospheric circulation between the two 20-year epochs. (Correlation co-efficients between the two series of pentad mean pressure values for (1) the region of lowest pressure near Iceland, (2) highest pressure in the Azores region of the North Atlantic and (3) pressure over Greenland near 70° N were all highly significant in the conventional statistical sense—whether the pentad values were considered as departures from the annual mean or from a smoothed 21-pentad mean which removed the main seasonal trend. Agreement over central Europe was only slightly less impressive. But in the region affected by 'blocking' anticyclones over Scandinavia there were important differences between the two sample 20-year periods.)

The maps for the later period covered most of the northern hemisphere. Excerpts from this series are illustrated in the miniature isobar maps in fig. 27(a) and (b). It will be seen that they demonstrate the appropriate features of the singularity table (App. 1) about the dates in question. The first two maps, showing the 20-year average pressure fields for 21–25 May and 20–24 June, indicate the thorough reorganization of the atmospheric flow pattern between these dates that brings about the Return of the Westerlies and all that that means for the summer weather in this country and the continent. The next pair of maps, for 19–23 and 24–28 August, show the abrupt changes at the end of High Summer, which turn the depressions farther away from our shores and start the early autumn sequence of anticyclones passing across Europe from the Azores region. The map for 13–17 September, which is on average one of the driest weeks of the year in Britain, shows a fuller stage of this early autumn development. The next map, for 28 October/1 November illustrates the period of the Late Autumn Rains: the low pressure belt has shifted farther out from the Pole in all sectors as the October cooling proceeded, with the result that the main depressions are now very near to Britain and there is lower pressure than before even in the Mediterranean. The map for 22–26 November is an example of how high pressure tends to emerge again over central Europe just after the middle of each winter month. The map for 6–10 January shows the strongest development of the circulation in winter with the Atlantic westerlies pushing east over Europe with maximum vigour: in viewing this map it is well to remember that 1919–38 was the climatic period which produced the strongest general atmospheric circulation of which we have record—in earlier and later years the westerlies have not reached such intensity and passed their maximum on average about 10 days earlier. The map for 21–25 January, another anticyclonic phase in central Europe, shows the main circulation beginning to push farther south on the Atlantic—a late winter development linked with the

E.C.—6

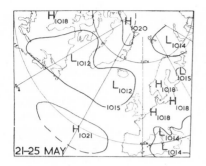

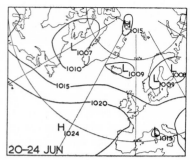

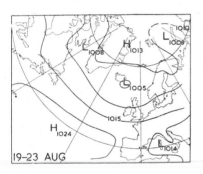

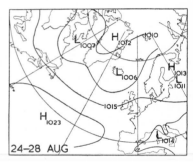

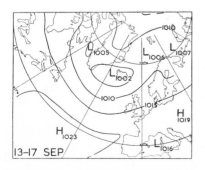

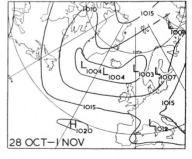

FIGURE 27 (*a*). Maps of Average barometric Pressure (in millibars) 1919–38 for selected 5-day periods ('Pentads') of the year.

beginnings of a seasonal tendency for fewer W and more E winds than before in Britain. The next map, for 12–16 March, illustrates one of the high points of the tendency for E or SE winds and anticyclones near England: it should be remembered that (because of friction) the surface winds blow across the isobars at an angle of 35 to 45° from high towards low pressure. The map for 1–5 April illustrates the spring shift of the westerlies back towards higher latitudes, at a stage when they commonly affect this country. But the circulation is already much weakened, and the variations from year to year include a proportion of cases influenced by anticyclones spreading northeast over this country from the Azores. The map for 16–20 April shows how later in the month the depressions tend increasingly to linger off Newfoundland, whilst others become more or less stationary near the British Isles and often let northerly winds through from the Norwegian Sea, where they are encouraged by the high pressure developing over Greenland.

Analysis of the seasonal developments over the hemisphere which under-lie both the Natural Seasons and the Singularity Calendar leads to identi-fication of the following classes of phenomena:

(i) *Master seasonal trends*, for which physical causes can readily be suggested and which are believed to operate in the same way every year.

(ii) *Main synoptic circulation processes*, such as characteristic depression and anticyclone tracks and sequences, which are common at particular times of the year. Their onset (and ending) may be sharply affected by geographical barriers which come into play when the seasonal trend has reached a certain point.

(iii) *Pulse phenomena*, apparently more or less regular oscillations of the pressure values over periods of 15–30 days or longer in the region of the main high and low pressure systems.

The most important examples of these phenomena for the seasonal progression of the weather in the British Isles appear to be as follows. It will be noticed that events even on the farther side of the hemisphere are believed to affect the course of our weather at certain times.

I. Master seasonal trends

1. Intensification of the wind circulation to its mid-winter maximum intensity and decline thereafter. (Physical basis: the greatest difference of effective heating between low latitudes and the widespread snow and ice-covered regions in the north is reached in winter. Energy derived from moisture exchanges declines as the winter goes on because of falling sea temperature and reduced evaporation.)

2. Late winter to spring displacement of the main polar high-pressure

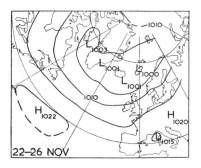

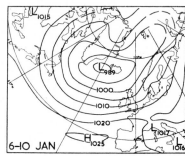

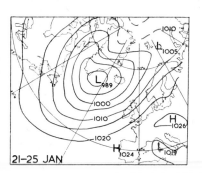

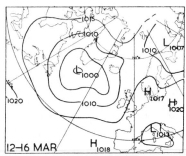

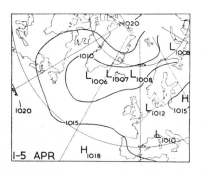

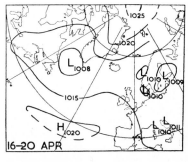

FIGURE 27 (b). Maps of Average barometric Pressure (in millibars) 1919–38 for selected 5-day periods ('Pentads') of the year.

region from Siberia towards northern Greenland and the Canadian Arctic Archipelago. (Physical basis must be connected with the warming of the continents and longest survival of a cold dense air layer over the region most remote (geographically protected) from warm air currents.)

3. Decline of the general circulation intensity to its annual minimum: this minimum is in May on the Atlantic side of the hemisphere. (Physical basis: general difference of heating between high and low latitudes is least in summer when the polar regions enjoy a 24-hour income of radiation. At the height of summer in July and August, however, the difference of heating between the largely frozen Arctic Ocean and northern Canada and Asia produces a source of energy which is not fully available in May.)

4. Northward displacement of the subpolar depression paths to high latitudes over western North America in high summer, in July and August, apparently accompanied by a shift of centre of the coldest region of the polar cap (and circumpolar wind circulation) towards our own sector—i.e. the Atlantic–European side. (Physical basis probably connected with the strong heating of Alaska, northeast Asia and the Canadian North-West after the snow is gone; also the Pacific Ocean does not bear an ice belt comparable with the areas of ice and cold water in the East Greenland and Labrador currents, not to mention Hudson's Bay and the Canadian Archipelago. Extension of the main circumpolar vortex towards, and sometimes over, Europe must be related to the dynamics of the circulation after rounding the cold region over northeast Canada and the northwestern Atlantic: the extension towards Europe shows notable differences from year to year.)

5. Southward displacement of the depression paths over the Atlantic–European sector in high summer (limited to the western Atlantic in the years which give the best summers in Europe), culminating in a southernmost position about end of July to beginning of August and some retreat northwards thereafter. (This somewhat surprising seasonal trend does not seem to have been clearly recognized before. It seems to be part of the dynamical process involved in 4 above.)

6. Early autumn sharpening of the cold trough in the upper westerlies over Northeast Canada, with strengthening circulation and turning of the depression tracks over the Atlantic farther to the northeast—towards the Barents Sea rather than Scandinavia and north Russia. (Physical basis: the beginnings of autumnal cooling become effective first in the sector where much cold water and some sea ice survives the summer.)

7. Late autumn and winter southward progress of the main zone of depressions (expansion of the circumpolar vortex aloft)—noticeable from October onwards, this culminates in southernmost positions about February or March. (Physical basis: increasing distance from the pole of the zone of strongest temperature contrasts—partly associated with the limit of snow and ice-covered surface.)

II. Main circulation processes

1. Main winter depression tracks from south of Greenland to the Barents Sea and Northwest Siberia—notably large systems about the time of the

mid-winter climax of circulation intensity. (Nevertheless the track fails to become established in a minority of winters—the coldest years, when the Atlantic circulation is weakly developed or the systems advance in the wrong latitude to make their way across Europe when cold air is established there.)

2. Spring northerly outbreaks in the Norwegian Sea, largely governed by the high pressure over Greenland.

3. Spring concentration of the main Atlantic low-pressure systems near Newfoundland–Labrador, and a less steady focus of cyclonic activity anywhere between the British Isles and the Baltic.

4. Summer isolation of the Mediterranean from North Atlantic cold air.

5. Summer depression sequences over, and north of, the northern Rocky Mountains and across Arctic Canada. Towards the end of the season some of these centres may pass north of Greenland into the Spitsbergen–North Norway area.

6. Summer depression tracks across, or near Scandinavia, towards North Russia. (This fails in some years—the finest summers in Europe—or is replaced by depressions travelling farther north into the Barents Sea or Arctic Ocean.)

7. Tropical cyclones (West Indian hurricanes and similar weaker centres) turning north and northeast over the western Atlantic in the late summer and autumn, producing some of the most violent storms on the North Atlantic in August, September and October.

8. Autumn depression tracks from near south Greenland to the Barents Sea and north coast of Asia, later in the season 'plunging' southeast into central-northern Asia. These tracks generally begin suddenly about the end of August or early September, replacing 6.

9. Autumn development of the circulation over the Pacific most characteristically starts with depressions frequently becoming stationary in such a position as to maintain southerly winds over Alaska. A ridge of high pressure develops farther east from the Arctic towards central Canada, with northerly winds which hasten the seasonal cooling over central, northern and eastern Canada. About the end of October the Pacific depressions become more liable to forge their way across the Rocky Mountains and rather more erratic sequences follow over Canada and the Atlantic for some time thereafter.

10. Cyclonic activity develops in the Mediterranean in autumn and winter, starting after incursions of cold air from the north, as the main Atlantic depressions get near enough and big enough to cause cold air to enter the Mediterranean.

11. Far southward penetration of cold air over the Atlantic in late winter leads sometimes to circulation developments that show little zonal (eastward) motion. This allows 'blocking' patterns with anticyclones and east winds to develop over northern and central Europe. It is sometimes caused by anticyclones already existing over Greenland. Such developments only become prominent in a minority of (the coldest) winters.

III. Pulse phenomena

It is more difficult to demonstrate the physical reality of these phenomena conclusively, or to suggest the mechanisms at work; nevertheless there is a good deal of evidence for a tendency to characteristic pulsations in the various main anticyclonic and cyclonic regions that affect the weather in this country. Maximum intensity of development apparently tends to occur at about the following intervals:

1. *North Atlantic depressions:*
    Summer 22–24 days,
    Autumn and winter 15–20 days.
2. *High pressure over Greenland and the Arctic Ocean:*
    Summer 55 days,
    Winter and spring 45 days.
   Greenland is affected also by sub-periods agreeing with those of the North Atlantic depressions.
3. *High pressure over Scandinavia*
    At all times of the year 30 days.
   Affected also by the pulses of Atlantic depression activity at about 15- to 20-day intervals in late winter.
4. *High pressure over central Europe*
    At all times of the year 30 days, but especially from about the September equinox to March.
5. *Azores anticyclone*
    No obvious pulsations.

The Antarctic pressure surges at about 45-day intervals described 50 years ago by Sir G. C. Simpson after Scott's expedition are probably similar to the Arctic phenomenon in the above list.

Thus we find suggestions of pressure oscillations with periods of approximately 15 (or 15–22), 30 and 45 days from various parts of the world, which may be recognizable over very long periods of years; though the phenomenon is as yet not altogether satisfactorily defined. It is plainly near the limit of the resolving power of our methods of analysis. Brooks already noticed—what is apparent from Apps. 1 and 2—that most of the severest storms of wind in the past are clustered around the dates which are still marked by a cyclonic tendency and the highest frequencies of gales. Similar remarks apply to the dates of onset and breakdown of many historic spells of weather—in some cases even to the dates of interruptions of the main spell. Good examples of this are provided in the great winter of 1739–40 and in many seasons in the 1690s, although the prevailing temperatures were materially different from today's. Yet we cannot demonstrate beyond suspicion of subjectivity oscillations which are never clearly marked throughout a whole year and some of which (as with the bouts of storm activity on the Atlantic) seem to quicken their pace (shorten the period between pulses) from summer and early autumn to January.

We need an explanation also of why the preferred dates—for instance, the dates of highest average pressure over Greenland and over the European continent—seem so narrowly fixed from century to century as may be deduced from the Zürich observations of 1550–76 used in App. 1. This is all the more surprising because of the change of a degree or more in the level of world temperature since the 1700s and 1800s, with corresponding changes in the extent of ice and snow. The aptest suggestion (due to Professor H. Flohn of Bonn) is probably that the oscillations start afresh each autumn in high latitudes when the effective heating from the sun is cut off there. Flohn and Scherhag have found evidence that the approximately 30-day oscillation through the winter months reaches its greatest amplitude in the stratosphere—i.e. its greatest amplitude relative to the pressure values ruling there. This might explain why the dated phenomena (e.g. the intensification of the low pressure belt on the northern Atlantic and its turning northeastwards towards the Barents Sea at the end of the summer) appear most regular in the higher latitudes and in autumn. By contrast, the date of onset of the southwest monsoon in northern India varies by more than a month.

The normal year and its seasonal round: practical significance of our meteorological understanding

No part of Britain has a climate with seasons of such strongly defined character as the wet and dry monsoons of India, the winter snow of Canada and Norway, or the dry Mediterranean summer. Yet some sort of natural seasons do exist and certain briefer episodes in the seasonal progression occur with enough regularity to be worth knowing. Indeed the *dates* of our seasons and singularities may be more regular than those of countries in lower latitudes like India and Egypt.

What use can one make of recognition of the division of the year into five broad natural seasons and the finer division represented by the singularity calendar? We cannot predict more than a day or two ahead what the weather will be on any particular day, but it is clearly wise to take account of the tabulated experience of past years whenever it is necessary to plan long beforehand an event such as a garden fête which is very dependent upon good weather. If it is a regular event to take place annually about the same date, its success in the majority of years may be directly affected. (This is only a special case of the long established use of climatic tables.) The Wimbledon tennis championships in the last ten days of June seem to have benefited from the weather patterns associated with the Return of the Westerlies, which tend to bring southeast England lee-side fair weather, and often some influence from the anticyclone belt to the south, just then. For the weather forecaster concerned with particular days in a particular year the problem is more difficult, especially as the pressure systems associated with the singularities often develop quickly and sometimes after preceding situations which make them surprising—as in the case of the early October anticyclone in 1962. Here the best hope is to probe beyond the statistics of particular weather situations in any one country towards physical understanding of the seasonal development of the large-scale atmospheric circulation which produces them. This we have attempted in the previous section.

The vagaries of our climate, in common with most others in the temperate zone, are such that in some particular year a whole season may fail, through the failure or displacement of its most vital controlling feature in the general atmospheric circulation. There have been years of ill memory when there was really no summer in the ordinary meaning of the word in this country, because the Azores anticyclone persistently extended towards southern Europe, or even spread a bit northwards in mid Atlantic, but never towards our shores. There have been years, too, in which the Siberian winter anticyclones kept so far away to the east that there was no real winter in Britain. Nevertheless it is normal for some influence to be felt in these islands from the Azores anticyclone in summer and from occasional shifts of the Siberian anticyclone towards Scandinavia or central Europe in winter. And this happens oftenest about the dates of anticyclonic tendency noted in the singularity calendar (App. 1) and in fig. 26. (Northerly cold weather in winter is most liable to come in cyclonic periods after depressions have crossed the country and halted over the North Sea–Baltic region.)

A tendency for unlike weather sequences, some of them clearly anticyclonic and cyclonic, to alternate at about 15–16 day intervals in China was apparently recognized by Chinese farmers as early as 250 BC. A division of the year not into months but into 24 half-month units was adopted.[1] This system was long used by the farmers for practical purposes, but not by officialdom, which was wedded to a lunar calendar. The 24 sections of the farmers' year were named according to typical weather or natural events—e.g. 'Spring showers' around 19/2, 'Awakening insects' 6/3, 'Spring equinox' 21/3, 'Clear and bright' 5/4, 'Grain rains' 20/4. This seems to show some parallel to the tendency for alternation of periods of expanded anticyclones and periods of cyclonic influence at 15-day intervals in the European winter. A subsequent development in China was a further elaboration of the year into 72 periods each of 5 to 6 days' duration. Each

1. Chu Ko-chen, 'The pulsation of world climate during historical times', *New China Monthly*, June, 1961.

was named after some phenological phenomenon—e.g. 'Awakening insects' or 'First blossom of the peach' 6/3, 'The oriole sings' 11/3, 'The falcon turns into the dove' (a primitive description of the reappearance of migrant doves) 16/3—making a calendar which served as a guide to the farmer even in years when the expected events were early or late, since the time to plough or to sow could be related rather to the phenological designation than to the actual date. This elaborate calendar of pentads was upset by the shifts of date occasioned during the centuries of cold climate around the 1600s AD. The basic division of the year into 24 terms seems to have survived and probably retained its usefulness: it was in any case understood that the *temperature* of any half-month term could vary in different years.

The division of the year into natural seasons and singularity periods in England may be looked upon as a description of the 'Normal Year'—possibly as useful an abstraction as the 'average man'. Much of this seasonal structure can be recognized in most years and parts of it in every year. We begin our calendar in summer because that is when several features occur with a rather high degree of regularity after the variability of spring. The following short list may be useful for reference to those features which occur in the highest proportion of the years studied[1]:

1. The *June Return of the Westerlies* prepares the way for the *High Summer season* in which long spells, mostly involving frequent W or NW winds, occur in about 70% of the years. Types W, NW and AC together exceed 70% around 20/6.

2. The *Late July–early August Thundery period* culminates with types other than AC, S or E in 70–75% of the years around 26–28/7, types other than anticyclonic 80%.

3. The *End of Summer Turning Point* in late August produces types W or NW in about 70% of the years, often combined with cyclonic tendency about 17–28/8, but becoming increasingly inclined towards fair anticyclonic weather in the southwest.

4. The *September Anticyclones* period is seen in the statistics by total frequencies of AC, W and NW types exceeding 80% on most days 6–19/9.

5. The *Late September Stormy episode* is more marked over the Atlantic than any part of Britain: the chief points are about 23–26/9 types other than anticyclonic 80%; peaks of C, S and W together about 70%.

6. The period of the *Early October Anticyclones*—it might be called the time of Golden Leaves—gives types AC, S or E 2–8/10 50–60%, but W about 40%.

7. The *Late Autumn Rains* stormy period—the Fall of the Leaves, if we were to adopt a phenological name—brings types other than AC 24–31/10 over 80%, 90% on some days.

8. The *November Anticyclones* period produces anticyclonic type in Britain just 25–30% 17–20/11, but types other than W or C about 70%.

1. Turn to App. 1 for more details and for the full table of singularities.

9. The *Early Winter Return of the Westerlies* brings W or NW type 70% 3–11/12, types other than anticyclonic 85–90% 3–8/12.

10. The *December Continental Anticyclones* affect Britain with AC, S or E type in just 50% of the years 17–21/12.

From this stage on there are no more clear-cut cases affecting Britain in a similar manner in over 50% of the years, except

11. *Mid-March Anticyclones*—the Spring Drying period—giving AC, N or E types 12–22/3 about 70%.

12. The *Time of the Spring Northerlies* giving combined frequencies of N, E and either C or AC types 25/4–3/5 about 70%; types other than W 29/4–9/5 over 80%.

13. The *Fore-monsoon Fine Weather Period* is related to frequencies of AC and S types together 60–70% 21–31/5.

Nevertheless, Keats, who was a sensitive observer of the seasonal round, seems to have noticed even the January Continental Anticyclones:

> 'St. Agnes' Eve*—Ah, bitter chill it was!
> The owl, for all his feathers was a-cold;
> The hare limped trembling through the frozen grass,
> And silent was the flock in woolly fold.'

>   *St. Agnes Eve i.e. 20th January.

(The words were written at Chichester.) But Keats lived in an epoch when the continental influence was unusually prominent in our climate.

An aspect which has not been much stressed, but which appears to promise results of some practical value from further research, is the identification of certain singularities as turning points in the course of the seasonal development and possible indicators for the season ahead—rather as the St. Swithin 'rule' suggested. In this connexion Baur[1] has found indications that in those summers and winters where the return of the westerlies, in late June and early December respectively, is particularly well marked and sustained over many days, with strong effects upon the temperatures in Germany (cooling in the summer case and warming in December), there is a strong tendency for the westerlies to continue or appear repeatedly during the season that lies ahead. The contrary cases of years when the westerlies are weak just at those moments do not appear to be of much significance: the characters of the summers and winters that follow can vary. This may be a warning against glib conclusions: no very straightforward rules of thumb can be expected. There will be no substitute for an understanding of the physical reasons for the different

1. Baur, F., *Physikalisch-statistische Regeln als Grundlagen für Wetter und Witterungs-Vorhersagen*, Frankfurt/Main (Akademische Verlag), Vol. I, 1956; Vol. II, 1958.

circulation patterns, their pulsations and their shifts from one year to another. But there are some other cases that may point the way forward a little. Certainly anticyclonic situations which manage to survive the dates of usually cyclonic tendency in late August and September seem particularly liable to last some days or weeks longer, as happens also at the end of some winter months. For instance, between 1898 and 1962 there were 12 years[1] when north European anticyclones giving AC, E and S types in Britain, established on or before 24/1, continued to prevail (with not more than a single day's break) until 1/2: in 11 of the 12 cases the anticyclone continued over northern, northwestern or central Europe for most of February with prolonged cold weather lasting most of the month in this country. Even in the twelfth case (1949) a long frost gave a spell of skating weather in eastern England throughout the first week of February. In one other case (1959) the average temperature for February was only slightly on the cold side, and only in the *east* of England; and the month ended with very warm sunny weather with light southerly breezes.

1. 1899, 1912, 1917, 1919, 1929, 1932, 1940, 1947, 1949, 1954, 1955 and 1959.

11

Our Climate Down the Ages

IT is about 10,000 years since the last glaciers of the ice age disappeared from this country. The swift warming that followed carried the average temperatures here and in most parts of the world by 5,000 BC to about 2° C above present levels. And, as the great accumulations of ice over Europe and North America melted, the level of the seas rose 100–150 feet between about 8000 and 3000 BC. (The total rise from the lowest sea level earlier in the ice age was a good deal greater than that, about 300 feet.) Most of the lowlands that had existed where the North Sea now is were then flooded, though appreciable losses of coastal lowlands around the southern part of the North Sea have continued even since Roman times, both by gradual erosion and sudden storm floods. The cutting of the Straits of Dover is also tentatively ascribed to the time of quickly rising sea level around 6000 BC.[1]

The warmest epoch, often called the Postglacial Climatic Optimum, lasted from about 5000 to 3000 BC. That was the time when forests grew much higher on the hills of Britain than they now do. The many tree-stumps of those woods, preserved in the peat, even on exposed ridges high above the present limit of trees, have been seen by many hill walkers. Amongst the woods at lower levels the more warmth-demanding species like the elm and lime spread farther north, and were more abundant, than they have been since. Woods even grew in the Orkneys and near the northwest coast of Scotland, indicating a less windy, as well as a milder, climate than that of today. On the coast of Wales at Ynyslas near Borth, Cardiganshire, one may see the stumps of a forest including elm and oak and pine that grew somewhat below present sea level, presumably in the earlier part of the warm epoch. To go into all the evidence, and into how the dates of the major climatic changes have been determined, would take us beyond the scope of the present book.[2]

1. Shotton, F. W., 'The physical background of Britain in the Pleistocene', Presidential Address to Section C of the British Association 1962, *The Advancement of Science*, Vol. 19, pp. 193–206, London, 1962.

2. The interested reader should consult Professor H. Godwin's great work on *The History of the British Flora*, Cambridge (University Press), 1956 or H. M. Steven's, *The Native Pinewoods of Scotland*, Edinburgh, 1959. For an introduction to dating methods see F. E. Zeuner, *Dating the Past*, London (Methuen), 4th edition, 1958.

The climate began to become cooler some time about or after 3000 BC, and between about 1000 and 500 BC the deterioration was sharp and accompanied by increased storminess. The woods died out on the uplands and near the exposed coasts. Since that decline the extent of woodland in this country seems to provide little further indication of the course of climatic changes, because it has been mostly determined by the activities of man and his animals.

Warming set in again, however, and in Roman times the climate was apparently not much different from that we now live in. Later the general temperature level seems to have risen further and the seas became less stormy; so that in late Saxon times, during the Viking age and the Early Middle Ages, our ancestors enjoyed a rather more genial climate than we do. That was the time when many vineyards were established in southern England, providing in all large quantities of wine for the monasteries and the houses of the great. In the 1100s and 1200s, at least, some of the English wine was highly esteemed and bore comparison with any. It seems probable that the climate was more like that of northern France today with summer temperatures generally about $1°$ C higher than now. The health and prosperity of the community (in common with neighbouring countries in northern and central Europe) was probably affected, and both seem to have suffered in the deterioration that followed from about 1300 onwards. With health and well-being in the agriculture of northern Europe went confidence and a tendency for society to settle down and recover from its wars and disturbances: for the period of good climate was also the time of the spread of Christendom over northern and eastern Europe and of most active building of the great cathedrals and abbeys.

Variations of climate, particularly of prevailing temperatures and storminess, since 1300 have been important and have touched in some degree every aspect of human life and its environment. The effects of the deterioration from 1300 to 1500–1600 and after have commonly been ignored, presumably because they were heavily overlaid by the Black Death of 1349–50 and the recurring ravages of the plague thereafter. Moreover England, unlike more northern lands including Scotland, was in the happy position that the full range of variation of temperature level that occurred left her within the best area of Europe to live in. To some extent England, and English commerce and fisheries, even gained by the eclipse of other nations less fortunately placed. Nevertheless, the period from 1550 to almost 1900 saw the greatest advances of the northern hemisphere glaciers, and probably of the ice on the polar seas, since the ice age. A tongue of the sea ice showed a tendency to thrust along the east coast of Iceland towards the Faeroe Islands, and isolated large floes were once or twice reported close to the shores of the Hebrides and near Shetland. This was the era when our rivers were most liable to freeze. The freezing of the Thames in London has been more and more hindered since 1800 by the building up of embankments and bridges that quicken the tidal flow, and the closing over of tributaries in pipes and culverts; but the earlier records tell their story. The river in London does not seem to have frozen over more than once or twice a century until the 1500s: during that century it froze 4 times, in the 1600s 8 times, and in the 1700s 6 times. The only occasion in the nineteenth century was 1814, but it seems likely that if its banks had not been altered it would have frozen over in several other winters since, when there were extensive ice floes in the river or in the estuary, including 1838, 1879, 1891, 1895, 1929, 1940, 1947 and 1963. Observation of the River Thames in the very severe January of 1963 revealed a further stage in the development of our artificial city environments. Towards the end of the month, after 5 weeks with temperatures in London almost continuously below the freezing point and averaging as low as $-3°$ C ($27°$ F) in the country farther up river, the temperature of the river water near London Bridge was $+10°$ C ($50°$ F). At this time there was ice about in the southern North Sea and near the Goodwin Sands in the Straits of Dover, with a belt of ice a mile or more in width along the coasts of Kent. Explosives were used to free ships in an Essex port. Up-river at Hampton Court the river could be crossed on foot. The warm open water extended from just near the power station at Kingston to the reach below Tilbury, and from the temperatures measured in it, the effluent of factories, power stations and urban domestic systems must have played a big part in it. If this development goes much further, in any future winters of equal severity the old frost fairs of Westminster and Blackfriars could be revived at Hampton and the fun on the ice could be followed by a swim at Westminster, provided nobody minds the pollution!

The abrupt chilling of the climate from about 1530–60 seems to coincide with the general introduction of glass in windows—which had previously been of lattice and wicker. The late 1500s and 1600s were probably the worst time, and the 1690s saw the last serious famine anywhere on the mainland of Great Britain, caused by a run of harvest failures in the upland parishes in Scotland where the proportion of the population who perished from hunger rivalled the Black Death. Some of the gentry in late Tudor and Stuart times who found themselves in possession of the wealth and lands of the dissolved monasteries conceived the idea of reviving the cultivation of vineyards. But although they built handsome walled enclosures, such as appear not to have been necessary in earlier times, after very few years these were turned over to growing gooseberries and strawberries, which they did admirably.

Enthusiasm can work wonders, and there has probably never been a century since the Middle Ages without somebody achieving success with a vineyard some time somewhere in the south of England. Equally, there seem to have been no cases in which the success was carried on by another generation after the enthusiast was gone. However, there has been a notable climatic improvement since 1700, and most of all in the present century, so that it is not surprising that several efforts at the growing of grapes for wine, notably in Kent and Hampshire, have been in the news in recent years.

There is plenty of evidence that rainfall amounts have also undergone great variations since the ice age and smaller, but in some connexions important, variations in recent times. Space does not permit us to go into the details of the story here. Moreover, rainfall distribution depends on every detail of local land relief and is characteristically more intricate than that of temperature. But when epochs occur which leave the marks of dryness (drying out of the bogs, etc.) over all parts of these islands simultaneously, it is clear that the zone of frequent passing depressions must have moved far away to other latitudes. This seems to have occurred in the early part of the great warm epoch after the ice age and again during the early part of the sharp cooling around 1000 BC. To a less marked degree it also occurred around AD 300–400 and in certain centuries since.[1]

Several times within the past 2,000–3,000 years drastic increases of raininess have ended a dry epoch and renewed the growth of peat bogs. Instances of this around 600–500 BC and AD 1200–1300 are commonly found in botanical studies in this country and elsewhere in northern and central Europe. They presumably imply a marked increase in the frequency of depressions and storminess in these latitudes. Both the vegetation and the activities of man were strongly affected. Godwin and Willis[2] have reported evidence that wooden trackways were laid across the Somerset Levels and other flat lowlands between about 900 and 450 BC, apparently to avoid long detours around land that had become otherwise impassable mire and swamp. Relics of boats have been found from the worst stages of the flooding. Similarly, effects of the decline that set in about AD 1300 were by no means confined to the vineyards. All over northern Europe farms and farm villages began to be given up on marginal land in the northern and upland regions[3] and there are frequent reports of corn that stayed green and was dashed by the autumn storms.

1. A useful summary was provided by C. E. P. Brook's book, *Climate Through the Ages*, London (Ernest Benn), 2nd edition, 1949.
2. Godwin, H., and Willis, E. H., 'Radiocarbon dating of pre-historic wooden trackways', *Nature*, Vol. 184, pp. 490–491, 1959.
3. See, for example, Steensberg, A., 'Archeological dating of the climatic change in north Europe about AD 1300', *Nature*, Vol. 168, pp. 672–674, 1951.

The chief vagaries of the climate in England since the year 1100 may be conveniently followed in fig. 28. This shows indices of the prevailing character of the summers and of the winters for every decade. All Julys and Augusts for which known records indicate beyond doubt an extreme (wet or dry) character, severely affecting the state of the ground and crops and the level of the rivers, were counted. The index number increases downwards on the diagram, since a very dry month scored 0, a very wet one 1 and unremarkable or ordinary months scored $\frac{1}{2}$. Thus, unremarkable decades scored about 10, those with the driest summers scored about 5 and the wettest 15 or over. Dryness or wetness is a safer indicator of the

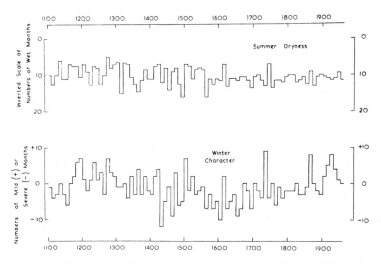

FIGURE 28. Numerical indices of Summer Dryness and Winter Mildness (or Severity) in England for each decade from 1100 to 1959.

nature of the summers than temperature, when using early manuscripts and chronicles, since reported effects on the condition of the ground have an unmistakable significance, whereas sparse records of terrible heat waves may refer to only a few days. Moreover, most dry summers are also warm, most wet ones are also cold (though exceptions do occur). Dry summer months in England are related to warm ridges in the upper air, wet ones to upper cold troughs. The winter index does use effects attributable directly to temperature. All Decembers, Januarys and Februarys with unambiguous reports of extreme mildness or severity were counted. The index is simply the number by which very mild months exceeded severe ones in each decade, a negative number if the severe cases predominated.

The impressions gained from the course of these indices agree well with the results of Professor Gordon Manley's careful work on the longest series of temperature observations in England. Manley's[1] average temperatures for central England give the following figures for comparison with twentieth-century experience:

Average temperatures °C		
	Summer June–August	Winter December–February
1680–1719	14·8	3·3
1900–1939	15·1	4·3

These temperature changes are believed to be very much in line with changes over most of the rest of the world. The question of causes cannot be entered into here, but there is a good deal of evidence that the North Atlantic storm tracks were generally farther south in the seventeenth century than nowadays and that many more depressions passed east across this country. Northerly and easterly winds were both commoner in England than at any time since.

The average temperatures in the 1680s and 1690s, the first two decades of Manley's record, were particularly low (summer months 14·4°, winter months 2·5° C, in central England). There is much circumstantial evidence of specially cold climate in those years. There was an abrupt change to higher temperatures during most of the time between 1700 and 1739, but after the great winter of 1739–40 the climate remained colder again. The big recovery has been since 1850, though even this was interrupted by colder years between about 1878 and 1895. However, from 1897 to 1937 the winters in Britain were on average milder than at any time for centuries past and probably equalled the best period of the early Middle Ages (see fig. 28). The general warmth of the summers of the present century has also surpassed any for long since, though not quite so outstanding as the prevalence of mild winters.

The corresponding variations of world temperature have resulted in a great recession of glaciers in every continent, and of the Arctic sea ice,

1. Manley, G., 'The mean temperature of central England 1698–1952', *Quarterly Journal of the Royal Meteorological Society*, Vol. 79, pp. 242–261, London, 1953. Also 'A preliminary note on early meteorological observations in the London region, 1680–1717 . . .', *Meteorological Magazine*, Vol. 90, pp. 303–310, 1961.

during the present century. Sea temperatures and sea levels have been affected. After being held more or less stationary for at least 150 years before 1830, the level of the sea relative to the land (which is sinking slowly) around the southern North Sea appears to have risen by 4 to 6 inches since. Even such small changes represent a threat to low-lying coasts and coastal defences, particularly at times of storms, and could become serious if continued indefinitely. The world's oceans could rise by more than 100 feet if the Antarctic ice cap, and all remaining ice on land were to melt. However, the Arctic sea ice in the sectors east of Greenland and north of Europe and Asia has staged a remarkable re-growth since 1958.

Perhaps it is as well that the notable warmth of the climate of the first half of the twentieth century has not been fully kept up in the last decade or two. Average January temperatures in England have fallen about 1° C from the extraordinarily high level (between 4·5 and 5° C) which they maintained in the 1920s and 30s. Between 1896 and 1939 there was no month in the English lowlands with mean temperature below the freezing point. There have been five since—in the winters of 1940, 1947, 1956 and 1963 (two months). This means the frequency has returned to what was quite normal in the nineteenth century. The winter of 1962–3, with mean temperature 0° C for the three months December–February and snow lying for about 60 days in most districts, was the coldest in central England since 1740—i.e. for 223 years—though in the 200 years before that the same degree of severity seems to have occurred 5 to 10 times. Summer temperature averages have also fallen a fraction of a degree since 1950. But the twentieth-century warming in the other seasons has only shown signs of coming to a halt in the very latest years. It is too early to say whether a new downward trend is setting in. Nevertheless, we are quite sensitive to small changes of climate and many people have noticed the deterioration of recent summers and winters since the best decades. The frequency of snow lying (the figures given elsewhere in this book exclude the winter of 1962–3) has increased notably since the mildest years in all lowland districts and has increasingly often affected communications in places as far apart as the north of Scotland and Kent. There is a sense in which we have been spoilt by the good summers of the 1930s and '40s and by the long run (broken only in 1917 and 1929) of mild winters between 1897 and 1937. This was the era when plumbing was introduced to the vast majority of houses in this country, and the mild years probably encouraged the belief that elaborate lining of roofs and lagging of pipes against frost was a bit unnecessary—an acceptable risk. It is less acceptable now. And the good summers of the 1930s and '40s encouraged the cult of the sun— hill-top sites for houses and the beginnings of the fashion for excessive glass in the architecture of schools, etc. They also brought success with peaches and other southern fruits grown in the open at favoured sites. But those years were a group without parallel for generations past, and the expectations have been slightly 'watered down' since.

Yet, the average summer in England is still a very pleasant affair, especially when bright weather in May, September and early October is reckoned in. Taken over all the year, the evidence suggests that, given sensible houses, our climate is one of the best in the world to live and work in, and that it has been so for longer than the English have been in England.

12

Weather Maps

IN this book we have looked upon the climate as something to be under-stood in dynamic terms, produced by the shifting patterns and sequences of depressions and anticyclones and the steering currents aloft that make up the atmospheric circulation, together with the slow, steady, seasonal changes of radiant heat received from the sun. It will be useful to include a look at some examples of the weather maps themselves which are one of the chief tools of weather forecasting and advice to the public.

Surface weather maps show the weather observations made simultane-ously at numerous stations on land and ships at sea, plotted with the use of a set of standard symbols. The maps are analysed by the drawing of isobars (lines joining places having the same barometric pressure when reduced to sea level) and entry of the fronts between the main airstreams at sea level. Such maps are available to the general public in the Daily Weather Report, published at the Meteorological Office, Bracknell. Two examples are given here in figs. 29 and 30. The isobars are at 4-millibar (4 mb.) intervals. The figures beside the plotted weather symbols are air temperatures in °C. Arrows show the wind directions, blowing generally clockwise around the anticyclones and counter-clockwise around the depressions, but generally somewhat across the isobars from the high towards the low pressure side. The number of flecks or barbs on the wind arrows indicates the strength of the wind, each full-length fleck represent-ing 10 knots (10 kt.) and a sharp triangle for 50 kt. when this occurs. The lines inside each station position circle indicate the amount of the sky covered with clouds. The main symbols used for the weather are in the keys at the foot of figs. 29 and 30. On some of the maps printed (but not in the illustrations here given) the names of the places where the ob-servations are made are included, and the Ocean Weather Ships are identified by the letters by which their stations (or proper positions) are known. The normal positions of the isotherms of sea surface temperature 5, 10, 15, 20° C in the month concerned are printed on the maps: this is most useful in revealing where the air is being heated and cooled by the sea.

The map for 31 December 1961 shows a small depression travelling north-northeastwards over the continent with its warm sector over central Europe. Rain is falling ahead of the warm front over Holland, and in the

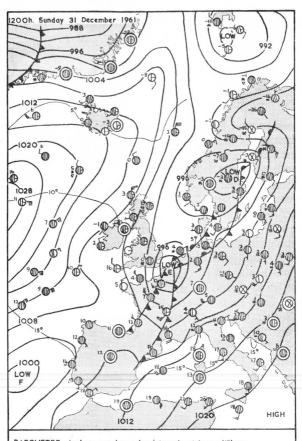

BAROMETER. Isobars are drawn for intervals of four millibars

WIND. Arrows fly with wind. A full length feather indicates ten knots and a short feather five knots. Calm is indicated by a circle outside weather symbol.

TEMPERATURE is given in degrees C.

CLOUD SYMBOLS ◯Clear sky ◔Sky 1/8 covered ◑Sky 2/8 covered ⊕Sky 3/8 covered ◕Sky 4/8 covered ⬒Sky 5/8 covered ⬔Sky 6/8 covered ⬕Sky 7/8 covered ⬤Sky 8/8 covered ⊗Sky obscured

WEATHER SYMBOLS • Rain Falling ✴ Snow ⚹ Sleet △ Hail 🖠 Drizzle ☰ Mist ≡ Fog ☈ Thunderstorm

FRONTS or boundaries between masses of air of different origin are indicated, wherever their characteristics are well pronounced:- ●━●━ Warm front on surface ▲━▲ Cold front on surface ▲━●━▲ Occluded front. The symbols are placed on the side of the line towards which the front is moving. Identification letters are given to the individual pressure systems.

FIGURE 29. Daily Weather Report Map for 12 hr. G.M.T., 31 December 1961.

cold northerly airstream over SE England snow is falling from the frontal cloudsheets overhead. Farther north over the British Isles snow showers are reported, where the cold air is deeper and has been rendered unstable for vertical motion by heating as it passed over the warm sea water of the North Atlantic Drift. The air in the Faeroe–Shetland–N. Scotland area appears to be 5 or 6° C colder than the sea. As the depression moved to Sweden during the next 24 hours, deepening cold air spread over the whole of Britain, the Low Countries and Germany behind the cold front.

The map for 7 June 1962 shows a strong anticyclone covering the British Isles. The air is moving only sluggishly round the centre. Cloud amounts are small, and the weather warm. The biggest depression is far away to the north in the Norwegian Sea. Small waves on the front over the Atlantic west and north of the British Isles represent disturbances travelling northeast: one of these 'deepened' (developed enough wind circulation as the pressure at its centre fell) during the following 18 hours to bring the cold front forward past Shetland to the coast of Norway and the tip of Caithness, with skies becoming overcast and some rain falling. The rest of the British Isles continued to enjoy fine weather.

The forecaster also uses charts of the winds at various upper levels, which reveal the more powerful and steadier windstreams that steer the surface weather systems and cause them to develop and decay. A variety of diagrams indicates the actual and potential development of vertical motion.

Simplified versions of the surface weather maps are shown daily on television screens and in most newspapers. Their variety is too great for any useful purpose to be served by illustrations here. Captions rather than symbols are commonly used to indicate the prevailing weather. Forecast maps for some time during the following day are usually shown as well as the latest map of observed weather. Those who wish to understand the why and wherefore of expected developments are bound to consider both maps —the latest actual and the forecast situation—as essential. And, of course, understanding is essential if the intelligent recipient of the forecast is to be able to apply adjustments and mental reservations to the forecast from his knowledge of local effects upon the weather. This is equally true if he is to follow what is happening if slowing down or speeding up of the weather systems, or some other new trend, makes the forecast begin to go wrong.

The most useful weather maps published are those that cover a considerable area of the hemisphere. The particular areas chosen by different newspapers and television stations vary; but, as the quickest travelling weather developments come to this country from the west and north, it is most important to be able to survey the existing systems over most of the Atlantic and the polar seas as far as the area near Spitsbergen. The

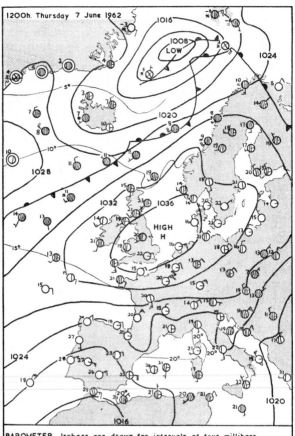

FIGURE 30. Daily Weather Report Map for 12 hr. G.M.T.,
7 June 1962.

average progress of a travelling depression is some 500 miles a day, but the distances covered range from 0 to 1,500 miles or more. Small frontal wave disturbances in a strong SW to W wind situation are liable to travel fastest: this type of situation may be recognized by closely packed isobars (i.e. strong pressure gradients) in the warm airstream running almost straight over great distances. Usually there is also a specially strong contrast between the temperatures in the warm air and those in the heart of the colder areas far from the front. These are situations where the fast-moving surface warm air and the waves on the front travel in line with a strong jet stream overhead at heights of 10 to 12 km.

Anticyclones in general travel more slowly than depressions. Identification of the actual position of the centre may be difficult within the wide area of weak pressure gradients commonly found in the central regions of large anticyclones: it also matters little, except from the point of view of the directions of the light local breezes and the gentle transport of local mists and fogs, haze and patches of cloud cover. Since the typical life cycle of large anticyclones is longer than that of most frontal depressions, the anticyclones are a more persistent feature of the pattern of spells of weather.

The enduring features of the regions of low surface pressure in any spell of weather that lasts a few days or more are the zones affected by the centres and passing frontal rains of successive travelling disturbances. Apart from these there are just one or two regions where rather large centres of low pressure are maintained almost stationary. The energy of the circulation of these central lows is fed by the arrival of the travelling disturbances slowing down at the end of their independent 'lives'. These central lows are sometimes regarded as 'depression graves', the end of the journey for travelling disturbances after their greatest vigour is spent. The weather in the region of the stationary centres is by no means uniformly bad, though the barometer is low: it is usually rather cold and liable to quite severe showers and storms, but much of the area may be bright. The strongest winds are round the periphery of these big low pressure regions rather than in the centre. The pattern of the massive windstreams, extending throughout the depth of the lower atmosphere, that control the steering of the fronts and travelling disturbances is related to the positions of the main stationary low pressure regions and the large stable anticyclones. These types of low and high pressure systems extend to great heights—i.e. concentric wind circulations are found through a great range of layers of the atmosphere. As this description implies, it is a common feature of spells of weather that successive systems follow much the same paths, and slow up and finally come to a standstill in the same areas—hence the constant features that make the spell recognizable as such.

The observation reports used in constructing the synoptic (i.e. as it were, 'bird's-eye view') weather maps, which are the basis of applied meteorology, are collected and passed to the central forecast office by an elaborate network (and timetable) of telephone, teleprinter and radio links. Development of this communications system has gone steadily forward since the first use of the electric telegraph to collect simultaneous weather reports from all over Britain for the maps which were an interesting novelty displayed at the Great Exhibition in Hyde Park in 1851. Nowadays the communications network is one of the most successful examples of international collaboration, and reports come streaming in, mostly by land-line teleprinter and radio teletype, from all over the world within an hour or two of the observations being made.

Within this country another, somewhat similar teleprinter land-line network, served by observers who send in their reports by telephone to area collecting centres, provides another type of weather map of great value to the public. These are the maps of road weather conditions compiled at frequent intervals by the A.A. and R.A.C.

The A.A. patrolmen are each responsible for regularly checking weather conditions on a stretch of road or on the roads within a district, reporting by telephone or radio to the area office the existence of snow, ice, fog or floods. Indications of condition and depth of snow or flooding, and of visibilities in fog, are included as far as practicable. An abbreviated code is used for certain details. At the area office the reports are marked on illuminated maps, summarized and transmitted by teleprinter to neighbouring area offices and to London. At the headquarters the latest maps are photographically copied and copies put in the hands of staff manning the telephones and receiving callers inquiring about conditions on the roads. About 300,000 inquiries are dealt with in the course of a winter (November–March). Additionally in the main towns an automatic telephone inquiry service, similar to the dial telephone weather forecast service, is provided by the A.A. in collaboration with the General Post Office. This caters for a further 300,000 callers. By dialling the appropriate number the caller is tuned in to a recording giving an up-to-date report on the state of the roads within a 50-mile radius. These tape recordings are changed as often as necessary. Road weather maps prepared by the motoring organizations are also transmitted by the B.B.C. and independent television at times and seasons when they have something to show.

Appendix 1
Calendar of Singularities

KEY TO ABBREVIATIONS

British Isles Weather Types quoted are defined on pp. 55–56.

F.H.C. means that the Flohn and Hess criterion (p. 143) for regularity of occurrence of similar weather patterns was satisfied within the dates quoted in $x\%$ of the years 1881–1947. The weather patterns involved are indicated by the most characteristic wind directions, etc., over Germany.

Periods of years

    I = 1873–97
   II = 1898–1937,   IIa 1900–30 approx.
  III = 1938–61
   IV = 1890–1950 $\pm$ 10 years approx.
    Z = Zürich observations 1550–76.

Weekly rainfall, sunshine, etc., averages quoted for various parts of the British Isles are for 1881–1915.

Singularity	Dates affected	Typical circulation development	Significant details (Statistically tested figures exceeding the level of 5% probability of occurrence by chance in *italics* 1% probability of occurrence by chance in **bold print**)
RETURN OF THE WESTERLIES (Onset of the 'European summer monsoon')	June	Spring period of highest mean pressure of the year in Greenland ends with ridges and offshoot Highs moving towards Britain and central Europe. Azores High spreads ridge towards Biscay and the Alps (towards Britain and Scandinavia in a minority of years—the finest summers).	Frequency of W and NW types approximately **doubled** between 1 and 20–30/6 (periods I, II and III). C type peak about *30*% on 31/5–2/6 (most noticeable in periods I, III and IV). W type peak frequency **52**% on 20/6; W, NW and AC together exceed 70% on 18–22/6; AC type rise from 25% on 20/6 to *35–40*% on 30/6–1/7 (period IV).
THUNDERY, CYCLONIC WEATHER (Height of the 'European summer monsoon')	Mid July to Mid August	Slow-moving depressions common in the region British Isles–Baltic–S. Scandinavia. Atlantic depressions travel towards this region.	Year's highest frequency (broadly dated climax) of C type (periods I, II and III) 30–35% on most days: sharp peak *35*% + 31/7–4/8 (II), replaced by twin maxima around 20/7 and mid August (I and III). (Tendency in some years for a fair weather break between stagnant cyclonic situations in mid–late July and early–mid August.) Highest av. pressure of the year at the Azores and lowest av. in eastern Europe.
END OF SUMMER TURNING POINT	17/8–2/9	Summer development of zonal westerlies about 50–60° N reaches its climax with some invigoration of the North Atlantic depression sequences by colder air than formerly arriving from Arctic Canada. In some years this gives an autumnal strength to the winds. On average the depressions are faster moving than in July–early August. In most years cooling of Arctic Canada from this point on leads to steering of the Atlantic depressions farther to the northeast (Barents Sea) away from the British Isles.	W type reaches one of the two highest frequency periods (broad climax) of the year (periods I, II and III). Types W and NW together about 70% (IV). C type peaks about *30*% 19 and **28**/8 (IV) followed by **fall to half** this frequency by 12/9.

Weather tendencies in			Constancy of date, regularity, etc.
Scotland and Ireland (often including N.W. England and Wales)	England central, east and south	Central Europe	
Sharp fall in av. sunshine. Av. weekly rainfall 18–24/6 twice that for 4–10/6. Frequency of thunder-storms in Edinburgh around 30/6 equals year's highest peak.	Av. rainfall amounts low and decreasing, sunshine high and increasing. Setback to the seasonal warming 11–17/6. 12–29/6 year's highest frequency of dry days in London (IV). 25/6–1/7 sunniest week of the year and one of the three driest weeks.	Year's highest peak of thunder frequency in S. Germany 1–5/6 (periods 1812–80 and IV), at Milan 12–14/6 (IV); highest peaks rainfall frequency about 5, 15 and 22/6 (Z), representative Alpine stations 2, 12 and 24/6 (IIa). Seasonal mean temperature rise interrupted by cooling 1–20/6.	F.H.C. Maritime airstreams invading central Europe 9–18/6 89%. Tendency for 3 bursts of the 'monsoon' about 2, 13 and 24–29/6 in central Europe. The rainfall peaks in Central Europe are separated by days with little more than half as great rainfall frequency (Z and IIa).
23–29/7 wettest week of the year in some British districts, notably wet on average in all districts except N. Scotland; year's maximum frequency of thunderstorms in London. Sunshine averages in southern Britain 20% less than 25/6–1/7. Highest peaks of frequency of thunderstorms in Edinburgh (1763–1897) around 21/7 and 8/8.		Notably high peak frequencies of rain-fall (IIa and Z); 67–80% in Hamburg 18–23/7 (IV). Thunderstorm frequency nearly equals June peaks, especially around 20/7 (IIa). Very low frequency of warm days around 6/7 and 1/8 (Z).	F.H.C. Maritime air invasions of Germany, mostly pronounced zonal circulation (westerlies in 45–55° N) 21–30/7 (89%) and 1–10/8 (84%). Tendency for 3 further 'monsoon' bursts around 6–8/7, 24/7 and 1–6/8.
20–26/8 one of the 3 wettest weeks of the year.	27/8–2/9 rather notable rainfall peak.	Notable rainfall peaks 18–24/8 (Z and IIa); in N. Germany 1–5/9 (IIa) and (Z). Much drier 25–31/8.	Sharply preferred date (a) may apply to climax of cyclonic vigour on N.E. Atlantic in late August, though interfered with by effects of tropical hurricane cyclones turning NE into the subpolar belt—broad climax around 1–10/9; (b) does apply to establishment of depression paths NE towards Barents Sea about 24/8, though this development also tends to falter around 1–3/9 and become re-established after 7/9.
Thunderstorms show slight frequency peaks in most areas 15–25/8, but the frequencies attained are little more than half those of late July–early August. The frequency and intensity of rainfall in Iceland increase markedly from 15/8 onwards.			

Singularity	Dates affected	Typical circulation development	Significant details (Statistically tested figures exceeding the level of 5% probability of occurrence by chance in *italics* 1% probability of occurrence by chance in **bold print**)
SEPTEMBER ANTI-CYCLONES	6–19/9	Anticyclones passing across Biscay and southern Britain over Europe into Siberia. (S'ly windstreams and cyclonic weather tends to affect Britain increasingly as each major anticyclone passes away east.)	One of the two highest frequency peaks (broad climax) of AC type (periods I, II, III) 30–40% on many days. Minimum frequency of C type *under 20%*, especially 6–12/9 (I, II, III). W type remains about 40%, much more frequent in Britain than during the other main period of anticyclonic tendency in May (IV).
LATE SEPTEMBER STORMINESS	21–30/9	Further intensification of the Atlantic depressions about 15–20/9 spreads across or affects much of Britain, especially the west and north.	Brief peak of C type 25–30% around 23/9 and minimum of AC type (25%) about 24–26/9 in Britain (period IV). S type 15–20% (IV).
EARLY OCTOBER ANTI-CYCLONES (Old Wives' Summer)	30/9–15/10	Renewal of the September anticyclone sequences commonly results in a stationary anticyclone affecting the region between these islands and eastern Europe and southern Scandinavia.	Marked peak frequency of AC type, reaching *40%* about 5–7/10 with low frequencies of C type; first autumn prominence of E type (10–20%); S type (5–15%), (period IV). Sharply increasing frequency of break-down of anticyclonic situations over Britain and the continent after about 7/10.
LATE AUTUMN RAINS	24/10–13/11	Cyclonic, often stormy, period with depressions passing close to the British Isles, especially about 24–29/10 and 7–12/11. The earlier systems have a tendency to pass across or even skirt the south of England. Cold N'ly and E'ly outbreaks are liable to affect Britain in these late October depression sequences. Cyclonic development is also common in the western and central Mediterranean. Pressure tends to remain high over eastern, and sometimes central, Europe and extend its influence westwards between the cyclonic sequences to give some interludes of fair, mild S'ly weather in Britain and western Europe around 1/11.	**Great decline** of AC type **to one half to one quarter of** the frequencies in late October that it presented in mid Sept.–early Oct. (periods I, II, III). Year's minimum frequency of AC type (*10%* or less) around 28–31/10 (I, II, III). Year's second climax (broad peak) of E type (20%) with main peak about 25–27/10 (I, II and III). Minor frequency peak of W type (about 40%) 5–11/11 (I, II and III).

Weather tendencies in			Constancy of date, regularity, etc.
Scotland and Ireland (often including N.W. England and Wales)	England central, east and south	Central Europe	
10–17/9 one of the 2 or 3 driest weeks of the year in E. and central England on average, notably dry in all districts. Year's minimum frequency of rain days av. only 2 in the week 10–16/9 in E. districts. Rainfall averages generally halved since 20/8–2/9.		Dry days exceed 70% on various dates 6–11/9 (IV, also Z).	F.H.C. Anticyclones affecting central Europe 3–12/9 (79%).
Sunshine averages increase 3–16/9 in the N. and W. and seasonal decline arrested everywhere.			
First autumn peaks of frequency of gales ('Equinoctial gales') at both Edinburgh and London (1763–1896), but neither so frequent nor usually so severe as those of mid winter. Rising frequency of rainfall. Steepened seasonal cooling trend.		Anticyclonic tendency continues throughout this time in the average year (period IV), but notable peak of rainfall (Z) 25–27/9.	Peak frequency of W and C types in Britain (periods I, II and III within these 10 days).
First prominent occurrence of rainfall in western Mediterranean after summer drought.			
Little effect on the Atlantic fringe, where av. rainfall has largely recovered from its mid-September minimum.	Gale frequencies temporarily low again. Modest pauses in seasonal trends of sunshine and rainfall in some districts. First major peak frequency of fog in London (1763–1896) about 15/10.	Dry days 70–80% 28/9–1/10 (IV).	F.H.C. Anticyclonic and S and E wind situations affecting central Europe 21/9–2/10 (76%).
Av. temperatures register a slight check to the seasonal cooling.			
22–28/10 is one of the 3 wettest weeks of the year, though the average numbers of rain-days nowhere exceed 5; in N. and E. Scotland av. rainfall does not become outstanding till 29/10–11/11.		26–29/10 cyclonic situations and frequency of raindays in Hamburg reach 66–70% (IV).	F.H.C. Fair weather situations, anticyclonic and S'ly in central Europe 28/10–6/11 (69%).
Fog frequency in London lower than in mid October or mid November. Steep fall of av. temperatures in all districts in late October, temporarily halted or reversed (warming) in first days of November. Considerable peak frequency of gales in Edinburgh (1763–1896) over these dates.		About 25–28/10 Zürich was affected by a sharp peak of rainfall frequency, equalling the highest of the year (Z).	
		Dry days rise in frequency to 77–81% in Vienna and Berlin on 2–3/11 (IV).	
Year's greatest peak frequency of rainfall in the western and central Mediterranean (e.g. Rome 50–60% 8–10/11) falls within these dates (IV).			

Singularity	Dates affected	Typical circulation development	Significant details (Statistically tested figures exceeding the level of 5% probability of occurrence by chance in *italics* 1% probability of occurrence by chance in **bold print**)
MID-NOVEMBER ANTI-CYCLONES (Early winter fogs and frosts)	15–24/11	Anticyclones, often forming first in maritime air over or near Britain, affect much of Europe. (The development is inclined to emerge rather gradually after the energy of the early November circulation appears spent, but tends to break down swiftly before renewed Atlantic storms advancing in the last days of the month.)	Sharp recovery of AC type to frequency peak (**about 30%**) and **decline** of W type (**to rather below 30%**) for several days about 17–20/11 (periods I, II and III).
EARLY WINTER STORMS AND RAINS (Winter return of the westerlies after autumn anticyclonic episodes)	26/11–10/12	Intensification of the Atlantic depressions and westerlies, now approaching their strongest seasonal development, usually pushes waves of mild air eastwards until blocked and lifted over the stagnant cold air in the heart of the Eurasian continent. There tend to be 2, sometimes 3, bouts of cyclonic activity affecting Britain around 28/11, 4–8/12 (and 14–17/12).	Sharp recovery of W type brings big peak (**over 50%**) around 5/12 (period IV), W and NW together reach 70%; sharp peaks 3–11/12 (I, II, III). C type peaks around 27/11 and 9–12/12 (I, II, III). AC type low frequencies (10–15%) around 3–8/12 (I, II, III), the decline being abrupt (II, III).
DECEMBER CONTINENTAL ANTI-CYCLONES (Before Christmas frosts: first phase of 'continental winter monsoon')	17–24/12	Anticyclonic development over central, and sometimes northern, Europe tends to occur through spread (or movement) of the Siberian winter anticyclone towards N. Russia (and Scandinavia) from 9/12 onwards and development of Highs over France–central Europe in former maritime air about 20/12.	Year's highest average barometric pressure over region London–Rhineland 17–21/12 (IIa). AC type recovers to shortlived peak around 25% on 17–21/12 (periods I, II and III). AC, S and E types together exceed 50% 19–23/12 (IV).

Weather tendencies in			Constancy of date, regularity, etc.
Scotland and Ireland (often including N.W. England and Wales)	England central, east and south	Central Europe	
Sunshine averages higher than for previous week.	Foggiest period of the year.	Dry days 76–80% frequency on 19–20/11 in Vienna (IV).	F.H.C. Fair weather situations in central Europe 11–22/11 (72%).
Av. rainfall decreases to a minimum 12–25/11 in all districts, amounts only ½ to ⅔ of those for the immediately preceding and following weeks in S. and central England.		Notable peak frequency of subsiding air on Alpine summits 19–26/11 (IIa).	
Gale frequencies notably lower than in preceding and following weeks.		Zürich (period Z) had frequencies of cold days and dry days mounting to big peak 25–30/11, then swift decline	
Cold anomaly shown by the av. temperature curves for most places north of the Alps, including London and Edinburgh (1800–1950 approx.).			
3–9/12 is on average the wettest week of the year with 5–6 rain days in most districts, but some recovery of sunshine in E. Scotland (lee effect).		High, but not outstanding, peaks of rainfall and rain frequency (IIa and Z).	F.H.C. Oceanic airstreams reaching central Europe with markedly zonal westerly circulation 1–10/12 (81%).
Frequency of gales rises abruptly to a high peak, which in Scotland is sustained through December. Main winter peak of thunderstorms. Fog frequency inland and in S. less than in preceding and following weeks.		Frequency of mild air about 1–10/12 checks or reverses seasonal fall of av. temperature (1800–1950 approx.).	
Halt or reversal of av. seasonal fall of temperature (i.e. warming) in most districts 3–9/12.		Lowest frequency of cold days at any time during the winter on 4–6/12 (Z).	
Rainfall peak also affects Mediterranean (Florence).			
Notable rainfall minimum 17–23/12.	Av. rainfall amounts 17–23/12 halved since 3–9/12 in the S.E.	Notable peak frequency of subsiding air on Alpine summits 18–23/12 (IIa).	F.H.C. Continental anticyclone situations affecting central Europe 14–25/12 (67%).
		Highest frequency of cold days at any time in the winter (50–60%) on 17–22/12 (Z).	
Peak frequencies of frosts in most inland areas of Europe in 45–60° N. Fog frequencies high, but lower than in November.			

Singularity	Dates affected	Typical circulation development	Significant details (Statistically tested figures exceeding the level of 5% probability of occurrence by chance in *italics* 1% probability of occurrence by chance in **bold print**)
STORMS OF MID WINTER (Mid-winter mildening)	26/12–12/1	Renewed intensification of the Atlantic cyclonic activity brings the westerlies on average to their strongest development of the year and the depressions to their biggest size. 2, sometimes 3, bouts of this activity affect Britain around 28/12, 6–8/1 (and 15–18/1). In epochs of vigorous circulation the later bouts are normally the most intense, but in quieter epochs only the end of December bout may press far to the east: there is at all times a tendency for the later bouts to fail to penetrate the continent.	Year's highest frequency of W type 60% about 8/1 in period IV, notably high peaks in the other epochs examined though peak dates around 28/12 in I and III and values not quite as high as early Dec. and late Jan. C type rises to a brief peak (*25–35%*) about 28/12 (IV) as secondary depressions tend to cross Britain. Frequency of AC type drops to low values (10% approx.) around 1–8/1 (II, III, III).
JANUARY CONTINENTAL ANTI-CYCLONES (Phase of the 'continental winter monsoon')	19–25/1	Anticyclones cover much of Europe, especially eastern, central and SW Europe, but also sometimes Scandinavia, reaching maximum extent when the energy of the preceding bout of Atlantic storms appears spent.	Frequency of AC type recovers to about *25%* 20–21/1 in periods II and IV, but this peak not noticeable in England in I and III. Types AC, S and E together 50% 20–23/1 (IV). Year's lowest frequency of C type (*10–12%*) around 24–26/1 (IV), similar minimum in periods I, II and III, values being low through most of Jan. but particularly around these dates.
RENEWED STORMINESS, GALES AND RAIN OR SNOW (End of January turning point)	27/1–4/2	Fresh intensification of cyclonic activity on the Atlantic brings the last notable peak of average intensity of the winds over the ocean. The main zone of the westerlies is by now farther south than before, so that the situations produced in Europe by this bout of cyclonic vigour vary from year to year and decade to decade.	Modest peaks of C, E and NW types (period IV, not exactly reproduced or date varies in other periods). Great decline in frequency of W type now begins or **has begun** since mid Jan. in periods I, II and III.

Weather tendencies in			Constancy of date, regularity, etc.
Scotland and Ireland (often including N.W. England and Wales)	England central, east and south	Central Europe	
Gale frequencies high but decrease after New Year (1763–1896). Rainfall maxima in most districts: probability of taking the form of snow increases. Av. amounts of rainfall no longer comparable with the maxima between July and early December in inland and S.E. districts. 25–31/12 least sunny week of year. Year's lowest av. temperature values correspond with the coldest W'ly winds in average and mild winters about 11/1 (and end of January). Notable frequencies of very mild and of very cold days in London 28/12–3/1 (1841–1936). Year's peak frequency of snow in London about 1–5/1 (1763–1896).		Frequencies of rain days show peaks of **66–81**% 28–31/12 (IV). Frequency of rain and/or snow at Zürich increased gradually from 21/12 to its highest winter peak 5–15/1 (Z). Av. temp. curves show a small mid-winter maximum at most stations around 27/12–5/1, the so-called 'Christmas thaw'. Thaw in Berlin 28–31/12 (**66–76**%) (IV).	F.H.C. Oceanic airstreams reaching central Europe 23/12–1/1 (72%).
Minor maxima of av. rainfall in most W. and N. districts. The only more or less regular feature in England seems to be a lull in the cyclonic activity, rather variable in date.	Sunshine averages increase sharply. Rainfall averages low.	Peak frequencies of dry days and of night frosts commonly reaching **65–80**% 19–25/1 on lowlands in Germany and Austria (IV). Year's greatest frequency of subsiding air on Alpine summits 22–23/1 (IIa). High frequencies of dry days especially about 16–19 and 25–27/1 (Z).	F.H.C. Continental anti-cyclones dominating much of Europe 15–26/1 (78%).
5–6 raindays in the week 29/1–4/2 on average. By far the year's greatest peak frequency of gales in Edinburgh about 25/1–4/2 (1763–1896). Nearly the highest winter peak frequencies of rain and snow at Edinburgh 23/1–4/2	Year's highest frequency of gales around 26/1–1/2 and third highest peak of snow frequency in London (1763–1896). Fog frequency lower than for many weeks past. Tendency for the depressions to break up established frosts. Several famous glazed frosts have occurred with the first depressions arriving on a southern track, preceded by cold E wind.	Peak frequency of rainfall (or snowfall) reaches **68–71**% at Hamburg on 27–28/1, lower frequencies at inland places (IV). Frequency of rain or snow at Zürich was again high 30/1–11/2 mounting to nearly its highest peak level about 10/2 (Z).	

Av. temperatures at most places in Europe 31/1–4/2 rather higher than in previous or following weeks.

Singularity	Dates affected	Typical circulation development	Significant details (Statistically tested figures exceeding the level of 5% probability of occurrence by chance in *italics* 1% probability of occurrence by chance in **bold print**)
FEBRUARY ANTI-CYCLONES (Phase of the 'continental winter monsoon') Late winter decline of the westerlies	7–22/2	As the Atlantic cyclonic activity again weakens and in general proceeds to still lower latitudes, anticyclones commonly form over central–western–northern Europe or Highs which have survived from earlier in central-eastern Europe tend to spread towards Britain and Scandinavia.	Moderate peaks of AC type in Britain around 7–12/2 (periods I, II and III). The main seasonal decline of W type is in progress but as the frequencies still exceed 35–40% till 22/2 this type readily re-appears as dominant if the anticyclones weaken in any particular year (IV). AC, S and E types together about 50% 8–13/2 (IV). Around 20–24/2 Britain rather commonly came under the influence of renewed anti-cyclones over central Europe, Scandinavia or Greenland (IV).
EARLY MARCH COLD PERIOD, SOMETIMES STORMY (March winter)	26/2–9/3	The most prevalent feature is probably high pressure over Greenland, but sometimes also over Scandinavia. N winds in Norwegian Sea and E winds over Europe common. A fresh bout of cyclonic activity on the Atlantic presses east, though usually weaker than the mid-winter bouts and in such various latitudes in different years that there are few if any regular features of the outcome in Europe.	First notable peak of N type; N, NW and E together 50% approx. 1–9/3 (IV), but S 15% at end of Feb. and W still 30–40%. Peak of C type, well marked (periods II, III only). Average upper air temperatures everywhere between Spits-bergen and England reach lowest values of the winter.
MID-MARCH ANTI-CYCLONES (Early spring anticyclones in Britain: late phase of the 'continental winter monsoon')	12–22/3	Anticyclones commonly form over or near Britain and become stationary in the area or over central-northern Europe. These anticyclones are less extensive in the W–E direction than those earlier in the winter. The depression tracks over the Atlantic continue mostly in rather low latitudes. The average level of barometric pressure in Greenland con-tinues to rise.	Sharp peak (**35%**) of AC type about 12–14/3 (period IV). Frequencies of AC and S types rising but peak dates vary in periods I, II and III. Peak frequency of E type (about 20%) 17–19/3 (I, II and III). AC, N and E types together about 70% **12–22/3** (IV). The anticyclonic period is inclined to end with a N'ly outbreak.

Weather tendencies in			Constancy of date, regularity, etc.
Scotland and Ireland (often including N.W. England and Wales)	England central, east and south	Central Europe	
Only slight effects. Gale frequencies somewhat lower than before. Rainfall averages begin to fall but not till after 12/2 in W. Scotland.	Progressive decline of gale frequencies to low values for winter by 20/2. Setback to upward trend of av. temperature 5–11/2. Greatest frequency of extreme cold days (produced by coldest days in severe winters) around 10–12/2. Last high peak of fog frequency in London (1763–1896). Sunshine averages improve, especially about 20/2.	Greatest frequency of good winter sports conditions on hills and mountains. Night frosts on German and Austrian lowlands 6–8/2 67–79% (IV). Equal highest frequency of subsiding dry air on Alpine peaks 8–12/2 (IIa). Low frequencies of rain or snow 13–25/2 (Z)	F.H.C. Continent dominated by anticyclones 3–12/2 (67%).
Peak frequencies of gales, though less frequent than earlier in the winter. Fog becomes unusual. Av. rainfall amounts higher than in preceding or following weeks, especially in E. and S. England. Year's highest peak frequency of snow in Edinburgh and second highest peak in London (1763–1896).		Few if any regular features. Accumulated snow in S. Norway normally reaches its greatest depth. Well defined but only moderately high peak frequency of rain- (and snow-) fall 27/2–2/3 in Zürich (Z).	
Depressions commonly form after N'ly outbreak in the western Mediterranean, leading to year's greatest frequency of rainfall in the Adriatic 3–9/3.			
No pronounced features apart from steady seasonal decline of rainfall and increase of sunshine.	Notable rainfall minimum. Also a minimum frequency of rain days, av. 3 in the week 12–18/3. Modest peak of night fog frequency in London, abrupt decline in frequency of gales (1763–1896).	Last main peak of frequency of days with dry subsiding air on Alpine summits 15–20/3 (IIa). Dry days 60–70% in S. Germany and Austria (IV). Low frequency of rain 15–20/3 (Z).	F.H.C. Anticyclones or anticyclonic northerly windstreams over central Europe 12–25/3 (69%).
Cold N winds rather prominent in Greece and S.E. Europe.			

Singularity	Dates affected	Typical circulation development	Significant details (Statistically tested figures exceeding the level of 5% probability of occurrence by chance in *italics* 1% probability of occurrence by chance in **bold print**)
SPRING RETURN OF THE ATLANTIC DEPRES- SIONS	30/3–15/4	With the spring warming of the United States and lower lati- tudes over the ocean and Africa, most Atlantic depres- sions now tend to cross the ocean in rather higher latitudes than in Feb.–early March and approach Europe near or over the British Isles. These are usually smaller depressions than in winter. The sequence normally ends with depressions becoming more or less station- ary off Newfoundland and over the regions near the British Isles, especially North Sea– Baltic, commonly with N'ly winds over Britain. The average pressure level remains high in Greenland. At times Britain comes under extensions of the Azores and Greenland anticyclones with dry, sunny weather—warm or cold as the case may be.	A secondary peak of W type (*40%*) 31/3–3/4 (period IV). Peaks of C, W and N discern- ible in most epochs but the dates wander by almost half a month. Probably because the key feature is a swift change of latitude of the mainstream of the circulation over much of the hemisphere, together with weakening of this circulation and longitude shifts of the main cold trough and low pressure axes, there are few constant features of the out- come in western Europe. Lowest av. barometric pressure of the year in N. France and S. Germany.
THE SPRING NORTHER- LIES	16/4–20/5	The Atlantic cyclonic activity and belt of westerly winds reach their weakest develop- ment of the year; the depres- sions are mostly rather small and the main ones tend to linger off Newfoundland. Pressure is usually high over Greenland. Over the North Sea, Scandinavia and the Baltic anticyclonic periods alternate with slow-moving depressions.	Year's greatest frequency of N type 20–30% on most days, reaching 30% around 12–18/5; also of E type 20–25% on 30/4– 3/5 (periods I, II, III). Noteworthy **increase** of C type to *25–30%* about 5–7/5 and lower preliminary peak about 25–30/4 (IV). AC type also **increases sharply,** prominent but peaks vary in date (I, II, III). Combined frequency AC, N and E, also of C, N and E, often 70% (IV). Year's lowest frequency of W type (I, II, III) about 15% around 1–7/5 and 21–24/5 with suggestions of a phase of rather higher frequency in between (II, III), possibly connected with a temporary weakening of the Greenland anticyclone (which seems to change from a cold to a warm anticyclone **about this time**).

Weather tendencies in			Constancy of date, regularity, etc.
Scotland and Ireland (often including N.W. England and Wales)	England central, east and south	Central Europe	

Few if any constant features apart from the first (abrupt) seasonal increase in frequency of showers and thunderstorms inland.		Rainfall frequencies 50% higher than in mid March (IIa).	
Fog becomes rare.		High frequencies of rainfall at Zürich 22/3–2/4 and about 10 and 15/4 (Z).	
The first noteworthy seasonal peak of av. sunshine duration in most districts (1881–1915) 2–8/4, followed by lower values 9–15/4. This may indicate a tendency for the stormy episodes to come in two bouts separated by a quiet and warmer anticyclonic interlude.			

23–29/4 av. rainfall and rain frequency greater than in any other week in April or May in E. districts. Late spring snowfalls may be particularly liable to occur in this week.		Cold outbreaks with N or NW winds affect Germany on at least 3 days 1–16/5 75% (IV), though the dates seem to vary rather widely within this period.	
Thunderstorm frequencies in London (1763–1896) increase abruptly about 1–3/5.			
7–13/5 one of the five driest weeks of the year in the extreme south, where it is also one of the sunniest on average.		Frequency of rainfall in N. Germany rather low, especially about 15/5 (IIa).	
14–20/5 sunniest week of the year in Ireland.			
Clear nights liable to give late frosts when the weather becomes calm after N winds.			

Singularity	Dates affected	Typical circulation development	Significant details (Statistically tested figures exceeding the level of 5% probability of occurrence by chance in *italics* 1% probability of occurrence by chance in **bold print**)
EARLY SUMMER ANTI-CYCLONES (Fore-monsoon fine weather period)	21/5–10/6	Reorganization of the barometric pressure pattern over the hemisphere produces anticyclonic interludes in western and central Europe including Britain, partly through stationary anticyclones centred over this region lingering from earlier in May and partly through anticyclones moving or spreading from the Azores and from Greenland.	Year's greatest frequency of AC type (*40%* or over on some days) over most of this period, but especially around 21/5 and 5/6 (periods I, II and III). A peak of S type (about 20%) 21–31/5 (I, II and III). AC and S together 60–70% 21–31/5 (IV). N winds still rather prominent and W type still rare till 31/5 (IV). E type has its last spring peak (10–15%) broadly over this period (IV).

Weather tendencies in			Constancy of date, regularity, etc.
Scotland and Ireland (often including N.W. England and Wales)	England central, east and south	Central Europe	
Sunniest weeks of the year 14/5–17/6.	Few regular features. Sunshine averages generally near the highest of the year and rainfall averages low, but considerable year-to-year variations.	Dry days at lowland places between Vienna and N.W. Germany 66–83% about 28/5–1/6 (IV). Year's lowest frequency of rainfall in N. Germany (II*a*).	F.H.C. Anticyclones influencing the region between central and northern Europe and the British Isles 22/5–2/6 (80%).
Driest weeks of the year 21/5–10/6.			
Lowest frequency of rain days, 3 per week on average in most districts.	Further peak of thunderstorm frequency in London 21–30/5, to some extent prolonged into June, equalling frequencies of early May (1763–1896).		

Appendix 2
Calendar of Historic Weather Events since 1500

Dates before 14 September 1752 have been corrected to the Gregorian (New Style) Calendar. The great majority have been checked back to early sources to eliminate possible 10–11 day errors due to confusion over the calendar change.

JANUARY

1. 1537   Thames frozen in London: King Henry VIII, with his queen, rode on the river.
5. 1552   Great wind storms all over W. Europe, repeated again 8–15 January with thunder, hail, snow, North Sea storm surges and sea floods.
   1814   Snow and strengthening NE wind 5th and 6th ended the foggy spell which since 26 December had crusted the vegetation in thick rime. From 6 January the frost became more severe, especially the nights, until 23rd.
6. 1666   Thaw broke the ice on London's river: water traffic moving by 10th. A mild January followed.
   1839   'The Great Wind': many ships wrecked, houses blown down in S. Scotland and N. England, Menai Bridge damaged.
   1928   NW gale: North Sea storm surge produced sea flood in Thames, people drowned in their homes in London.
7. 1709   50-day great frosty period began, during which Thames froze.
   1838   2-month frosty period set in with light SE wind and fine day with hoar frost in London; on 5th it had been SW with gentle rain.
8. 1697   NE gale renewed the frost after brief intermission with rain and drizzle in London area on 6–8th.
11. 1740   Record cold day in spell which began on 4th. Afternoon temperatures in Holland −20° C, in London about −9° C (+15° F) E gale.
12. 1697   Rain with W wind and thaw 12–18th interrupted the frost in London.
   1818   Severe W gale damaged buildings in Edinburgh; repeated with SW–NW gale on 14–15th.
13. 1565   Thames flood accompanied thaw: river in London clear of ice by 15th. A notably unhealthy fog followed for 7 days.
   1725   Very dry period began: only 15 days with rain at Wells, Somerset in next three months.

14.	1938	Widespread gale damage.
	1963	Period of severest frost began. No thaw in much of the South for 12 days.
15.	1820	−23° C (−10° F) reported at Tunbridge Wells—no details of exposure known.
	1952	Severe gale damage in N. Scotland; gusts to 127 m.p.h. at hill site in Orkney.
18.	1881	Worst snowstorm of 19th century in London: E gale of 73 m.p.h. at Great Yarmouth, snowdrifts 12 feet deep in Isle of Wight.
19.	1942	Great snowstorm all over Britain: aircraft dropped food to snowbound train S. of Wick.
	1963	Coldest day: afternoon temperatures of −7° C in Surrey with E gale.
20.	1608	Thames frozen over: the severe weather set in on 21 Dec. 1607 and lasted in England till about 20 Feb.
	1838	Lowest temperatures of 19th century in London: −16° C reported at Greenwich about sunrise, −20° C at Blackheath, −26° C (−14° F) at Beckenham. Temperature in Greenwich −11° C at midday.
23.	1891	End of skating spell in London and on Fenland rivers, which had lasted all Dec. and nearly blocked Thames with ice in London.
	1947	Onset of long frosty spell with E winds, period of over 50 days with snow lying in London.
24.	1868	Gale blew down parts of stone buildings in Edinburgh ('Windy Friday').
25.	1716	Ice on Thames in London lifted 14 feet by a flood tide but did not break.
	1741	Violent WSW gale in Scotland: widespread damage to buildings.
	1795	Coldest night in an extremely severe month: temperature alleged to have fallen below −20° C in London.
26.	1809	SW gale and temperature quickly rising to +8° C (47° F) in Scotland after snowstorm ended severe frost period with E winds which began in Dec. 1808.
	1884	Lowest barometric pressure ever recorded in Britain, 926·5 mb. at M.S.L. at Ochtertyre, Perthshire in storm centre.
	1940	Great snowstorm in SE. England with violent gale and deep drifts 26–29th. Depth of level snow 1–2 feet in many districts.
	1963	Slight thaw after 12 days of continuous and often severe frost. Most rivers and several harbours frozen.
27.	1920	Violent gale: gust of 111 m.p.h. in NW. Ireland.
	1940	Glazed frost paralysed traffic N. Wales–Hants, spreading to all SW. England by 29th. Freezing temperatures persisted.
28.	1927	Widespread gale damage.
29.	1701	Severe S gale after period of frost; many ships wrecked, trees blown down and buildings damaged in S. England.

30.	1945	Rain and thaw ended severe frost period which began 3 Jan.
	1950	Glazed frost preceded thaw in S. England.
31.	1644	8-day snowfall 31 Jan.–7 Feb.
	1901	Highest pressure ever observed in Britain, 1,055 mb. at Aberdeen.
	1953	Disastrous NNW gale, gusts to 126 m.p.h. in Orkney: forests destroyed in N. and E. Scotland, North Sea flood and drownings in East Anglia and Holland.
	1956	E gale brought in exceptionally cold air from continent starting 4-week frosty spell. Midday temperatures in London $+8°$ C on 30 Jan., $-4°$ C on 1 Feb.

FEBRUARY

1.	1697	Rain and SW gale interrupted frost for one day only near London.
	1814	Last Frost Fair held on Thames in London 1–4th.
2.	1740	Rain and thaw 2–4th interrupted the long frost.
	1776	End of severe spell affecting all Europe since 9 Jan., with Thames frozen for some time; intensely stormy cyclonic February followed.
	1887	Onset of notable drought.
3.	1666	'A most furious storm' (Pepys), houses blown down in London.
	1838	Thaw began gently with NW wind in London and became rapid in sunshine on 5th, but rain with S–SE wind on 6th preceded renewal of E winds and frost on 7th.
5.	1814	Rain and thaw rapidly broke up the Thames ice in London 5–6th, though frosts continued frequent till 20 March. Brief spell of very mild days with winds mostly between W and S 6–13 Feb.
7.	1911	Notable drought began.
8.	1698	Ice 8 inches thick on the sea coast of Suffolk.
	1823	Great snowstorm in N. England: the ways subsequently opened by tunnelling through drifts.
10.	1579	Thames flooded by melting snow, deposited fish in Westminster Hall.
11.	1895	Lowest temperatures in spell of prolonged frost: $-27°$ C ($-17°$ F) at Braemar, $-24°$ C at Buxton. Thames blocked 9–17th by ice floes 6–7 feet thick, ships only able to enter Port of London with the tide.
12.	1855	Cricket match played on the ice at Ely.
13.	1695	Thaw broke the long frost, though frost returned with much snow and N and E wind in March.
14.	1579	4-day snowfall 14–18th with N wind, deep drifts: many people and cattle lost.
15.	1900	All-day snowstorm in N. England with drifting and lives lost; rapid thaw followed.
	1929	Coldest day in the long frost which began on 11th.

16.	1962	W gale of exceptional strength all over Britain, unverifiable measurement of 177 m.p.h. gust on hilltop in Unst, Shetland. Widespread damage, especially in Sheffield.
17.	1962	Disastrous North Sea flood at Hamburg.
18.	1684	Rain and thaw after 8 weeks with Thames frozen: ships could reach Port of London by 20–22nd.
20.	1608	Approximate date of end of exceptionally severe frost in England which had lasted more or less since 21 Dec. 1607.
21.	1697	Rain reached London area on 4th day of W wind and ended long frost.
	1861	Gale destroyed Chichester cathedral tower and part of Crystal Palace, London.
	1903	Saharan dust fell from dry air all over S. England and Wales.
22.	1692	Freezing NE gale and heavy snow in Highlands ended mild fair weather and brought renewal of long wintry spell as in Dec.–Jan. 1691–2, thereby providing cover for escapes from the Massacre of Glencoe.
	1962	E wind brought renewal of long spell of wintry weather after mild conditions since 6 Jan. Exceptionally late spring followed for blossom and leaf.
23.	1933	Gales 23–26th and snowstorm dislocated traffic in England.
	1955	−25° C at Braemar.
27.	1903	Disastrous gale as deep depression crossed Scotland: train blown off viaduct in Lancs.
28.	1937	Great snowstorm with N gale, drifts 13 feet deep in Wales and Scotland lingered through March.
	1959	Record February warmth, shade temperature reached 19° C (66° F) at Greenwich with S wind and sunshine.
	1963	Succession of dry sunny days between 24 Feb. and 3 March brought a gradual end to the 9-week period with snow lying in the South. Night frosts severe until 3 March.

MARCH

1.	1636	Approximate beginning of long dry period. By September serious drought effects.
5.	1838	Rain and thaw in London; all snow gone by the 8th.
8.	1674	13-day snowfall and blizzard—'The Thirteen Drifty Days'— in the Scottish Borders began about 5–8 March (New Style). Most of the sheep perished.
9.	1740	SW wind 'with gentle rain like the month of May' brought the end of a great winter.
	1891	Great snowstorm in the west of England, trains buried for days: E–NE gale, shipwrecks, many lives lost.
10.	1929	Day temperatures reached 21° C (70° F) in Lake District in calm sunny weather whilst skating continued on the thick ice preserved by cold nights.

11.	1947	Rain in S. England began thaw which slowly spread to the whole country by 22nd: floods lasted till mid May on low ground.
16.	1947	Gale damage, gust nearly 100 m.p.h. in Suffolk (Mildenhall).
18.	1886	End of spell of frost and snow which began on 5 Jan. Skating possible for 67 days at Weybridge, Surrey.
19.	1812	Snow fell 1 foot deep about Edinburgh, followed by drifting in NE gale 21–23rd.
20.	1814	The long spell of E winds and severe weather in London ended with high day temperatures and a SE breeze, and from the 22nd winds were more variable in direction.
24.	1878	Sudden NW gale, with violent squalls, and sleet and snow, wrecked training ship HMS *Eurydice* off Isle of Wight with all hands lost.
	1895	S gale ('worst gale of 19th century' in Midlands), 100 m.p.h. probably exceeded: stone buildings demolished.
27.	1812	Skating on Good Friday in Edinburgh area.
28.	1916	Snowstorm in S. England: gale produced drifting, traffic dislocated.
29.	1901	Heavy snow and drifting in Scotland, N. England and Wales.

APRIL

1.	1917	Great snowstorm in N. Ireland and in N. England.
5.	1911	Freezing all day at Hampstead: latest known date for this in London.
12.	1725	End of 3-month dry spell at Wells, Somerset.
14.	1921	Snow in many districts 14–18th: colder than January of that year.
16.	1949	85° F (almost 30° C) in London, earliest known date for this.
18.	1850	Thunderstorm with tornado and exceptionally big hailstones in Dublin.
19.	1849	Great snowstorm in S. England: Westerham coach buried in drift.
20.	1893	Early heat wave: 28° C in London.
21.	1695	Strong SW winds and rain ended exceptionally long severe and snowy winter, almost the first rain for several months near London. NE and E winds had been almost continuous since 21 March; variable winds now followed, though frequently N and E in May and early June. (This April and May the greatest extension of the Arctic sea ice ever known was spreading round the entire coast of Iceland.)
24.	1600	A deep snowfall.
	1921	End of unsettled weather of March and April: months of mostly fine, dry, warm weather followed.
25.	1725	Beginning of exceptional prolonged rainy spell with winds between NW and SW (after a mild winter). Rain fell in London on at least 60 of the 75 days between this and 8 July.

	1908	Heaviest recorded spring snowfall in England, roads and railways blocked: secondary depression in the Channel.
	1950	Deep snow damaged trees and telephone lines in the South.
27.	1919	Snow fell all over Britain, heavy in the Southeast: 8 to 12 inches deep in the Home Counties.
29.	1882	Violent SW gale destroyed spring foliage in S. England.

MAY

1.	1698	Snow fell 6 inches deep in Yorks with keen frost: some of it lay till the 5th.
4.	1579	Snow 1 foot deep in London after 5-hour fall.
5.	1959	Beginning of long spell of fine anticyclonic weather, which soon became rather warm, lasting till June and renewed later.
6.	1911	Beginning of predominantly fine anticyclonic weather, which lasted till mid June and was later renewed.
	1939	Violent thunderstorm in Bedfordshire, hailstones 1 inch diameter.
10.	1891	Snow in Bath and London.
12.	1947	Beginning of long spell of mainly warm, anticyclonic weather, renewed again in July after breaks in June.
13.	1698	Much snow in London area and in Yorks: corn and fruit crops damaged.
14.	1698	Severe frost and icicles in Yorks. Weather mostly poor till 20 August.
16.	1740	Snow fell in London at night 16–17 May.
	1935	Snow 3 inches deep at Cambridge; record May frosts 16–17th −12° C at Rickmansworth: much damage to fruit blossom after heat wave on 6th.
17.	1891	Snow in Bath and London.
	1955	Snow fell in London and lay in many parts of England, blocking roads in Peak District and S. Wales.
19.	1698	Deep snow in Shropshire.
	1868	32° C (90° F) at Tonbridge: earliest known date for this temperature in England.
20.	1729	Tornado destroyed buildings along track through Sussex and Kent.
21.	1950	Tornadoes accompanying severe thunderstorms in E. England: £50,000 damage; part of Linslade, Beds, destroyed. Big hail also in Beds.
22.	1922	33° C (91° F) in London, hottest day of the year: earliest known date for this.
25.	1846	Hot dry spell began.
27.	1821	Snow in London area: latest known date.
	1860	Snow at night 27–28th on northern Pennines blocked the roads over the hills: drifts 4 feet deep.
	1879	Thundery rain, with depression over the Channel, began long rainy summer, with S and W winds prevailing.

29.   1920   Thunderstorm and cloudburst near Louth, Lincs: £100,000 damage; people drowned in their homes.
      1944   Cloudburst in N. Wales, roads blocked with fallen rock.
30.   1692   Warm thundery spell set in and lasted 3 weeks.
31.   1740   Moors at Eskdalemuir frozen too hard for peat cutting.
      1911   Severe thunderstorms in many parts of England: 17 people and 4 horses killed at the Derby on Epsom Downs.

JUNE

1.   1924   Severe flooding in central England after 2-day downpour.
2.   1938   Depression crossing England on 1–3rd produced W gale in the English Channel, snow on Helvellyn and at low levels in N. Scotland.
      1953   Coronation Day N'ly outbreak with frequent showers in E. England. Afternoon temperatures 2–3rd 8–10° C in English Midlands, 7° C in Aberdeen.
3.   1962   Record June frosts: −6° C (22° F) at Santon Downham, Norfolk on 1st and 3rd.
4.   1944   W–NW gales 4–6th (D. Day Gales), gusts over 60 m.p.h. on coasts between Pembroke and Hebrides.
6.   1954   Depressions crossing the country ended the changeable thundery weather and started long spell of cool rainy weather with W–NW winds lasting till late August.
7.   1697   Severe flood caused by lake burst in bog near Charleville, Co. Cork, the spring having been uncommonly wet in England and Ireland with frequent rain and hail.
      1768   Beginning of wettest part of a record wet summer in England. Rain on at least 36 days out of the next 44; thundery.
9.   1910   Large hailstones in heaps 2–3 feet deep after thunderstorms between Wales and Surrey.
10.   1903   Extremely wet spell began: all districts affected.
11.   1667   Beginning of long dry spell lasting until mid August: great heat in June and July.
      1768   2-day deluge 11–12th.
13.   1903   Uncommonly persistent rain in E. and SE. England 13–15th, depression centred in Channel.
14.   1914   Floods and hail damage in London.
      1949   Start of prolonged fine summer weather.
15.   1869   Sudden NE gale on E. coast of Scotland, shipwrecks cost many lives.
17.   1815   Thunderstorm rains in Belgium delayed Napoleon's army before Waterloo.
18.   1764   Severe thunderstorms: lightning destroyed churches and naval ship. (Helped decision to introduce lightning rods.)
      1846   End of 25-day exceptionally hot dry spell in Ireland.

19. 1676 Exceptional heat 19 June to 1 July, long remembered.

     1692 Wind and rain stripped trees of their leaves, climax of 3-day rainfall around London. Continual rains and floods went on through July and August, though with little more thunder.

22. 1799 Beginning of long rainy spell: only 8 days without rain till 17 Nov.

23. 1783 Hot dry weather set in after continual rains. The fine weather was marred until 20 July or later by persistent thick smoky haze and pall, apparently from Iceland volcano.

24. 1897 Hail damaged crops, glass and Diamond Jubilee decorations in and round London.

27. 1666 Heat wave began: mostly dry in London since 12th.

     1933 An anticyclone spreading across after a cold N'ly outbreak began a long dry spell, which soon became notably warm and lasted till 27 Aug.

28. 1788 Probably the wettest day ever recorded in Suffolk.

     1917 9·56 inches rain at Bruton, Somerset.

29. 1957 35·5° C (96° F) in London: peak of heat wave from 28 June to 6 July.

JULY

1. 1960 Night frosts in several parts of England on 1st and 3rd—e.g. −1° C in Norfolk.

2. 1893 Cloudburst on Cheviots, bridges washed away.

    1946 Thunderstorms of tropical intensity over S. and E. England 2–4th: gales, floods and large hail.

4. 1681 End of 4 months spell of dry E winds in Scotland.

    1696 W winds and frequent rains and gales set in, after warm thundery June, and lasted till 15 August.

    1959 Renewal of fine anticyclonic weather after stormy interlude since 23 June.

    1960 Rainy weather set in and lasted till 6 Sept.

5. 1666 'Extremely hot ... oranges ripening in the open at Hackney' (Pepys).

    1955 Beginning of 2-month fine spell.

6. 1666 Beginning of period with occasional showers and heavy rains, though often warm.

8. 1893 Thunderstorms and whirlwinds in N. England, hailstones 2 inches across.

    1923 Flood at Carrbridge, Inverness-shire.

9. 1725 Intermission 9–12th in very prolonged rainy period.

10. 1923 Spectacular all-night thunderstorms 9–10th over London and SE. England.

11. 1596 Period of frequent severe gales in Scotland set in and lasted till 16 August: many ships lost on the E. coast.

    1923 Heat wave began, temperatures reaching 32° C (90° F) in England on 3 successive days (11–13th).

12.	1900	Flood disaster at Ilkley, Yorks.
13.	1725	Renewed rains with SW–W winds predominant till 4 Sept. with continually cool weather.
	1808	'Hot Wednesday': shade temperatures 33–35° C in E. and SE. England, 37° C (99° F) reported in Suffolk (exposure details unknown).
	1921	The weather became unsettled and wet with frequent strong winds in W. and N. districts after the dry spring—early summer: dry weather continued in the E. and S.
15.	1888	Hailstones 2·8 inches (7 cm.) diameter at Gloucester.
16.	1847	Cloudburst on Bodmin Moor, Cornwall: flooding rivers destroyed bridges.
17.	1948	End of 3-week spell of exceptionally cold northerly winds.
18.	1953	Widespread thunderstorm damage in the South.
	1955	11 inches rain in 24 hours in Dorset: heaviest fall ever reliably measured in England (occurred in a dry month).
19.	1707	'Hot Tuesday': many heat wave deaths in England (temperatures uncertain).
20.	1930	4-day persistent rain 20–23rd on N. Yorks moors (12 inches in all).
21.	1826	The only day with considerable rain in a long dry summer from June onwards: the earth now parched from Suffolk to Aberdeen, cattle suffering.
22.	1868	38·1° C (100·5° F) at Tonbridge, Kent: highest shade temperature ever observed in England (in long, dry, hot summer).
	1907	Widespread thunderstorm damage in the South, great depths of hailstones.
25.	1738	Severe hailstorms in many districts, in Herts and Wilts lumps of ice up to 9 inches across fell (in mainly dry summer).
26.	1565	Severe thunderstorms with hail.
	1666	Hail 'as big as walnuts' in London and 27th on Suffolk coast.
28.	1948	Warmest night recorded: temperature 28–29 July did not fall below 23·3° C (74° F) at Westminster. Day temperatures in London reached or exceeded 32° C (90° F) on 3 successive days 28–30th.
29.	1588	Spanish Armada entering the Channel with SW wind after repeatedly stormy, often NW–N winds on the Atlantic coasts between England and Portugal since 9 May.
	1875	Whirlwinds in Dublin.
	1911	Exceptional thunderstorm and hail (in fine summer).
	1956	Violent gale in Channel, wrecks cost many lives; landslides and floods inland in S. England and Wales.
31.	1588	Squally WNW wind: thereafter mostly light W winds in the Channel till 8 August.

AUGUST

1. 1846 Violent thunderstorms. Hail smashed glass arcades over Regent Street pavements in London beyond repair. Potato blight famine in Ireland following humid heat and frequent thunderstorms in June–July, as in 1845 also.

    1938 Exceptionally thundery spell 1–12th, widespread damage.

2. 1906 Widespread violent thunderstorms in SE. England, tornado in Guildford.

3. 1879 Great hailstones smashed roofs in W. London.

    1931 Thunderstorms and flooding in London 3–5th.

4. 1829 Disastrous floods of all rivers between Moray and Angus, after torrential rains 2–4th with NE wind and waterspouts. Stone bridges and houses washed away in 5 or 6 counties, coastline altered at river mouths. (July had been very thundery in the South, but cold with night frosts in Scotland.)

6. 1952 Thunderstorm floods near London.

    1956 Violent thunderstorms in SE. England, hailstones piled 6 feet deep blocked streets in Tunbridge Wells.

7. 1949 Widespread heavy rain interrupted the long dry spell: $3\frac{1}{2}$ inches in Ayrshire.

8. 1588 Armada, defeated off French coast (Gravelines), carried northwards by strong SW winds in the North Sea.

9. 1911 37·8° C (100° F) at Greenwich.

11. 1938 Thunderstorm and tornado damage in Scotland.

    1948 Heavy continuous rain 11–12th in S. Scotland caused £1 million damage.

12. 1582 Severe thunderstorms and very big hail in Norfolk.

15. 1952 10 inches rain on Exmoor, Lynmouth flood disaster: many drowned.

17. 1588 Winds in the North Sea turned NE. Spanish fleet heading west around the north of Shetland.

    1784 Sleet near coast of Moray Firth.

18. 1696 End of the rains in the South, where W winds brought mostly fair weather over the next month; dearth of food becoming serious in Scotland.

    1924 9·4 inches rain at Cannington (Quantock Hills), Somerset.

19. 1867 Intense heat followed by thunderstorms in SE. England.

    1932 37° C (99° F) at Greenwich.

20. 1698 Beginning of a short period of fine weather which saved some of the harvest in Yorks: later a long wet autumn ruined most of the crops, which sprouted.

    1932 37° C again at Greenwich: third successive day over 32° C (90° F).

21. 1695 N wind and night frost at the end of a cold summer with continual rain and W gales. 'Greater frosts were not always seen in winter' (John Evelyn at Wotton, Surrey). (This summer

was one of the first of a sequence of disastrous harvests in Scotland, where famine ensued.)

22. 1850 Snow on the Cairngorms nearly down to Braemar. A week of very cold weather.

24. 1588 Severe Atlantic SW gales 24 Aug.–3 Sept. completed the break up of the Spanish Armada, now northwest of Ireland and west of the Hebrides.

  1905 Exceptional rainfall in E. Ireland 24–26th: total about 10 inches.

  1940 Ground frost in London ($-3°$ C): earliest known frost in modern times.

25. 1891 10 inches rain in 2 days 24th–25th at Seathwaite (Lake District).

  1954 Beginning of a week of warm dry weather between the summer and autumn rains.

26. 1692 Beginning of fair warm weather which lasted till 14 Sept., after the summer rains.

  1912 Exceptional rain (over 8 inches) in East Anglia: floods.

27. 1695 Renewed rain and gales (winds mostly between NW and E) set in till 12 Oct.

  1829 Further floods in the same districts in NE. Scotland as on 3–4th.

  1933 Heavy rain and floods in Ireland, Scotland and NW. England ended the main dry spell, but fine weather soon returned and dominated September.

31. 1879 Fine anticyclonic weather ended long rainy spell.

  1912 Anticyclonic weather spreading from SW. ended the summer rains and began a period of drought lasting in many districts till 28 Sept.

  1949 Approximate end of main fine spell of the summer.

  1955 W winds broke the long fine spell in W. districts, breakdown in the E. followed about 5 Sept.

SEPTEMBER

1. 1883 Former West Indian hurricane storm brought heavy rain and violent gale in W. and S. England.

  1906 $35 \cdot 5°$ C ($96°$ F) in London.

2. 1741 First general rainfall after heat and drought since 12 June.

  1773 First rain in N. Scotland after long dry summer with waterfalls dried out.

  1816 Sharp frost: ice on water near London (Luke Howard). (This was described as 'the year without a summer'; there were snowdrifts still on Helvellyn, Lake District, on 30 July.)

3. 1906 Last of 4 successive days with temperatures above $32°$ C ($90°$ F).

5. 1725 Beginning of drier weather and a mild autumn after prolonged raininess since April.

  1958 Tornadoes and giant hail accompanied a thunderstorm across Sussex: hailstones the size and shape of half grape-fruit and weighing $6\frac{1}{2}$ oz. near Horsham.

7.	1773	Very wet and stormy in NW. Scotland and Hebrides: autumn continued rainy till 3 Nov.
	1960	Beginning of 5-day fine spell between the rains of summer and autumn.
13.	1903	Anticyclone over Britain 13–22nd after notable wet summer.
15.	1666	Foul weather in the southern North Sea began the breakdown of the long dry warm summer weather. (The Great Fire in London broke out on the 12th. The smoke reached Oxford.)
16.	1935	Severe gale: 100 m.p.h. gust at Scilly, 88 m.p.h. at Bedford.
	1961	Former tropical cyclone produced hurricane damage in the west of Ireland.
17.	1954	First snowfall covered the Cairngorms down to 2,500 feet. (800 m.) above sea level.
18.	1696	Stormy wet weather returned.
19.	1666	The first considerable rain quenched London fire: rainy autumn followed.
	1926	32° C (90° F) in London: the latest known date for this.
20.	1773	Rain and gales in the Hebrides.
	1846	Beginning of period of violent gales in Ireland, lasting till 21 Nov.
	1919	Snow 19–20th covered the hills in Scotland and as far south as Dartmoor: earliest known date for widespread snow in Britain.
23.	1863	2·4 inches rain in 2 hours at Edinburgh.
	1872	Air temperature fell to −2° C (29° F) in London: the earliest known date for this.
	1893	Shower of sleet and snow in Edinburgh: perhaps the earliest known date.
24.	1895	Temperature over 30° C (87° F) in London: the latest known date for this.
25.	1692	NE gale introduced long spell of stormy NE–NW winds, mostly dry but very cold day and night: frosts around London from 9 Oct. prevented fruit ripening.
	1885	Heavy snowfalls on the Scottish and Welsh mountains.
	1907	Warmest day of the year (25·5° C in London): latest known date for this.
26.	1903	Depressions again began to pass across or near Britain: beginning of wet autumn.

OCTOBER

3.	1959	29° C (84° F) in the shade in London.
6.	1921	29° C in London: latest known date for temperatures over 80° F.
7.	1829	Snow lay for a while in the London area and elsewhere in the South: earliest known date.
8.	1739	Beginning of historic winter: E wind set in with frequent frosts.
9.	1740	N wind brought uncommonly severe, early, night frost, after cold summer: ice on many rivers in England. (This was the coldest October on record.)

10. 1555 Westminster flooded after great storm of wind and rain.
     1959 First general rain in England after long summer drought broken only by occasional thunderstorms in July and August.
11. 1916 8 inches rain near Loch Hourn in W. Highlands: the heaviest known rainfall in a day in Scotland.
12. 1740 Ice ½ inch thick in Kent.
14. 1829 Severe NE gale 13–14th in Scotland: ships lost.
     1881 Severe gales 13–14th as depression crossed Scotland: many ships wrecked.
15. 1571 Gales and sea flood in Lincs and in the Fens: many ships wrecked, houses destroyed, cattle perished.
     1886 Severe gale damage in the S. and W. as depression crossed Ireland and England.
18. 1954 2–3 day rainfall 17–19th in Scotland and NW. England, after wet summer, destroyed crops: floods dislocated traffic; landslides.
19. 1665 Cold weather and rain in London: death rate from plague began to fall off.
     1870 Tornado damage in Devon and Somerset and at Stratford.
     1880 Snowfall in London.
20. 1846 Violent storm in Ireland, probably former tropical hurricane.
25. 1859 Severe storm wrecked the *Royal Charter* off Anglesey (500 drowned) and destroyed Brighton pier: led to introduction of gale warnings by the then rather new Meteorological Office.
27. 1913 Tornadoes of exceptional violence in Devon, SE. Wales and Cheshire: several deaths.
28. 1836 Snow lay in Edinburgh 4–5 inches deep: earliest date.
     1927 Widespread severe gale, gust nearly 100 m.p.h. at Southport.
29. 1954 Renewed flooding in the same areas as on 18th damaged roads and buildings.
31. 1638 Tornadoes in Devon and Somerset: church at Widdicombe destroyed during service.

NOVEMBER

1. 1785 Tornado damage in Notts.
2. 1931 Prolonged rains and flooding: 9·6 inches rain in 2 days near Brecon.
3. 1739 Brief wet spell 3–10th interrupted the course of the long, dry, and already often frosty, winter.
4. 1946 Warmest November day on record: 20·5°C (69°F) at Edinburgh, 22°C (71°F) at Prestatyn, North Wales.
    1957 Gale destroyed new houses at Hatfield, Herts.
5. 1926 Violent SW gale in all districts.
    1938 21°C (70°F) in London: the warmest November day known.
6. 1771 Heavy rain and floods at Kings Lynn.
7. 1665 Deep depression probably brought the lowest barometric pressure ever measured in London (about 931 mb.).

8.   1954   Severe floods in Ireland after heavy rains.
9.   1931   Violent S gale in Channel 9–10th: heavy seas damaged build-
            ings on shore along S. coast.
10. 1739   Cold E winds re-established.
     1810   E gale: sea floods round Boston, Lincs.
11. 1570   The greatest North Sea storm and flood after that of 11 Oct.
            1250: coastal changes; cities drowned on the continent.
12. 1740   N gale with rain, snow and hail.
     1901   Gale 11–13th, as deep depression crossed Ireland, Wales and
            N. England.
     1915   Gale 11–12th with heavy rain and some snow, as deep depression
            crossed the south of Ireland and England.
13. 1696   Mostly fair weather, but with severe frosts near London, set
            in 13–20th after frequent stormy winds and rain since 18 Sept.
16. 1771   Heavy rains flooded the rivers Tyne, Wear and Tees, washing
            away most bridges.
     1928   Gale: widespread damage to telephones.
17. 1799   End of period of continual rains since 22 June.
     1893   Severe N gale after depression crossed Ireland and Scotland.
21. 1696   W winds and rainy weather returned till 10 Dec.—at times gales.
22. 1948   Beginning of 10-day fog in E. and central England.
23. 1928   Gale: barometric pressure in Edinburgh 950·7 mb. at sea level.
25. 1829   ENE gale in Scotland: many ships lost.
26. 1739   Beginning of longest break in the prevailing E winds of this
            long cold winter: many rainy days between 26 Nov. and 4 Jan.
            1740, though still rather cold.
     1948   Smoke fog deaths in London 26–1 Dec.
27. 1954   Disastrous S and SW gales: Goodwins lightship wrecked.
28. 1890   Temperature at Kew never rose above $-4°$ C ($25°$ F).
30. 1665   Climax to a month of wind and rain, the roads very bad. English
            ships trapped by ice in port at Hamburg (Pepys).
     1788   Earliest known case of a long unbroken frost began, lasting
            till early Jan. 1789. (The frost fair on the Thames in London
            during this spell was the first since 1740.)

DECEMBER

2.   1665   Severe frost in London 2–7th.
3.   1909   Gale caused many shipwrecks, including the Manx steamer:
            depression crossed Ireland and England (949 mb. on Yorks.
            coast).
4.   1879   Exceptionally severe frost: $-30·5°$ C ($-23°$ F) unofficially
            recorded at Blackadder, Berwickshire. People frozen to death;
            many trees, especially holly, killed.
5.   1687   Boats plying in the streets of Dublin after heavy rains 4–5th.
     1695   An interval of snow and frost in the London area after mild
            dark misty weather and before a long wet spell which lasted till
            Feb. 1696.

	1906	NW gale in Scotland.
	1952	Smoke fog in London, visibility under 12 yards for 3 days 6–8th: heavy death rate.
7.	1564	Severe frost set in: the court later indulged in sports on the ice at Westminster (probably one of the first occasions a great frost had been treated in this way).
	1703	Most violent gale ever known in the S. of England 7–8th: wrecks, Eddystone lighthouse washed away, destruction in New Forest, Portsmouth town, woods, parks and buildings in London, Cambridge and elsewhere.
	1873	Dense smoke fog in London 7–13th: many deaths.
8.	1954	Severe thunderstorm and tornado in London.
9.	1886	Very intense storm crossed N. Ireland and England: barometric pressure fell to 927 mb. at sea level in Belfast.
11.	1657	Beginning of one of the longest periods with snow lying in England, lasting reputedly till 21 March 1658.
	1696	E wind brought in spell of snowy weather lasting till Feb. 1697.
12.	1901	NE gale and snowstorm cut communications in all parts of England: depression in the Channel 12–14th.
14.	1890	Coldest known December day in London, temperature never rose above −6° C (21° F).
15.	1683	Onset of great frost in England and central Europe: Thames frozen to London Bridge by 2 Jan. 1684 (booths on the ice by 27 Jan. and for more than a fortnight thereafter).
17.	1663	Sea flood inundated Whitehall: exceptional tide with gales.
	1938	Onset of extreme frost period, lasting till early Jan. 1939.
	1952	Severe gale damaged buildings in Scotland and N. England: 111 m.p.h. gust in Lincs.
18.	1961	Onset of period of severe frosts lasting till early Jan. 1962. Skating began in the South on 25th.
21.	1607	Onset of long frost.
	1665	Severe frost set in again, the Thames blocked by ice in London by 30th. The plague much reduced, but flared up again in the mild weather after 6–10 Jan. 1666.
22.	1962	Frost set in in evening after some milder foggy days and became severe: skating began in the South on 24–25th.
25.	1796	Very severe frost in London: −21° C in Marylebone, −19° C in Mayfair.
	1836	Great ENE gale and snowstorm 25–26th, many lives lost: roads throughout England impassable for several days, snow 5–15 feet deep in many places, a few great drifts 20–50 feet.
	1927	Heavy snowstorm 25–26th with E wind in London and the South: general depth 2 feet, drifts 10–20 feet deep blocked roads and buried vehicles.
26.	1813	Early example of a thick smoke fog in London 26 Dec. 1813–2 Jan. 1814, visibility under 20 yds.

	1906	Heavy snowstorms 26–30th in S. and E. Scotland.
27.	1694	Long frost began: Thames frozen in London during January 1695.
	1696	W wind 27–29th brought more snow but did not break the long frost near London.
	1962	The first of a succession of 4 heavy snowfalls in the South with depths of up to 18 inches of level snow in the Weald by New Year.
28.	1879	WSW gale: Tay Bridge disaster, train blown into the firth as bridge fell.
30.	1900	Unusually heavy winter rainfall: 3–$3\frac{1}{2}$ inches and extreme floods at Worcester.
	1951	Violent gale, widespread damage in N. Scotland.

Appendix 3
Units and Conversions

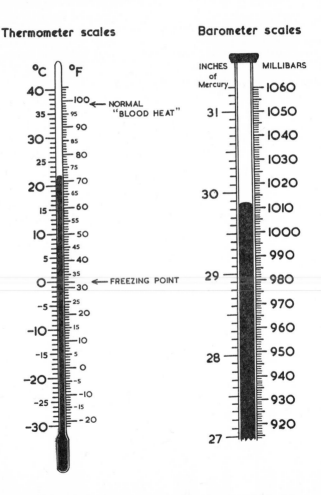

Thermometer scales

Barometer scales

To convert Fahrenheit temperatures to Centigrade (Celsius) beyond the range of the scale shown, subtract 32 from the Fahrenheit figure and multiply the remainder by 5/9.

Rainfall scales

Rainfall is measured in inches or millimetres. The range of values occurring is too great to be covered by a picture such as those shown for temperature and atmospheric pressure.

Inches are converted to millimetres by multiplying by 25·4. Many readers wishing to convert rainfall figures in millimetres to inches will find it sufficiently near to divide by a hundred and multiply by four.

Scales for wind speed

In this book wind speeds are given either in miles per hour or in knots (nautical miles per hour). The international units are knots and metres per second. Conversions are as follows:

1 knot = 1·15 statute miles per hour.

1 metre/second = 2·235 statute miles per hour or 1·94 knots.

1 km./hour = 0·62 statute miles per hour or 0·54 knots.

In addition the scale of wind force devised by Admiral Beaufort in 1805 is still in use. It is repeated here, with its equivalents in wind speeds measured by an anemometer at the standard height of 10 metres (33 feet), partly because its descriptions give a useful idea of the effects of various wind speeds on land and sea. (A scale of this type, but on which the numbers only went up to 4, was in use as long ago as the 1690s.)

SCALE OF BEAUFORT WIND FORCE

Scale Number	Name	m.p.h.	Effects on land (abbreviated)	Effects on sea (abbreviated)
0	Calm	0–1	Smoke rises vertically	Sea like a mirror ('oily calm' to use an older description).
1	Light air	1–3	Direction of wind shown by smoke drift, but not by vanes.	Ripples with the appearance of scales but no foam crests.
2	Light breeze	4–7	Wind felt on face, leaves rustle, vanes turned.	Small wavelets, crests look glassy but do not break.
3	Gentle breeze	8–12	Leaves and small twigs in constant motion, light flags extended.	Large wavelets, crests beginning to break.
4	Moderate breeze	13–18	Raises dust and loose paper, small branches moved.	Small waves, becoming longer; fairly frequent white horses.
5	Fresh breeze	19–24	Small trees in leaf begin to sway, crested wavelets on inland waters.	Moderate waves and more pronounced length, many white horses, chance of some spray.
6	Strong breeze	25–31	Large branches move, whistling in telegraph wires, umbrellas used with difficulty.	Large waves begin to form, white crests more extensive, some spray.
7	Moderate gale (Not counted as gale in statistics)	32–38	Whole trees move, hard to walk against the wind.	Sea heaps up, foam from breaking waves begins to be blown in streaks.
8	Fresh gale	39–46	Breaks twigs off trees, impedes progress.	Moderately high waves of greater length, edges of crests begin to break into spindrift, streaks of foam.
9	Strong gale	47–54	Slight structural damage to chimney pots, slates, etc.	High waves, dense streaks of foam, crests topple and roll over.
10	Whole gale	55–63	Rare inland, trees uprooted, considerable structural damage.	Very high waves, whole surface of sea white, heavy tumbling seas, visibility affected.
11	Storm	64–72	Widespread damage.	Exceptionally high waves may hide moderate ships from view temporarily.
12	Hurricane	73–82	—	Air filled with foam and spray.

Additional scale numbers have been added in recent years to define winds up to force 17 (126–136 m.p.h.), formerly all classified as force 12.

Index of Names

Subject Index